675

D0101839

אוריון

THIS TIME
OF CRISIS

Also available by the same author:

This Dangerous Menace: Dundee and the River Tay at War, 1939 to 1945
*This Present Emergency: Edinburgh, the River Forth and South-east Scotland
and the Second World War*

THIS TIME OF CRISIS

GLASGOW, THE WEST OF SCOTLAND AND THE NORTH WESTERN APPROACHES IN THE SECOND WORLD WAR

by ANDREW JEFFREY

MAINSTREAM
PUBLISHING

EDINBURGH AND LONDON

First published in Great Britain in 1993 by
MAINSTREAM PUBLISHING COMPANY (EDINBURGH) LTD,
7 Albany Street, Edinburgh EH1 3UG

ISBN 1 85158 582 6

A catalogue record for this book is available from the British Library

Typeset in 11/13 pt Sabon by Origination, Dunstable
Printed in Great Britain by Butler and Tanner Ltd, Frome

Contents

Chapter One

For God's Sake, Save my Baby!

At 1930 hours on Sunday, 3 September 1939, Adolf Hitler was about to leave Berlin for eastern Germany in his special train, the *Führersonderzug*. There he would visit the Fourth Army, already striking deep into northern Poland.

In London, the first meeting of the newly constituted War Cabinet had just closed after discussing reconnaissance photographs which showed that a strong German naval force was at sea off Wilhelmshaven. An air attack was ordered. Winston Churchill walked across Horse Guards Parade to the Admiralty. He had been recalled from the political wilderness to the post of First Lord of the Admiralty in Neville Chamberlain's wartime administration.

Aboard the Donaldson Atlantic liner *Athenia* dinner was being served in the dining-rooms, already blacked out against the possibility of submarine attack. A number of passengers feeling the effects of the Atlantic swell forebore to eat, preferring to lie in their bunks as the ship ploughed her way westwards at a steady 15 knots.

All through that extraordinary, unhappy day, and for the two preceding days, Glasgow's railway stations had been filled with lines of children boarding trains for the countryside. It had been estimated in April 1939 that 317,000 children, mothers accompanying under-fives, teachers and helpers would be eligible to leave Glasgow under the official evacuation scheme.

The figure for Clydebank, the west of Scotland's other evacuable area, was 12,385. The receiving areas were to be Ayrshire, Dumfriesshire, Kirkcudbrightshire, Wigtonshire, Argyll, Bute, Perthshire, Kinross, Stirlingshire and Fife.

A survey of these receiving areas carried out that spring showed that, in general, better-off areas were markedly less willing to accept large numbers of

THE CORPORATION OF GLASGOW

EDUCATION DEPARTMENT.

EDUCATION OFFICES,
129 BATH STREET,
GLASGOW, C.2.

March, 1939.

TO THE PARENTS OR GUARDIANS
OF CHILDREN IN GLASGOW.

DEAR SIR (MADAM),

Evacuation of Children from Glasgow in the Event of a National Emergency.

It will already be known to you that the Government are making plans to enable parents who live in the crowded areas of large cities to have their children transferred to safer places if war should ever break out.

The city of Glasgow is included in the plans, and all parents in Glasgow, particularly those who live in the crowded parts of the city, will want to consider whether their children should be included in the arrangements

Under the arrangements which are being made the children would gather at the primary school nearest their home and the older and younger members of each family would as far as possible be evacuated together. They would go to the chosen places in the care of teachers who would remain with them. They would live in the country in houses where they would be welcome. Arrangements would be made to let you know their new addresses as quickly as possible. Children under school age would also be allowed to go if the mother or a woman friend went with them, and all the children of one family would be sent to the same place.

In any case, I have to ask you to show on the attached form whether or not you would wish your children to be included in the scheme. This question is being put to you now, so that the Government may be able to complete, in peace time, their plans for the evacuation of children from this city, if, unfortunately, war should break out.

I am,

Yours faithfully,

Rm Allardyce

Evacuation Officer.

children than were less well-off areas. Though Perthshire households were willing to accept a total of 63,568 evacuees, only 24,068 of these could be children. Dumfries would accept 25,353 but only 8,982 children. Denny, on the other hand, would take 652 evacuees of whom 540 could be children. Kirkcudbrightshire would accept 9,498 children in a total of 10,944 evacuees.

The available accommodation for 273,439 people, of whom only 150,115 could be children, fell far short of that for the 330,385 required. In June 1939 the Scottish Office discovered that 116,922 people could be accommodated by evacuating into, rather than out of, suburbs such as Pollokshields, Cathcart and Knightswood.

The evacuation scheme was based on a fine piece of social distinction. It was believed in official circles that the destruction of working-class areas in the heavy bombing expected within hours of the outbreak of war would result in widespread social unrest. More affluent areas, on the other hand, could be expected to 'take it'.

Some 338 trains were arranged to carry 237,523 evacuees out of Glasgow on 1, 2 and 3 September. In the event, only 118,833 people turned up, many of the trains ran half empty and 35 were cancelled. In Clydebank, arrangements had been made to cater for 11,700 evacuees; only 5,159 appeared.

Clyde steamers were pressed into service: 23 trips being run to cater for 21,000 evacuees from Glasgow and 3,700 from Clydebank. Some 11,000 people from Glasgow and 2,000 from Clydebank actually travelled. Many of the Glasgow children had never seen the sea before.

Over 250 mothers and children from Polmadie School found themselves in Eaglesham, and 860 from Fairfield School in Govan arrived in Lanark. Some 124 children from the Blind Asylum were taken to Glen Nevis Youth Hostel at Fort William and children from the Southern General Hospital were moved to wards specially set up in Culzean Castle by the Marchioness of Ailsa. Around 400 patients at the Victoria Infirmary had been sent home or to other hospitals to make way for the flood of air-raid casualties expected hourly. Cars supplied by members of the Royal Scottish Automobile Club assisted in the evacuation of the Western Infirmary. Mothers and children from Shettleston and Tollcross were sent to Stirlingshire, 900 evacuees from Dennistoun went to the Largs area and 2,500 arrived in Dunoon. Of the 350 evacuees expected in Strathblane, only 106 arrived and just 73 arrived at Killearn where 369 were expected.

Evacuees arriving in Oban were taken from the railway station to Rockfield School where they were fed and assigned to billets. Many of the children, it was discovered, had never travelled in a motor car before and had to be coaxed to get in. When a second train arrived with 500 mothers and children from Govan, problems were experienced after some of those who had offered billets withdrew at the last moment.

Billeting officers in Drymen found that apprehensive evacuee families refused to be split up, notably one Maryhill woman and her seven children. This caused serious difficulties in finding suitable billets.

The initial response to the evacuation scheme in Glasgow and Clydebank, at around 50 per cent, was considerably better than that in Edinburgh where it was only 30 per cent. For most evacuees, the genteel rusticity of the receiving areas was totally alien. For receiving families, the pitiable condition of inner-city residents came as a severe shock. Middle-class families were catapulted into having to cope with ill-shod, ill-clothed, verminous and often diseased children who had little or no experience of modern personal hygiene. Incompatibility, particularly among adults, was an immediate problem and led to billeting officers being bombarded with complaints. Discontent and loneliness led to a flood of early returns to Glasgow and Clydebank,.

The parents of evacuees visiting their children in Perthshire caused resentment by 'expecting hospitality and lodging'. Householders in Renfrewshire who took in private evacuees were threatened with legal proceedings for contravening the overcrowding clause of the Housing Act (1935).

A number of luckier children did find themselves accepted in a happy and stable environment where they formed enduring and loving relationships.

Renfrewshire County Council had, for some days, been receiving telegrams from the Home Office ordering them to take action on a series of Local War Instructions, known as LOWIN for short. LOWIN 7 was received in mid-afternoon on 23 August and was concerned with measures to ensure that a blackout could be immediately enforced. Entitled 'Wireless Communication', LOWIN 9 stated that 'a receiving instrument' was to be established at the Air-Raid Precautions (ARP) headquarters and that an official was to be posted, armed with pencil and paper, to take down details of any official announcements.

The Council's Emergency Committee met for the first time in the County Buildings, Paisley, at midday on Saturday, 2 September. The minutes of their discussions on that last, tense afternoon of peace betray a certain lack of urgency. The only decision of any importance reached was that the County Clerk should send prepaid telegrams to local Air-Raid Precautions controllers asking them to 'supervise in a general manner' all ARP services in their area.

Daly's of Sauchiehall Street announced, in Saturday's *Glasgow Herald*, the immediate cancellation, 'owing to the crisis', of their demonstration of country-life wear, planned for the following week. Campbell's, 'the Great National Furnishers' of 60 Union Street, advertised that 'All furniture purchased between August 27th and September 30th 1939 on Campbell's helpful period payments CAN BE RETURNED in case of emergency BY MUTUAL CONSENT WITHOUT FURTHER PAYMENT other than the rental up to date.'

Readers of the *Daily Record* could take comfort from a report that, according to a member of the War Office team at the International Motorcycle Trials at Salzburg, Germany was in the grip of an acute petrol shortage. Glasgow's lamplighters were threatening to go on strike to force the Corporation to accede to their demand for overtime payments for emergency duties in connection with the blackout. The city's vets were experiencing what one described as '. . . the hectic rush of a large section of the public to have

ANCHOR ~ DONALDSON CABIN SERVICE

The "Athenia" as seen from the top
of the Quebec Bridge

LETITIA ATHENIA

their dogs and cats humanely destroyed'. The disposal of carcasses would, over the next few days, become a serious problem.

Ladies' hairdressers were proudly advertising 'Hair to suit tin helmets'. It was said that pre-war styles did not suit a tin helmet or peaked cap. 'Now the hair is cut clean around the nape of the neck, with crisp little curls at the front to make a frame for the face.'

At 1115 hours that Sunday Neville Chamberlain, in probably the most notorious broadcast made by any politician, informed the nation that '. . . this country is at war with Germany'. As he finished speaking, a thunderstorm broke over the west of Scotland and provided a fittingly Wagnerian finale to the uneasy truce of the inter-war years.

The *Athenia* had sailed from Princes Dock in Glasgow just after midday on Friday, 1 September. As she passed slowly down the Clyde in the care of two tugs, passengers were shaken by workers in Fairfield's shipyard yelling, 'Cowards! Cowards!'

The ship anchored off Belfast that evening and picked up 136 passengers. She then set sail for Liverpool where another 546 passengers boarded. From the Mersey, she sailed north, back up the Irish Sea, and out through the North Channel.

Passengers, already apprehensive at the deteriorating international situation, had been positively alarmed when, shortly after the news of the declaration of war had spread round the ship, the lifeboats were prepared for launching. This nervousness was to some extent allayed by the appearance at dinner of the *Athenia's* master, Captain James Cook. Cook seemed relaxed and in good spirits as he went to his table.

First Officer Barnet Copland had just been relieved on the bridge by 28-year-old Third Officer Colin Porteous and went round the decks to check on the ship's blackout before himself going below to dinner.

Around the hatch over number 5 hold at the after end of the tourist deck, a group largely made up of women and children were enjoying the fresh air, having escaped the overcrowded and oppressive atmosphere in the blacked-out liner. Not far away some children were standing in a circle, singing 'Down Mexico Way'. None of those aboard the *Athenia* were aware of the single, unblinking eye of a periscope observing their ship from around a mile away to the south.

Fritz-Julius Lemp had taken his type VII Atlantic U-boat, *U30,* to sea from Wilhelmshaven in the early hours of 22 August. Following the German invasion of Poland he took *U30* into her allotted operational patrol area 200 miles west of the Hebrides. The inshore patrol area off the Scottish coast was occupied by *U27*. At lunchtime that Sunday he received the signal to commence hostilities against Britain and retired to his cabin to open his sealed orders. On one thing these orders were specific: that he was to operate within

The Tourist Third Cabin Dining Saloon in the Athenia. *All of the liner's accommodation had been blacked out the night before war was declared. When, following the explosion of U30's torpedo, the lights failed, this room was plunged into complete darkness. One witness described the terrible screaming which broke out as crockery and food crashed to the floor and diners crowded towards the staircase. Cordite fumes from the explosion heightened the panic and a number of fainting passengers had to be helped on deck by stewards.*
(RALSTON COLLECTION, STRATHCLYDE REGIONAL COUNCIL ARCHIVES)

the Prize Rules and not wage unrestricted submarine warfare. This meant that he could not sink unarmed, unescorted merchant vessels without warning.

The transatlantic sea lanes, which *U30* was prowling, seemed strangely deserted on that first afternoon of war. In fact, all of Britain's merchant fleet had been sailing under the orders of the Admiralty trade division since 23 August, and many ships were already in the throes of being hastily converted into armed merchant cruisers. Shortly after 1900 hours and just after sunset, *U30*'s lookouts sighted a lone vessel approaching on a westerly course.

13

Lemp immediately ordered his boat to dive and manoeuvred her into an attacking position. Later, he was to admit that excitement clouded his judgment, causing him to ignore the orders not to attack unescorted merchant vessels. At a range of something under a mile he ordered, 'Torpedos los!'

Two of the torpedoes missed the *Athenia,* and one stuck in its tube. The fourth torpedo slammed into the liner's hull on the port side directly under the mainmast. It exploded inside number 5 hold, against the engine-room bulkhead, and a huge spout of water rose up the ship's side. Much of the blast inside the hold took the easiest route of escape – through the hatch covers. The deck reared upwards and, with a roar, a cloud of blackened debris, smoke and lethal splinters flew upwards, carrying with it many of the tourist passengers who had been enjoying the evening air only seconds before. When the smoke subsided, carrying with it a number of grotesquely spinning bodies, one young passenger, Roy Barrington, stood blackened and naked, his clothes blasted from his body. Nearby, his mother lay dead, killed instantly by a splinter. Ten-year-old Canadian Margaret Hayworth had been sitting near number 5 hold with her mother and her sister Jacqueline. When her mother screamed at her to move away she remained horribly still, a bright reddening gash across her forehead.

Though at least one passenger was blown overboard, others had remarkable escapes, being blown against the ship's rails. Down below, however, in the third-class accommodation, the blast wreaked utter havoc. Bulkheads buckled and collapsed and mirrors shattered sending glass splinters flying through the air. The galley was wrecked and two of the cooks were severely scalded by escaping steam. Two of the ship's engineering staff were instantly blown to pieces and water thundered through from number 5 hold into the engine-room. The engines stopped almost immediately as did the turbo-alternators which provided the ship's electrical power.

On the bridge Third Officer Porteous heard the explosion and felt the ship lurch first to starboard and then settle back to port with a pronounced list. Instantly, he reached for the button which closed the watertight doors and, to the accompaniment of the loud ringing of bells, they slammed shut. He was sounding emergency stations on the ship's whistle when his eye was caught by a puff of smoke about 800 yards away on *Athenia's* port side.

Many witnessed the same puff of smoke, some claimed to have heard the crack of a gun and others saw the outline of a submarine shrouded in the smoke. As the U-boat was on the ship's weather side, some claimed to have smelt cordite as the smoke drifted down onto the *Athenia.* None of the survivors later interviewed by an American naval officer could confirm absolutely that the U-boat had indeed used its deck gun to fire on the liner. What is certain is that no shell struck the ship, nor was there any sign of a shell hitting the water anywhere nearby. First Officer Copland thought the smoke to have been caused by water getting into the exhausts of the U-boat's diesels which would have been started immediately on surfacing. He too saw the U-boat on the surface just over half a mile from the *Athenia* where it stayed briefly before submerging again less than four minutes after the torpedo struck.

In the dining-rooms chaos reigned as passengers crowded towards the stairways to the upper deck; crockery smashed to the floor and the lights flickered out, plunging the blacked-out accommodation into darkness. Passengers, many of them weeping with terror, stumbled up the darkened stairway to the promenade deck guided by the feeble glow of lighted matches held by Chief Steward Reginald Rankin and a passenger, Nancy Bishop of Toronto.

The third-class accommodation aft on D deck started to flood almost immediately following the explosion. Here, nine-year-old Daniel Wilkes watched his mother crushed to death when a bulkhead collapsed. Swirling water picked up luggage piled in cabins and corridors, and swept up the bodies of passengers killed in the blast.

For third-class passengers the situation was made even more desperate by the fact that the explosion had destroyed the stairway from D deck up to C deck. Mr J. Curran of Dundee tried to get back to his cabin to collect his lifejacket but found his way barred by the debris. Mr J. Bigelow found himself faced with the collapsed stairway as he ran down to D deck where he had left his wife and children. He jumped down into the flooding corridor below where he found his wife and daughter had become separated from their son, David. Bigelow waded chest-deep among the bodies floating in the corridor and found his son, close to drowning, near their cabin door.

It was some minutes before the crew were able to restore order on deck and set about launching the lifeboats. Stewards with torches guided passengers towards the promenade deck, all the while encouraging them to take their time and get their lifebelts on.

A group of Eastern European refugees proved impossible to reassure. Few spoke any English and many were quite unable to understand the orders of the crew. Being from largely agricultural communities, most had never seen the sea prior to their flight from the Nazis. Panic-stricken, they ran from side to side on deck, clutching their pitifully meagre possessions in baskets or suitcases. Most gathered on the starboard side which, owing to the list, was furthest away from the sea. Still clutching their suitcases, they filled many of the boats on that side, throwing the carefully rehearsed lifeboat drill completely out of gear.

One refugee shouting, 'Let me on that lifeboat,' and pushing his way through a group waiting to board a boat, had to be threatened with an axe. Other passengers, angered to find their places had been taken up, were further incensed to see valuable space in the boats being taken up with luggage. Prompt action by the crew avoided what could have become an ugly scene; they took the bundles from the weeping refugees and threw them into the sea. One unfortunate side-effect of this was the anti-Semitic sentiment evident among many survivors.

Although there was plenty of room for all the passengers and crew in the boats, there were distressing echoes of the *Titanic* disaster of 27 years before. At almost every boarding station, husbands stood back as their distraught wives climbed, or were pushed, aboard. Children were thrust into boats, screaming for their parents who stood quietly on deck. Thornton Mustard,

Cabin Class accommodation in the Athenia. *Above the mirror is a notice informing this cabin's occupants that their lifeboat station is No. 4 on the promenade deck. With almost 60 passengers on board it, lifeboat No. 4 was successfully launched under the command of Quartermaster MacLean. Two young men cowered with their wives on the bottom boards and refused all MacLean's entreaties for help at the oars. A group of women in the bows stared at the lilting* Athenia *and quietly began to sing 'Nearer My God to Thee'.*
(RALSTON COLLECTION, STRATHCLYDE REGIONAL COUNCIL ARCHIVES)

an educationalist from Toronto, was about to take a seat in a boat next to his wife when a young woman rushed forward. He stood back and allowed her to take his place. Despite anguished appeals from his wife as the boat was lowered, he resolutely remained on deck. Mrs Mustard would never see her husband again. In the chaos other families became accidentally split up.

Terror-stricken passengers were seen jumping straight into the water instead of climbing down the rope ladders provided. Many were drowned. A mother stared in astonishment as a male hand came out of the crowd and grabbed the lifebelt she was putting on her child. Meanwhile, members of the crew were giving up their lifebelts to passengers. Thomas McCubbin of New Jersey was helping some women and children down a ladder when, to his astonishment, a mother thrust her infant child into his arms with the anguished words, 'For God's sake, save my baby!'

Fifteen-year-old Brenda Chapman from Birlsmorton near Malvern had been in bed when the torpedo struck. She rushed to her young brother's cabin and got him to their boat. By the time Quartermaster Graham was ready to launch boat 11 A, it was overcrowded with almost 90 people. The ship's list to port made the launching of this, one of the starboard boats, difficult enough even were it not so heavily laden. Graham shouted for assistance and crew members including First Officer Copland fought to get the boat off its chocks and over the side.

When the boat was still suspended a short distance above the sea, the strain became too much for the exhausted crew members and the stern of the boat fell into the water. One woman was flung into the sea and others suffered bruising and broken bones as they were pitched into a heap at the stern. The forward fall was hurriedly let go and the boat got away half full of water. Barnet Copland was later found to have suffered four broken fingers and serious rope burns in his attempts to halt 11 A's dizzy descent. Despite being clad only in pyjamas and being badly bruised, Brenda Chapman took a turn at the oars during the night.

All the boats had been launched by 2130 hours and were standing off, riding to their sea anchors, a short distance from the ship. Faintly across the water came the sound of children reciting nursery rhymes. Frightened passengers prayed and sang hymns including 'Abide with Me' and 'Eternal Father, Strong to Save'. Porpoises played unconcernedly among the boats and were often mistaken for submarine periscopes. On the *Athenia*, an emergency generator had been started and the deck lights had come back on. In number 5 hold the blackened and naked bodies of the initial victims of the explosion floated ever higher as the ship slowly filled. Some 22 people, including five passengers, remained aboard and had gathered round Captain Cook near the bridge. On hearing the explosion, Cook had hurried to the bridge from where he ordered the sending of distress signals. He then went to his cabin to gather the ship's secret code books which he placed in a weighted bag and threw over the side.

Signals staff at the Admiralty could scarcely believe their eyes when they received the following message:

From Malin Head Radio   THI 2217   3/9/39   received 2230
Addressed: Admiralty Naval Wireless

Important.
Important Admiral Rosyth. Intercept 2059. Jamming near. SSSS SSSS SSSS
Athenia GFDM torpedoed 5644 1405.
to:
1st Lord
1st SL
DCNS
CSO 1st SL

The *Athenia's* chief radio officer, David Don, had sent his SOS in naval code and had some difficulty in getting the message through. Captain Cook then ordered him to send it in plain language. One of the first vessels to pick it up was *U30*, which had surfaced some distance away from the *Athenia*. When the news was brought to Lemp, and he realised what he had done, he is reported to have said, '*So eine Schweinerei! Warum fährt der aber auch adgeblendet?*' ('What a mess! But why was she blacked out?')

The first ship to respond to the stricken liner's distress calls was the Norwegian tanker *Knute Nelson*, at the time 40 miles to the south-west of the *Athenia*. The Swedish yacht *Southern Cross* responded shortly afterwards as did the American steamer *City of Flint*.

Winston Churchill had spent his first evening at the Admiralty being introduced to the senior officers who would serve under him. On his being given the news of the *Athenia's* plight, the destroyers *Electra*, *Escort* and *Fame* were detached from the Home Fleet, at sea west of the Hebrides, and ordered to her aid.

Just as the three destroyers worked up to full speed, the brightly lit *Knute Nelson* was approaching the scene of the disaster and the relieved survivors in the boats pulled towards her. Two and a half hours later the *Southern Cross*, once the property of Howard Hughes and then owned by the Swedish industrialist Axel Wenner-Gren, also ablaze with lights, hove into sight. Wenner-Gren, a friend and confidant of the Duke and Duchess of Windsor, had flirted with fascism during the 1930s and was in the process of abandoning Europe, which he believed doomed, for the United States.

One of the Athenia's *lifeboats alongside a destroyer.*
(TRUSTEES OF THE IMPERIAL WAR MUSEUM, LONDON)

Lifeboats filled with exhausted, seasick, injured and frozen survivors crowded round the two rescue ships. The body of an elderly woman who had died in one boat was tossed over the side to avoid upsetting other passengers. At around 0330 hours, the survivors in boat number 5A paid no heed to shouts from the *Knute Nelson's* deck to keep well clear until the last of a line of boats alongside her had been emptied. Ignoring also the advice of Able Seaman Harry Dillon, they secured alongside *Knute Nelson* oblivious to the danger posed by the proximity of the tanker's slowly revolving propeller.

In an astonishing lapse of seamanship Captain Anderssen of the *Knute Nelson* ordered his ship to full ahead without taking account of the effect that would have on the boats alongside, in particular 5A. In the lifeboat, survivors, some of whom had been offering up prayers of thanksgiving for their deliverance, looked on with horror as first the painter snapped, then the boat was drawn into the Norwegian's whirling propeller; 5A was smashed and the passengers were pitched, screaming, into the sea. Some managed to crawl back onto the lifeboat's upturned hull which was kept afloat by its buoyancy tanks. Others tried to hang onto the lifelines. The tanker's crew had managed to get their ship stopped and were pulling gasping people from the water but, in the dark, many drifted away and were lost.

The small group on and around the upturned lifeboat had to wait for daylight when they were picked up by HMS *Escort*. In the intervening hours, actress Judith Evelyn and her fiancé Andrew Allan watched as the bitter cold of the North Atlantic took its toll and, one by one, frozen people slipped away to die. Among the victims of the tragedy of 5A were Nancy Bishop whose calmness on the dining-room stairway had been so exemplary, Thornton Mustard and Revd William Allan, Andrew Allan's father.

A similar tragedy was taking place alongside the *Southern Cross*. A panic-stricken survivor in boat number 8 made a personal bid for safety and, in doing so, dragged the boat under the yacht's graceful counter. It capsized three times, throwing 50 people into the sea. Again, a number were drowned before they could be rescued by the crew of the *Southern Cross*.

Survivors in other boats looked on in horror as children drowned in front of them. Patricia Farrow watched a mother float past her boat with a crying baby in her arms. She said later, 'We tried to reach them but they disappeared before our eyes – the baby crying. God, it was awful.' Some hours later, a woman who had been plucked from the sea by the *Southern Cross* was seen to stand up and scream, 'My baby!' before throwing herself over the side.

Commander P. N. Walter in HMS *Fame* arrived at the scene at 0640 hours to find *Electra* and *Escort* already there. He signalled to the latter that he would carry out an anti-submarine sweep of the area. Fifteen minutes later he closed the derelict *Athenia*. Still afloat with a 30-degree list to port, she appeared deserted. In fact, one person was still alive aboard the stricken ship. Barnet Copland, on being picked up by HMS *Electra*, discovered that, in the chaotic evacuation, one woman passenger had been left behind. On the first night at sea, Mrs Rose Griffin of Toronto had fallen down a ladder. Unconscious and with a broken nose and a fractured pelvis, she was carried to the ship's sick-bay on B deck, and there she remained. In one of Electra's boats, Copland, Bo'sun William Harvey and Able Seaman MacLeod re-boarded the *Athenia* where they found Rose Griffin, still unconscious, in the partially flooded sick-bay. Less than 30 minutes after this small party left her, the *Athenia* slowly lifted her bows to the sky and sank stern-first.

Some 222 survivors had been picked up by *Southern Cross*. The *City of Flint* arrived on the scene at 0930 hours and Wenner-Gren transferred these people across to her before continuing on his way to Bermuda. Captain Gainard then turned his ship back westwards for Nova Scotia. A small white coffin was brought down the gangway when she docked at Halifax. It contained the body of little Margaret Hayworth who had died after briefly regaining consciousness in the lifeboat.

20

The *Knute Nelson* took 430 survivors, including Captain Cook, to the port of Galway in Eire where she arrived on the morning of Tuesday, 5 September. The hospitality given to the weeping, half-clothed, injured and burned survivors by the people of that small town was limitless.

Illustration of the international ramifications of the sinking, if it were needed, was provided by the arrival in Galway, as the *Knute Nelson* was unloading, of John Cudahy, the American Ambassador to Dublin. He was followed by Captain Kirk and Commander Hitchcock, respectively the American Naval Attache, and his assistant, at their London embassy. Cudahy's first, brief telegram to the State Department, giving details of their questioning of the passengers and crew, was sent that afternoon.

Winston Churchill had not been slow to realise the event's political significance either. During the previous afternoon he had exchanged signals with Lieutenant-Commander Buss in HMS *Electra* in which he attempted to identify how many Americans had died. Commander Walter in HMS *Fame* opened his report on the events surrounding the sinking with the words, 'In view of the probable political importance of the sinking of SS *Athenia*, I have the honour . . .'

Owing to early morning fog in the Clyde, *Electra* and *Escort* were diverted from their intended destination, Old Kilpatrick, to Greenock. They secured in Albert Harbour shortly before 0700 hours on Tuesday, 5 September. Unfortunately, no preparations had been made at Greenock to receive the survivors.

Over an hour after the destroyers arrived, Donald MacLean, Greenock's public assistance officer, received a telephone message which indicated that '. . . a large number of survivors of the *Athenia* had been deposited on the Albert Harbour from HMS *Electra* and *Escort* and that the large majority of them were scantily dressed and many also required hospital treatment. When I tell you that these people were being landed at the same pier as where a sugar boat was busily unloading and that there was no shelter or lavatory accommodation, you can understand the utter confusion that existed. I do think that the survivors should have been retained on board the rescue ships until some accommodation had been provided. As it was many of the dockers who were employed unloading the ship shared what food they had with some of the survivors.'

The women of Greenock rose to the occasion with a will, securing food and clothing for the survivors who, according to MacLean, were in an 'awful condition'.

Thirty-five survivors were taken to the Western Infirmary in Glasgow, two to Greenock Eye Infirmary and nine to the town's Royal Infirmary. There the hapless Rose Griffin died, bringing the final death toll to 93 passengers, of whom 69 were women and 16 were children. Fifty of the dead passengers were British, 30 were American, seven were Polish and four were of German extraction; 19 of the *Athenia's* crew were killed.

Greenock was left with a sizeable bill for the feeding and clothing of over 500 survivors for which a parsimonious Scottish Office showed a dogged reluctance to give recompense.

By the evening of 5 September, all the survivors had been lodged in Glasgow hotels. One young man was seen, after a 30-hour vigil, to rush from the crowd around the Central Hotel to embrace his mother. Mary Lenehan of Gairbraid Avenue, Maryhill, suffered a heart attack on hearing of the liner's sinking. She died a few hours later, unaware that her sons John and James were among the rescued.

At the onset of war Lord Provost Paddy Dollan had instituted a fund for the relief of distress caused by enemy action. Among the thousands of donations, large and small, forthcoming when news of the *Athenia* disaster reached Glasgow, were £1,000 from the Donaldson Line, £500 each from the Clyde Navigation Trust and Glasgow businessman Hugh Fraser, and £250 from Fairfield's, the shipyard where *Athenia* was built.

Again, John Colville, Secretary of State for Scotland and a member of the famous steel-making family, refused to countenance any assistance from the Exchequer for the destitute survivors. On Wednesday, 6 September, Dollan telegraphed Colville requesting assistance in the return of those landed at Galway to Glasgow, where many had relatives. Families split up in the confusion of abandoning ship would thus be reunited. This too was refused.

Dollan's telegram was sent after he and Jack, the 19-year-old son of American Ambassador Joe Kennedy, visited 150 American survivors staying at the Beresford Hotel in Sauchiehall Street. Amid stormy scenes, the future American President tried to reassure them that they would be safe from attack if they sailed for home in an American ship. Hardly surprisingly, the survivors were far from convinced, one man shouting at Jack Kennedy 'You can't trust the goddamned German Government. You can't trust the goddamned German submarines!'

Eight German-Jewish refugees were locked up in Barlinnie Prison for a week until their bona fides could be established. Fifty-six Polish and Czech refugees remained in the Roberts Hotel in Bath Street at the beginning of October 1939.

Despite the story having been pushed from the front pages by the invasion of Poland, it refused to go away entirely. At first the German Government truly believed their forces innocent and denied all responsibility. They responded to an Admiralty press release, issued early on 4 September, which stated that the *Athenia* had been torpedoed and that destroyers were on their way, by stating that it was 'an infamous, shameless lie, a criminal attempt to influence US opinion'.

Even after it became apparent that *U30* had fired the fatal torpedo, and with the world's press finding ready comparisons with the *Lusitania* disaster in the First World War, the Germans continued to deny responsibility. Increasingly desperate explanations were offered from Berlin. German sources were quoted, in *La Nation Belge* on 26 September, as saying that Churchill had ordered the *Athenia* sunk by a British submarine in order to sway opinion in America. These statements were dismissed in London as 'opportunist fabrications'.

The Germans were seemingly handed a propaganda gift in mid-October when a survivor, Illinois travel agent Gustav Andersen, filed an affidavit with the State Department stating that he had been told by Chief Officer Copland that there were 'plenty of guns' in the *Athenia's* hold which were destined for the coastal defences of Halifax and Quebec. He further alleged that members of the crew had confirmed this and that Copland had told him that the ship was to be fitted out as a commerce raider on her return to Britain. Copland's vehement denials of this arrant nonsense were not enough to stop isolationist senators in America from taking up Andersen's case.

Paul Ferdonnet, the French version of Lord Haw Haw, broadcast the story, with some added colour, from Stuttgart on 19 October. It appeared under banner headlines in the Italian *Gazetta del Popolo* on 21 October, and inflamed anti-British sentiment in South Africa when it was broadcast on *Zeesen*, the German propaganda station transmitted to Africa and Asia.

Percy Sillitoe, Glasgow's Chief Constable, was asked by MI5 to undertake a discreet investigation into Andersen's contacts in the city. It turned out that Andersen was an accredited agent for the Donaldson Line in the western states of America. Sillitoe discovered that he had a history of mental instability and had 'never lost his nervousness of disposition'. Assistant Purser Andrew Taylor reported that, when the torpedo struck, Andersen had immediately become hysterical and had to be helped to a lifeboat.

Amongst other things, it was discovered from Ross Kennedy, a reporter on the *Daily Express* who knew Andersen well, that he 'seemed inclined to favour the doctrines of Hitler'. While in Scotland prior to sailing in the *Athenia,* Andersen had visited Edinburgh and St Andrews where, according to Sillitoe, 'he was continually photographing places to which an ordinary citizen would be debarred access'. When the ship called at Liverpool on Saturday, 2 September, he was observed photographing the balloon barrage over the city.

In the early months of 1940, George Nugent, a Washington lawyer who had represented American passengers in the *Lusitania* case, lodged claims amounting to the then considerable sum of $700,000 against the Donaldson Line on behalf of American passengers. In the *Washington Post* of 4 March he averred that his evidence would 'stand pat on Churchill's charges of German

Fritz-Julius Lemp (right) and his officers on the bridge of U30.

guilt'. He added that 'the sympathies of most of my clients are with the Allies, but they feel that the Admiralty has been afforded ample opportunity to establish a case against the Germans, if there be one'.

Although President Roosevelt and the State Department had never really entertained any doubts as to what actually happened, it was not until 3 September 1940, exactly a year after the sinking and with the Battle of Britain at its height, that the *Washington Post* finally announced that the US Government favoured the British version of events. In Montreal, a month later, Fifth Engineer Thomas Hastie of the *Athenia* gave a statement before a US Court Commissioner which confirmed, once and for all, that a torpedo had caused the sinking. This left Nugent's case dead in the water.

In the early hours of 4 September 1939, 140 miles to the south-east of where rescue operations at the *Athenia* were still being carried out, Kapitanleutnant Franz in *U27* stopped, and fired on, SS *Blairbeg*. The *Blairbeg* escaped unharmed when Royal Navy destroyers came to her rescue.

Three days later, in a marked change of policy, Lemp in *U30* allowed the crew of the SS *Blairlogie* to take to the boats before he sank their ship. On the morning of 14 September he sighted the steamship *Fanad Head* bound for Belfast in the North West Approaches. Again, he surfaced and ordered the ship's crew into the boats before he sank her. The *Fanad Head*'s wireless operator had, however, sent out an SOS as soon as *U30* surfaced. This had been picked up by the aircraft carrier HMS *Ark Royal*, then on an anti-submarine sweep west of St Kilda with the 8th destroyer flotilla.

U30 had been at sea for over three weeks and was short of food supplies.

Having got the *Fanad Head*'s crew away from the ship, Lemp sent across a boarding party to take off some supplies and then sink the ship. Confusion over labels led to some delay and, while this was going on, three Sea Skuas of 803 Squadron in *Ark Royal* came to the scene and attacked the U-boat.

The first two Skuas crashed after dropping their little 30lb Cooper bombs far too low and blowing their own tails off. The observers of both aircraft were killed. The pilots survived to achieve the dubious distinction of becoming the Fleet Air Arm's first prisoners-of-war.

Meanwhile *U30* had dived in such a hurry that one of her crew was left on deck and the boarding party was still on the *Fanad Head*. The third Skua's bombs missed. Lemp surfaced to find one of his party aboard the *Fanad Head* had been wounded and that he had two prisoners. He was also given the alarming news that a destroyer was bearing down on the ship. Lemp hid his submarine from the oncoming destroyer behind the *Fanad Head*, while manoeuvring to sink her with a torpedo before going deep and escaping.

The surviving Sea Skua had hardly been recovered when *Ark Royal* herself came under attack. At 1507 hours Kapitanleutnant Gerhard Glattes in *U39* fired two torpedoes which exploded in the British ship's wake. The destroyers *Firedrake*, *Foxhound* and *Faulknor* immediately pounced on the U-boat after gaining Asdic* contact and, 40 minutes later, with the submarine leaking and filling with chlorine gas, Glattes had no alternative but to order his boat to the surface where he and his 42 crew surrendered after scuttling the submarine.

On 17 September, west of Ireland, Otto Schuhart in *U29* sank the aircraft carrier *Courageous*. Taking 519 of her crew with her, *Courageous*, an old converted battle-cruiser, went down in 15 minutes.

Gunfire from *U27* sank the trawlers *Arlita* and *Lord Minto* west of St Kilda on 18 September. *U27* was still off St Kilda on 20 September when she was sunk by the destroyers *Fortune* and *Forester*.

After suffering damage during the depth-charging which followed the sinking of the *Fanad Head,* Lemp took his battered boat to Iceland where he put his injured crewman ashore before sailing for home. He arrived at Wilhelmshaven on 27 September to a distinctly frosty welcome from his superiors, markedly different from that afforded to Otto Schuhart. *U30*'s log was hurriedly and crudely faked to conceal her true actions.

On one of his last patrols in command of *U30*, in August 1940, Lemp sank six ships. In November that year he commissioned the new type VIIC boat, *U110*, and was on his second patrol in her when he attacked convoy OB318 outbound from the Hebrides at around noon on Friday, 9 May 1941. The

* apparatus for detecting and locating a submarine or other underwater object by means of ultrasonic waves

U-boat was spotted and depth-charged to the surface by the corvette HMS *Aubretia*. When *U110* broke surface, her crew swarmed out on deck and leapt over the side as it appeared that the destroyer *Broadway* was about to ram. The U-boat had also come under withering fire from *Broadway* and another destroyer, HMS *Bulldog,* and Lemp's orders to scuttle were not properly carried out. Lemp himself appears to have been caught in the crossfire and killed while his crew were picked up by *Aubretia* and *Broadway* and quickly hustled below.

With her crew out of sight, a boarding party under the command of 20-year-old Sub-Lieutenant David Balme from HMS *Bulldog* was put aboard the deserted submarine. In addition to what Balme euphemistically described as 'the usual art studies', a treasure trove of secret documents was found. To the delight of the Admiralty, Telegraphist Allan Long discovered a naval 'Enigma' coding machine in the radio room along with the daily keys valid until the end of June 1941. These were to prove of vital importance in the pursuit and eventual destruction of the German battleship *Bismarck* in May 1941.

On 27 September 1939, just as Fritz-Julius Lemp brought his battered command back to Wilhelmshaven, Bellochantuy Hotel in Kintyre was crowded with those who had come from as far away as Surrey, seeking sanctuary from the expected bombing. Large numbers of the well-heeled and, in particular, the elderly took refuge in Scottish hotels which were not slow to catch on to the late season bonanza this represented. Discreetly anodyne advertisements offered, as at Aviemore Hotel in June 1940, 'a haven of peace and rest. Here, among the tonic air of the pinewoods, you will find a sanctuary far removed from the rush and strain of the outside world'. These establishments were scathingly referred to at the time as 'funk-holes'.

Shortly after 1100 hours that September morning, the destroyer *Valorous* and the sloop *Hastings* were attacked by enemy aircraft near May Island at the entrance to the Forth. At least one particularly courageous Luftwaffe pilot appears to have made his way to the west coast in search of shipping targets. For some unknown reason the German aircrew sprayed Bellochantuy Hotel with machine-gun fire, making it the first building in Britain damaged by enemy action during the Second World War. A window was broken and the roof of a garage damaged in the first attack which took place as children played on the nearby beach. The aircraft returned 15 minutes later and a further three bursts of fire did more damage to the roof. Nobody was injured in either attack. Police took spent bullets, found outside the front door, away for examination.

Chapter Two

Measures to Meet an Airborne or Seaborne Invasion

In no respect was Britain as a whole, and Scotland in particular, less prepared for war than in the field of Air-Raid Precautions. The civil defence services, whose job it was to deal with the effects of bombing, were hopelessly ill-trained, ill-equipped and hamstrung by both public apathy and the petty jealousies of their political masters. This situation did not improve to any measurable degree in Scotland until the danger of attack was long past.

At the end of 1935, local authorities considered Scottish Office circular no. 3026, which required them to take the first tentative steps on ARP provision. The response from most authorities was to do precisely nothing. Labour-controlled councils in particular took the view, in line with party policy, that preparations for war would inevitably lead to war.

George Lansbury, the Labour leader, declared at the party conference in October 1935 that 'those who take the sword shall perish by the sword'. This strongly pacifist view was echoed by much of the party in Scotland including David Kirkwood, Clydebank's MP, who stated that he was 'all out for peace in the real sense and would not send a Clydebank boy to war on any consideration. No war for me under any circumstances.'

An electorate with bitter memories of the terrible cost of the 1914-18 War was only too willing to agree. Sadly, the idealism of Lansbury, Kirkwood and others took no account of the fact that, with the advent of long-range bombers, war could no longer be kept at arm's length.

Glasgow Corporation appointed its ARP committee in November 1936. The Corporation promptly refused its new committee free use of the city's halls for lectures by ARP and Red Cross instructors. Only in late 1937, when compelled by the Scottish Office, did most authorities fall into line. Some, including, ironically, Clydebank Town Council, continued to pay little more than lip service to the issue until the Munich Crisis erupted at the end of 1938.

Woefully inadequate intelligence combined with muddle-headed thinking by British military strategists to produce wildly unrealistic over-estimates of the strength and capabilities of the Luftwaffe. It was generally believed that the declaration of war would be followed, within hours, by massive air-raids and that much of Scotland would be laid to waste before a month was out. It was said that the enemy bombers would roam, unmolested, in Scottish skies, dropping bombs and spreading clouds of poison gas at will. The Scottish Home and Health Department sent coded telegrams to hospital officers requesting that, by the end of the first week of war, 12,000 beds should be cleared to accept air-raid casualties. Thousands of extra stretchers were provided.

An already jittery public had their fears heightened by the film 'Things to Come', H. G. Wells' view of the probable nature of air-raids. This fiction was widely taken too much to heart and popular support for the appeasement policies of Neville Chamberlain grew.

Expenditure on ARP in Glasgow in the year to 31 May 1939 was a mere £4,617 and had actually dropped in early 1939, following the Munich Agreement. In comparison, the city's parks budget during the same period was £18,500. Forecast expenditure on ARP for the period 1939-40 was almost £30,000, more than two-thirds of which would, in any case, be met by a government grant. This sum was required to cover the cost of training 11,412 mainly volunteer air-raid wardens, building shelters and equipping both first-aid parties and the report and control network.

Just one of the myriad problems about which the City Corporation did little or nothing, until it was too late, was the blackout of tenement stair lighting. In 1939 there were an estimated 94,000 close lamps in the city and confusion reigned over whether they should be screened, or blacked out entirely. Steel sheeting, bought at the time of Munich with the intention of making shades, lay untouched and rusting in a Lighting Department store.

Scottish Regional Civil Defence headquarters in Edinburgh stated, on the day war broke out, that Glasgow's close lights should be left on and windows blacked out. The Corporation pointed out that around 3,300 closes in the city had no windows, merely roof lights which would, therefore, have to be painted over. As the stair lighting only came on with the street lighting, the Corporation would be forced to leave street lighting burning permanently over wide areas of the city. Further confusion arose over gas-lit closes.

One of the LOWINs (Local War Instructions) received by Renfrewshire County Council's emergency committee immediately prior to the outbreak of war stated that all ARP personnel should be called out immediately. Members baulked at the prospect when it was pointed out to them that this would cost £15,000 per week. It took the committee almost a week to discover that these extra wages would be met by the Exchequer, not least because, rather than pick up the telephone, the County Clerk insisted on communicating by telegram with Western District Civil Defence headquarters in Glasgow. Chief Constable and Head Warden John Robertson reported that many volunteer ARP personnel, called out in addition to having to do their own jobs, had reached the stage of complete exhaustion by 11 September.

That the whole organisation had been hurriedly put together, without much thought as to how it would function, can be seen from the bitter rows which developed within days of the start of the war. Nobody had any clear idea of their own responsibilities, or to whom they were, in turn, responsible. Relations between the police and local ARP controllers, appointed for no other reason than that they were baillies, quickly deteriorated. John Robertson and the Renfrew County ARP controller, Major Michie, had a particularly acrimonious exchange towards the end of October.

Another bone of contention arose within days of the outbreak of war when local controllers in Renfrewshire discovered that they were expected both to assume considerable responsibility and to keep long hours without being paid. Many resigned, the first to do so being Provost Donald of Barrhead on 9 September 1939. Later, they were offered £3 per week – though this was only the same wage as that of full-time auxiliary firemen, whom they were expected, in part at least, to control.

The Auxiliary Fire Service (AFS) was formed largely by volunteers manning trailer pumps. It had the task of augmenting the cover provided by full-time fire services. The Renfrewshire Firemasters were quick to point out that, even if the other civil defence services were not, all of their full-time and volunteer personnel were on stand-by at the outbreak of war. All was not, however, quite as it appeared.

Four lightweight trailer pumps had been provided to cover the Giffnock Police district. These were stationed at Anderson's Garage in Newton Mearns, Eastwood Toll Garage, Linn Park Garage and Arundel School in Clarkston. Four full-time and 13 part-time AFS men were stationed at Newton Mearns. Bridge of Weir AFS station had its full complement of personnel – but no equipment. The large Coventry-Climax trailer pump sent to cover Gourock, Inverkip and Wemyss Bay had arrived without any fittings, though one old hose had been discovered in a shed.

Renfrewshire Councillors were somewhat taken aback to be told, on 15 September 1939, that the Army Council had requested the release of Royal Engineers from bomb disposal work. Regional Civil Defence headquarters suggested that an appeal should be launched for volunteers to be specially trained to fulfil this role. Giffnock Cleansing Superintendent James McMillan,

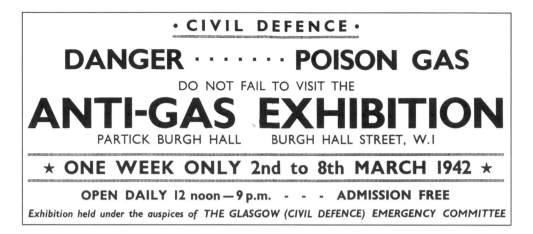

and Thomas Marshall, the Roads Surveyor at the Hurlet, volunteered along with four policemen. Their training course in bomb disposal was to last, in total, six hours. Fortunately for them at least, the Army Council had changed its mind by October.

Despite the perceived threat of immediate heavy raids, work on the construction of the Renfrewshire County Report and Control Centre – vital if there was to be any hope of coping with air-raids – was not authorised until the war was more than two weeks old. It was not completed until the end of January 1940.

The Council had also been somewhat less than diligent in the building of shelters, and most of those that were built proved to be inadequate. The first approval for the strengthening of closes in Renfrew, Port Glasgow and Gourock was only given at the end of September 1939. Shelters constructed at Woodhall in Port Glasgow were found to have been put up the wrong way round, with their doors opening directly on to the busy main road to Glasgow. Sub-standard shelters were also to be found in Maryhill, Lochwinnoch, Greenock and Bishopbriggs, many of which had been constructed by corrupt building firms.

Shelter provision was, at best, patchy. In October 1940 Renfrewshire County Council agreed to build shelters for just 20 per cent of those entitled to free shelters in Barrhead, Elderslie, Johnstone and Linwood. To qualify for a free shelter, a household had to have an income of less than £250 per annum.

Shelter provision in Port Glasgow was particularly poor, largely due to the Town Council having dithered between the strutting of closes (by far the cheapest method), the building of concrete surface shelters and the digging of deep tunnels. With regard to the latter, and even assuming that the plant and labour had been available, they would still have taken more than two years to construct. The diligence with which Port Glasgow Town Council applied themselves to shelter building after bombs fell on the town in May 1941 was widely commented on.

It was decided that Renfrewshire schoolchildren who could reach home in 15 minutes were to be sent there directly on the alert. This, however, completely contradicted the orders given to wardens, namely that they should clear the streets immediately on the sirens being sounded.

As late as March 1941, a mere ten days before the first of the heavy raids on Clydeside, the air of unreality persisted. There was still an unwillingness to take the issue of school shelters seriously. With reference to Inchinnan School, the Controller indicated that 'some of the public shelter provision now in the school *might* [author's italics] be available for the children'. All over Glasgow, carefully tended back-court flower-beds were dug up to take Anderson shelters and baffle walls were being erected across close mouths.

Vandalism of public shelters had become a particularly serious problem in the city by mid-1942. Regional Civil Defence Commissioner, Lord Rosebery, wrote that, 'In spite of numerous prosecutions for wilful damage to shelters, offences have continued over a long period. It is estimated that over 40 per cent of public surface shelters have suffered damage to fittings.' Newly replaced fittings such as doors, seating, lights and sanitary equipment were being stolen, damaged or destroyed.

To serve its population of 150,000, Renfrewshire established 13 first-aid posts at the outbreak of war which were manned by 116 paid personnel and 1,000 volunteers. Some 34 ambulances, seven specially converted buses and 200 cars were available for the transport of casualties. The vehicles serving Barrhead were said to be in particularly poor condition.

In Ayrshire, a converted bus and 11 cars with trailers were stationed at Pringle's Garage in Saltcoats and four casualty-carrying vans were kept in Allan's Garage, Main Street, Prestwick. A first-aid post was set up in the *Galloway News* building in Castle Douglas.

In August 1939, with war imminent and in anticipation of 1,500 fatalities from its first air-raid, Glasgow took urgent steps to increase its mortuary provision. The Kelvin Hall, Dennistoun Palais and part of Crossmyloof Ice-rink in Titwood Road were earmarked for the purpose. Around 500 cubicles were built in the Kelvin Hall, though this had to be given up in 1940 when it was turned over to the manufacture of barrage balloons. Dennistoun Palais was found to be unsuitable and Gavin McArthur, the city's ARP co-ordinating officer, requisitioned the area under the Barrowland Ballroom, next to the market. Some 65 cubicles were built and equipped with slabs. The Barrowland mortuary was never used, though considerable sums in compensation were handed over to the owners of the ballroom. Corporation officials, inspecting the mortuary after the heavy raids of mid-1941, were disconcerted to find that it had been stripped of its valuable fittings and was being used as a store for the market traders. There were also clear indications that horses had been stabled there.

Other, smaller, mortuaries were dotted around the city. These included one in a lock-up in Church Street, Johnstone. Another, in a hall next to the post office at Newton Mearns, was equipped with shrouds for 42 bodies. The Scottish Office set rates of payment for the handling of bodies at five shillings (25p) per attendant for the first three bodies. For each additional body, the mortuary attendant would be paid one shilling (5p). The owners of vehicles used to transport bodies were paid five shillings per hour.

The needs of the hour notwithstanding, local authorities proved incapable of shaking off the stultifying bureaucracy which had bedevilled their activities in peace-time. A number of fire appliances were damaged by shrapnel in the raids on Greenock. Before he could go ahead with repairs costing little more than £10, the West Renfrewshire Firemaster had to write to the County Council. His letter had then to be submitted to Council and minuted, whereupon a written reply authorising the repairs was then sent. During all this time, valuable fire appliances were out of action.

Permission to carry out a repair, costing just £12, to the siren at Giffnock Police Station had to be sought of both the County Council and the civil defence authorities in Glasgow. Lengthy deliberations were conducted on the advisability of buying groundsheets to protect bicycles used by boy messengers. Another protracted debate was conducted on whether the light switches in shelters should be clearly marked 'ON' and 'OFF'.

In Glasgow, Kelvinside wardens met on 10 August 1939 to discuss celebrating the forthcoming opening of their new Ward Headquarters at 1 Crown Avenue. Ever conscious of their social standing, it was suggested that, 'as we in Kelvinside have never taken part in the social side, or joined the Wardens' Association, we might make an exception on this auspicious occasion, the opening of our new headquarters, and have a social evening.' Catering was to be provided for 100 invited guests. Unfortunately, the date chosen was Saturday, 9 September 1939, six days after the outbreak of war. The first social evening of whist and dancing was not held at Crown Gardens until the end of May 1942.

A Kelvinside GP, Dr Ford Robertson, devised a new form of anti-gas training, rather grandly dubbed the 'Kelvinside Graphic Method of ARP Exercises'. According to Head Warden George Millar, high officials in Glasgow to whom it was demonstrated were suitably impressed. He wrote that 'It is expected that this method will become universal throughout the country.' Home Office ARP training officers at the Government Anti-Gas School at Easingwold near York appear to have been less impressed; they rejected Dr Robertson's method as being far too complex.

A Glasgow ARP Rescue Service Tender. It was the serious deficiencies in this service which aroused the greatest public disquiet during the Clydeside raids.
(GLASGOW MUSEUMS: THE MUSEUM OF TRANSPORT)

Regular exercises were held during which it was noted that civil defence personnel tended to stand around rather than take cover. This, it was said, 'was probably due to their anxiety to see what is happening'. To the intense chagrin of the army, wardens who had closed streets during exercises, because of supposed unexploded bombs, refused to allow military convoys through their roadblocks. Written orders were issued to the effect that 'It is not the responsibility of civil defence to interfere with any military movement.' It appears that during later combined exercises the army got their revenge as further orders had to be issued restraining them from 'appropriating' fire engines. It was pointed out that they might be needed for a real fire.

Shortages of adequately trained, young and active personnel, largely due to the demands of industry and recruitment into the forces, plagued the civil defence services during the war. MAGNA, or Mutual Aid Good Neighbour Association parties, were formed by merging stair wardens, shelter marshals and fire-fighting parties, and encouraging greater co-operation from local residents. By the time of the heavy raids of March 1941, over 9,000 people in the north-west of the city were involved in some capacity.

Further pressures on the available personnel were created following a particularly severe fire raid on London at the end of December 1940. This took place on a Sunday night when all the commercial premises were locked and the fires were able to spread almost unchecked. It resulted in the long overdue introduction of compulsory firewatching at offices and factories for all able-bodied men under 63 years and women aged 45 or under. There was the somewhat pious hope that this would persuade workers to carry on after the alert, secure in the knowledge that a firewatcher was on the factory roof. Two teachers were seconded to conduct firewatcher training in Glasgow in October 1940, but bureaucratic delays meant that the scheme did not come into operation until after the heavy raids had passed. It was therefore of little use.

The one aspect of civil defence which caused the greatest public furore in Glasgow was the inadequacy of the city's rescue service. There was a complete absence of competent supervision and, according to a police report on one incident, workers standing idly around while it was known that people were still alive and trapped, 'could be heard saying quite openly that everyone was in charge'. The report continues: 'Although a certain enthusiasm and drive was necessary to save life, there was none, and most of them lolled about as before without any apparent enthusiasm on the part of the leader.'

Deputy Regional Civil Defence Commissioner, Councillor William Quin, commented that rescue workers at one incident were 'haphazard, casual and slow'. The recovery of live casualties a week later lent weight to his criticism.

Although the performance of some of the individuals concerned was undoubtedly poor, there were many instances of extraordinary gallantry. The problems with the service stemmed from the fact that it was lacking in both funds and manpower. The Corporation had failed not only to purchase much of the heavy equipment required, but also omitted either to properly train existing staff or to recruit the 500 part-time staff required to bring the service up to the minimum recommended level. In September 1941, six months after these deficiencies had become horribly apparent, Regional Civil Defence Commissioner Lord Rosebery noted that 'The Corporation seem to have adopted a delaying policy and, by the end of this month, have still not agreed to take any definite action to improve this service on the lines recommended.'

The essential problem with civil defence was that it was organised along local authority lines and was, therefore, fragmentary and largely unco-ordinated. Standards of personnel, training and equipment varied considerably. In addition, councils frequently found themselves unable to cope with the conflicting demands of government departments.

Above all, wooden-headed councillors failed to comprehend that the Luftwaffe was not about to respect municipal boundaries. Petty political jealousies were allowed to stand in the way of proper co-ordination: Barrhead and Gourock Town Councils refused to co-operate with Renfrewshire County Council on mortuary provision; Ayr Town Council resolutely refused to maintain its scheme on anything other than a part-time, voluntary basis; on being asked to make available 24-hour emergency ration packs for civil defence personnel, the deputy ARP controller for Motherwell refused unless the cost was met by the Exchequer; and Clydebank's fierce independence from

Glasgow was responsible, at least in part, for some of the lapses which occurred during the heavy raids on that town.

Despite all the pre-war attempts at rationalisation, in September 1939, each of Scotland's 33 counties and 191 burghs still had its own fire brigade. These were not amalgamated into the National Fire Service until August 1941, a move which would eventually lead to the long overdue standardisation of fittings between the various brigades. The real drive towards the proper national co-ordination of civil defence did not start until October 1941. By then, however, the serious bombing was over. It was all too late.

The civil defence services could do nothing until the bombs had been dropped: it was the job of the anti-aircraft defences to deter enemy aircraft from attacking. Radar cover on the west coast was almost non-existent in 1941. Observer Corps posts at Fort Augustus, Salen, Alexandria, Brodick, Strathaven, Castle Douglas and on the roof of the J. P. Coates Factory in Glasgow were among those providing vital information for the RAF.

Fighter squadrons were controlled from the operations room at Rosemount on the Prestwick to Kilmarnock road. First to occupy the new fighter station at RAF Ayr, in April 1941, were the Spitfires of 602 (City of Glasgow) Squadron. Both the Hurricanes of 43 Squadron and 141 Squadron's Defiant and Beaufighter night-fighters operated from Ayr during that summer.

Barrage balloons were sent up around important factories, power stations and the like, to discourage more accurate, low-level bombing. When the RAF arrived to set up a balloon site on Glasgow University playing fields, next to the vitally important Barr and Stroud works in Anniesland, they were astonished to be given their marching orders by the University authorities who did not wish to see their precious pitches damaged.

Balloons were forever breaking loose, particularly in bad weather. Two balloons on the site next to Cowal Street Gas-works in Maryhill were struck by lightning on the night of Friday, 1 November 1940. They trailed burning fabric across the city towards Pinkston Power Station. Many locals thought the burning fragments were burning aircraft about to crash and armed parties combed the area looking for enemy pilots. That same night, another balloon dragged its heavy cables across Pollokshields, bringing down a chimney at 5 Terregles Avenue, severing electricity and telephone cables in Pollokshaws Road and Victoria Road, and damaging the roof of Johnstone's Garage in Garturk Street.

On another occasion, a shaken Giffnock resident watched pieces of fabric from a destroyed balloon drifting down over the South Side and was convinced that he was witnessing the invasion. His telephone report resulted in a heavily armed party of police and soldiers searching Maxwell Park for enemy parachutists.

On 26 June 1940, 321 Heavy Anti-Aircraft Battery, Royal Artillery, took

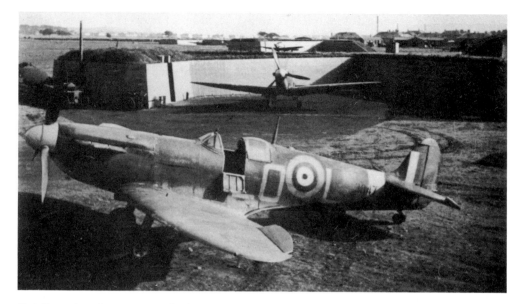

Spitfire IIAs of 602 (City of Glasgow) Squadron at RAF Ayr in the spring of 1941. The squadron returned from distinguished front-line service in the Battle of Britain, initially to Prestwick in mid December 1940, thence to the newly opened airfield at Ayr in April 1941.
(602 SQUADRON ARCHIVES)

up positions at Dykebarhill, Langbank, Linwood and Carmunnock. Only the Dykebarhill site was fully equipped; Linwood and Carmunnock had no guns at all and those at Langbank had arrived without vital equipment. When the first supply of ammunition arrived for Langbank, it was found to be badly rusted and some gun parts did not appear for over a month. In addition, much of the Battery's domestic equipment was found to have been sent, in error, to the Orkney Islands.

GSG3 site at Mid Netherton Farm, Carmunnock, had still not received its armament allocation at the beginning of August 1940. Telegraph poles masqueraded as guns until 5 October, when four 3.7" guns arrived at Cathcart Station for the site.

Trouble for 321 Battery was far from over. As Major Lewer, the Battery commander, recorded wrily, a court of enquiry was held at the end of July 1940, 'to enquire into a damaged cow, run into by the hired lorry of this battery'. No sooner had this crisis blown over than, on 24 August, 32 cases of acute diarrhoea were reported at Dykebarhill. This was initially thought to be due to contaminated milk, and, by the following morning, 50 men at the site were incapacitated. The site was placed in quarantine and the cooks instructed to wash their clothes every day.

A medical officer's inspection of the site revealed that the kitchen was full of flies and that there was a pool of swill on the ground outside. The 'dry bucket' latrines were full to overflowing, and many had broken seats. The latrine at another site was found to be an old workman's brazier, sunk into the ground, which was apparently never emptied.

Heavy rain caused the magazine at Langbank site to flood to such an extent that the fire brigade had to be summoned to pump it out. It was found that the contractors employed to build the site had left the main drain 35 feet short and simply blanked off the end.

Major Lewer records one incident which demonstrates that, even with the invasion threat at its height, there were still those in the Army desperately clinging to pre-war bureacratic attitudes. A special new 'Flowrex' oil was required for the machine fuse setters fitted to the battery's guns, without which they could not be used. Lewer telephoned a request for the oil to the Ordnance Corps depot at Bishopbriggs. The orderly officer there was absent but the foreman assured Lewer that two gallons of the oil were available for collection. A truck left for the depot immediately, only to return without the oil. The orderly officer at Bishopbriggs was finally tracked down the following morning. He informed Lewer that he was not going to accept chits from a quartermaster sergeant and that he was reporting the matter to headquarters. Patiently, Lewer said that he could report the matter to whomsoever he liked, but would he please send the oil right away as there was a war to get on with.

The dispersal of the Home Fleet from Scapa Flow to Loch Ewe and the Clyde at the end of October 1939 led to reinforcement of the Clyde Anchorages anti-aircraft layout. Eight guns from the Glasgow defences were brought west, along with 16 from Edinburgh and Rosyth, bringing the total establishment around the Tail o' the Bank to 40 3.7" static guns. This left just eight guns to cover Glasgow.

The redeployment of the guns was set to take place at first light on 19 October 1939. It soon degenerated into chaos owing to what one officer termed 'numerous breakdowns of gun-towing vehicles, due principally to the fact that they were a scrap lot collected at short notice from a variety of sources. Nearly all of them were suffering from a lack of maintenance.' There was also a lack of trained drivers. The shortage of daylight that winter day and the early blackout caused problems, as did the fact that most of the tracks to the gunsites were quickly churned into a sea of mud.

Gun Operations Room in Glasgow, after a brief period at 29 West George Street, was moved to Aikenhead House, Kings Park. Just some of the gunsites established around the city were those at Cardross, Kilcreggan, Irvine, Paisley, Hamilton, Blackhill, Uddingston, Lennoxtown, Garscadden, Clydebank, Old Kilpatrick and Dumbarton. Each co-operated with nearby searchlight batteries, such as 57 Searchlight Regiment which was deployed around Old Kilpatrick, Clydebank and Yoker. During the two nights of heavy raids on Clydeside in March 1941, Carmunnock site fired 321 rounds and Dykebarhill site 671.

Uppermost in the mind of the Admiralty in 1939 was the perceived need to keep Home Fleet movements away from prying eyes. To do so, they planned, in conjunction with MI5, to create two 'protected areas', the first of which covered the Orkney and Shetland Islands. The second included all of the mainland north and west of the Caledonian Canal, the Burgh of Inverness and the Western Isles.

The plans drawn up by Henry Waring of MI5 involved the setting up of control points at Fort William, Tobermory, Corran Ferry, Fort Augustus and the Kyle of Lochalsh, at each of which three MI5 local security officers were to be stationed. Further assistance was to be provided by local police, hotel managers and civilians who were to act as informants reporting on any suspicious characters.

Following the sinking of the *Royal Oak* and in an effort to drum up some enthusiasm for the scheme, Brigadier Eric Holt-Wilson, the Deputy Director of MI5, convened a meeting at the War Office on 25 October 1939 with representatives of the Scottish Office and Scottish Command. It was agreed that commandants should be appointed for each protected area and that they should be 'local gentlemen of considerable county standing'.

The regulations covering Orkney and Shetland came into force on 1 December 1939. The scheme for the mainland and Western Isles met with strong resistance from the Scottish Office, who could clearly see that it was unworkable and that it had been devised by people with little knowledge of the area other than that gained from looking at a map.

MI5's original plan stated that permits required to enter the protected area would be issued in London and Inverness. Wearily, a Scottish Office official pointed out that, as Inverness was itself a protected area, presumably all applications for permits would have to be sent by post. Military Permit Offices were then opened in Edinburgh and in the Broomielaw, Glasgow.

In November 1939, with the mainland scheme still not in operation and the Scottish Office continuing to drag its heels, MI5 sought War Office approval to have the regulations back-dated to the day war broke out. Tiring of the whole business, the Scottish Office pointed out that, technically, this would mean that thousands of people, including hundreds of evacuees, would have committed offences, some of them many times over.

War Minister Oliver Stanley signed the Defence Regulation which enforced the mainland scheme on 26 February 1940. Within three months, events in Norway and France were to make the whole thing obsolete.

On 13 July 1940 Brigadier Witts, the officer in charge of Glasgow Area

The Loch Lomond Motor Boat Patrol in August 1940. Manned by naval and military personnel, and fitted with Lewis guns, these launches were expected to give enemy seaplanes attempting to land troops on the loch 'a warm reception'. The launch on the right sports a sprig of lucky white heather.
(TRUSTEES OF THE IMPERIAL WAR MUSEUM, LONDON)

Command, wrote to local authorities in the area, to say that '. . . every village and town must be made capable of defence, and the Government have appealed to the public to offer voluntary labour to make this possible. We want to press forward with roadblocks, defence works, trenches and the immobilisation of possible landing grounds. Any works that you can put in hand will add to the protection of the country and you have my full authority to proceed with the utmost possible speed . . . I beg you to leave nothing undone.'

This letter did not go down well with authorities already trying desperately to cope with the conflicting demands of both civil and military defence. Frenzied anti-invasion preparations had begun some weeks before, after the defeat of France and Norway, when steps were taken to identify places where enemy gliders and aircraft might land. In general, the flatter country south of the Clyde was seen as being at the greatest risk. Straight stretches of road, at least 600 yards long and free of obstructions, were seen as particularly vulnerable. Stout poles were erected on either side of the A8 east of Red Smithy and along the A77 south of the Malletsheugh Inn.

Improvisation on such a grand scale as that surrounding the construction of defences in the summer of 1940 inevitably led to some spectacular misunderstandings. The confusions and contradictions which arose out of the construction of roadblocks are a prime example. At first steam-rollers and old buses or lorries were placed on the roadside at selected points, ready to be pushed across the road should the worst happen. These were replaced by more permanent brick and concrete structures, the recommended design of which was changed no less than four times during the months of May and June 1940. It was discovered that the blocks, as originally constructed with 11-foot echeloned gaps, were too narrow.

In an effort to halt the chaos, Colonel Norman Campbell, Officer Commanding Clyde sub-area, ordered that work on permanent roadblocks should cease on 18 June 1940. This was countermanded less than two weeks later when Scottish Command issued Instruction no. 33 entitled 'Measures to meet an Airborne or Seaborne Invasion'. According to this, every town and village was to make itself into a defended locality by building permanent roadblocks. These were to be constructed close to houses from where Molotov Cocktails, which people were being encouraged to manufacture at home, could be thrown. There were numerous cases where zeal triumphed over common sense, though an appeal for volunteers to help build anti-invasion defences in Renfrewshire brought forth a total of just three names.

A list of 'key points' to be defended against sabotage was drawn up which, by 1943, had grown to 150 different locations in Glasgow alone. Among them were important factories, shipyards, public utilities, the Post Office Wireless Station at Pinkston and, for some reason, the Acme Tea Chest Company at Polmadie. Dobbie McInnes, the instrument manufacturers, were somewhat surprised to discover that their office in Bothwell Street was designated a key point while their factory in Broomloan Road, in the city's Govan district, was not.

The first test for the Home Guard in the west of Scotland came early on Wednesday, 14 August 1940, and was obligingly provided by the Germans. Just after midnight a single enemy aircraft was reported over Lochwinnoch. It flew north to Dumbarton before returning south over Johnstone and was finally plotted over Galston at 0028 hours. Almost immediately, reports began to come in from Home Guard units that parachutists had landed on Eaglesham Moor, on open country in Ayrshire and near Castle Douglas. As one officer noted, 'Subsequent action by various units left something to be desired.' Garrison troops in Renfrewshire were the 24th Polish Lancers and their reaction to the incident was described by one observer as being 'too keen'.

The plane had dropped parachutes carrying cases of maps, wireless transmitters and various instructions to imaginary agents. According to the German High Command war diary, 'We dropped pack assemblies in order to feign a parachute landing, which caused great excitement in the British press.' Hysteria about the existence of a widespread fifth column reached fever pitch.

German efforts at espionage directed through the west coast of Scotland were, in fact, nothing if not hopelessly inept. Alphonse Timmerman, a Belgian merchant seaman posing as a refugee, landed from the Glen Line steamer *Ulea* at Rothesay Dock, Clydebank, on 1 September 1941. His story was that he had escaped across France to Spain, where he had been briefly interned, before securing passage on the *Ulea* from Gibraltar. His wallet was found to contain a considerable sum of money and an envelope discovered in his pocket held secret writing materials. Timmerman was hanged in Wandsworth Prison on 7 July 1942.

Another Belgian, Franciscus Johannes Winter, arrived by sea on 31 July 1942, this time at Gourock on the SS *Llanstephan Castle*. Like Timmerman before him, Winter was taken to the MI5 interrogation centre at the Royal Victoria Patriotic School in London where, for three months, he stuck to his story that he wished to join the Free Belgian Forces. His story was not believed and, eventually, he admitted that he had been recruited by Abwehr, the German secret service, to report on shipping movements. He was executed at Wandsworth on 26 January 1943.

John Francis O'Reilly, an Irishman captured after the German invasion of the Channel Islands, was parachuted into County Clare on 16 December 1943. His instructions were to make his way across the Irish Sea to Glasgow and foment anti-war sentiments among members of the Independent Labour Party and the Scottish National Party. He was arrested by the Garda shortly after landing and spent the rest of the war in prison.

The identity of a Free French naval officer arrested at Greenock after reputedly passing information on shipping to the collaborationist Vichy government remains a mystery.

The invasion warning code word 'Cromwell' was issued, by mistake, in Scotland on 7 September 1940. Church bells, the public invasion warning, were rung in Glasgow and armed guards appeared everywhere. By 0930 hours the following morning Dunbartonshire Home Guard reported that they had allowed 1,835 people not carrying identity cards to pass through their roadblocks.

At 2309 hours on Saturday, 10 May 1941, ploughman David Maclean heard a loud crash and rushed out of his cottage behind Floors Farm near Eaglesham to find a parachutist drifting down in the moonlight. The parachutist's aircraft had crossed the east coast near Durham, flown north-west to the Firth of Clyde, passing over West Kilbride at rooftop height. It went briefly out to sea and dropped an auxiliary fuel tank before turning back inland towards Glasgow. A Defiant night-fighter sent up from Prestwick failed to intercept it.

Watching the raider's progress on the plot at 34 Group, Royal Observer Corps Centre in New Temperance House, Pitt Street, Glasgow, was Major Graham Donald. Just after 2305 hours, post 34/H2 next to North Kirkton Moor Farm, Eaglesham, called in to say that 'One man has just baled out and looks like landing safely.' This was followed almost immediately by another call which stated that 'The plane has come down out of control and crashed in flames.' The aircraft, correctly identified by the Observer Corps as an ME110 fighter/bomber, had come down in a field at Bonnyton Farm beside the Humbie Road between Newton Mearns and Eaglesham.

After calling out the Home Guard, Major Donald set out to search for the wreckage and the pilot, saying, 'If they can't catch an ME110 with a Defiant, I am now going to pick up the bits with a Vauxhall!' Having examined the still smouldering wreck, he caught up with its pilot at the Home Guard company headquarters in Hawthorn Road, Busby, and was immediately struck by the strong resemblance he bore to the Deputy Führer of the Third Reich. When the prisoner asserted that he had a message for the Duke of Hamilton, Donald was convinced that he was talking to Rudolf Hess.

Hess was taken from Busby to the Home Guard headquarters at the Scout Hall in Florence Drive, Giffnock. At 0005 hours on the Sunday morning, Giffnock Home Guard telephoned Lieutenant Cowie, 14th Argyll and Sutherland Highlanders, at Paisley, to ask for what they termed 'disposal instructions' for their prisoner. Cowie contacted Captain Brunton, the Duty Officer, Clyde sub-area, and at 0110 hours Lieutenant F. E. Whitby of the 11th Cameronians was ordered to Giffnock to convey the prisoner, whose true identity was still unknown to the Army, to Maryhill Barracks. They arrived at Maryhill around 0230 hours.

Returning to Pitt Street, Donald used the Observer Corps teller line to Turnhouse, where the Duke of Hamilton was serving as Station Commander, to inform the Duty Controller of his belief that Rudolf Hess was in Glasgow. His report was greeted with incredulity and Hamilton did not see, and identify, Hess until 1000 hours the following morning.

Hess was moved that Sunday afternoon, in an ambulance, to the military hospital at Buchanan Castle near Drymen. Three buses were laid on to carry troops to 'protect' him during his stay there.

Reaction to Hess's arrival in Scotland was mixed. There were many who wanted to parachute him straight back into Germany. One woman, somewhat excited at the news, informed her husband that Hess had come to see Jimmy Maxton, the veteran socialist MP. Among the wilder rumours circulating in Glasgow was one which averred that Hess had been on his way to start a revolt in Ireland.

An impressive display of force from a patrol of Dunbartonshire Home Guard in June 1940.
(TRUSTEES OF THE IMPERIAL WAR MUSEUM, LONDON)

The truth about the Deputy Führer's mission has been the subject of endless, overblown debate ever since. The fact remains that it had little or no effect on the conduct, or outcome, of the war. As Lieutenant Cowie of the 14th Argylls wrote at the end of his role in the affair, 'A tremendous fuss was made about this, and the fact that he was one of the most notorious Nazi gangsters was almost forgotten.'

The Home Guard fulfilled a more mundane role with regard to the Forth and Clyde Canal, which was viewed as a possible defensive line and thus covered by machine-gun nests. It was planned that, in the event of invasion, all the swing bridges would be opened by the Home Guard and vital parts would be removed.

In June 1941 it was found that nobody in the 1st Battalion, Glasgow Home Guard, had been trained to operate the important bridges at Cloberhill, Temple or Lambhill, and no arrangements had been made to gain access to the control houses. Dumbarton Home Guard had been more diligent and had men trained to operate and immobilise all the canal bridges in their area. At Bowling Harbour, the railway bridges would be immobilised by railway personnel.

Of greater concern to the military authorities was the possibility that the canal would be subject to sabotage. At 35 miles long, it had 40 locks, 32 road crossings and six steel railway swing bridges. Seven railways, two roads and two rivers passed under it in tunnels. Furthermore, it was discovered that there were eight stretches of canal where breaches of its banks would cause extensive flooding. Ten emergency stop gates were installed on the top reach where, along with the Union Canal, a breach would have led to 21 miles of canal emptying on to the surrounding countryside. Five and a half miles of canal would deluge Maryhill Road should the viaduct there be blown, and both the LMS and LNER approach tunnels to Queen Street and Buchanan Street railway stations were thought vulnerable to flooding from Port Dundas.

An additional worry was the Admiralty oil-pipe, running from Grangemouth to Old Kilpatrick and buried mainly in the north bank of the canal with intermediate pumping stations at Hungryside and Castlecary. This was patrolled continuously by three men on bicycles.

Zone I (Glasgow) Home Guard headquarters was at Park Circus Place. In overall command (nominally, at least) was Colonel the Rt Hon John Colville MP, the former Secretary of State for Scotland. Over 23,000 men made up the city's 12 battalions, the largest being the 12th (Works South East) Battalion which had almost 3,200 men based at Leslie Street, Pollokshields. Two battalions, the 7th and 8th, were railway battalions. The 9th and 10th Battalions were formed of post office personnel responsible for the defence of telephone exchanges.

Zone II (Lanarkshire) Home Guard comprised 16,000 men and Zone IV (Dumbarton) Home Guard had 5,300 men including 1,900 in Bowling and Clydebank. Zone V (Renfrewshire) Home Guard had, in 1940, 9,683 men of whom 4,096 were in the 2nd (Paisley) Battalion. Battalions on the Clyde coast helped to man mine-watching posts, looking out for mines dropped into the river from aircraft.

Around 700 Home Guardsmen were entrusted with the defence of Kilmarnock. By 1941, half of them had rifles. They were to be aided by any other units which happened to be available at the time. It was hoped that, if still in town, the SMT could provide 75 men, none of whom would be armed. Armed with a few rifles, 25 men of the Pioneer Corps were supposed to hold a roadblock on Fardale Hill, thus denying the enemy the Troon to Kilmarnock road.

The Firth of Clyde was guarded by a number of fixed gun positions. In May 1941, 538 Coast Regiment, Royal Artillery, occupied the battery of Cloch Point. Two 4.7" quick-firing artillery pieces were manned by 153 Coast Battery at Toward Point. Limited space meant that the emplacement was so tight that, in spite of using ear-plugs, gunners used to bleed from the ears during practice shoots.

155 Battery had two 12-pounders on Castle Hill, Dunoon, from where they overlooked the Clyde anti-submarine boom running across the river to

HELP THE ROYAL NAVY !

VOLUNTEERS WANTED
(FULL OR PART-TIME)
FOR CLYDE ANCHORAGE NAVAL SERVICE

Base of Operations
GREENOCK HARBOUR AND ANCHORAGE

The aim of this Service is to relieve experienced Seamen for duty on the high seas.   Members will not be subject to Naval discipline.

All able bodied men who can give a minimum of 24 hours' continuous service per week are invited to write (marking envelope "C.A.N.S.") for particulars of allowances, conditions of service and Application Forms to :

Lieut.-Commander F. JEYES, R.N.R., Naval House, Clarence Street, GREENOCK

ROLL UP !

Published and printed for Clyde Anchorage Naval Service by Robertson & Scott, Edinburgh

Cloch Point. Ardhallow Battery contained two 6" guns and one 9.2" artillery piece. The latter was never fired on practice shoots as the concussion would have shattered windows over a wide area. Anti-submarine defence was provided by an Asdic loop which ran from Wemyss Bay to a point near Innellan.

Protection for Oban Bay was provided when anti-submarine nets were laid at the south end of Kerrera Sound in April 1940. A searchlight was played at intervals over aircraft parked at Kerrera which were inspected for signs of sabotage every two hours. The armed drifters *Appletree* and *Lydia Long* mounted patrols in the Firth of Lorn and the Sound of Mull. The *Appletree* was rammed and sunk by an RAF pinnace south of Lismore Light while on patrol on a miserable dark night in October 1940. Her crew was picked up, though much concern was expressed over the fact that her confidential books had not been saved and might fall into the wrong hands.

Free Norwegian Army headquarters was in Imperial Buildings, Great King Street, Dumfries. They were responsible for the defence of much of south-west Scotland. Abbotsinch airfield was guarded by 11 officers and 150 men of the 11th Cameronians. Four officers and 134 men of the 10th Royal Scots Fusiliers guarded Prestwick airfield. The anti-aircraft magazines at Bishopbriggs and Inchinnan were the responsibility of the Corps of Military Police.

The 14th Battalion Argyll and Sutherland Highlanders had, by early 1941, spent 18 months looking after vulnerable points south of the city, such as the Royal Ordnance factory at Bishopton. Guard duty had become 'a deadly monotonous task', and attempts to relieve this boredom included sending the men on refresher training courses and moving them around to different guard duties.

Numerous cases of men going absent without leave from the 14th Argylls had arisen during the end of 1940. This was due to the very poor condition of their barracks accommodation in former workmen's huts at Bishopton, and the particularly severe winter weather. In addition, most of the men lived in the immediate area. As the battalion war diary records in February 1940, the weather for the previous three months had been exceptionally bad. With the exception of the main Greenock to Renfrew road, itself particularly hazardous owing to frozen snow, all others in the area had been blocked. There were a number of cases of influenza, though 'considering the age of the men, poor quarters, severe weather and duty consisting of 24 hours on, and 24 hours off guard, the health of the battalion was remarkably good'.

The invasion scare of 1940, and the often ludicrous expediencies devised to meet it, arose largely from the bewildering ease with which the German Army and Air Force had brushed aside the British Expeditionary Force. Soldiers returning after evacuation from France brought exaggeratedly fearful tales of the capabilities of the enemy. Told repeatedly, either in an attempt to magnify the narrator's own part in the events, or as a means of rationalising the comprehensive nature of that defeat, these stories quickly grew out of all proportion.

In the overheated atmosphere of June and July 1940, an already shocked and jittery citizenry listened, awestruck, to tales of scarcely credible ingenuity on the part of the enemy. Before long, rumour had it that hairy-handed nuns were wandering the Borders and the Germans had a fleet of large flying boats, filled with soldiers, ready to land on Clydeside's reservoirs. This last led to the quaintly entitled 'Immobilisation of Water against Aircraft'. Trees were cut down and formed into booms topped with iron spikes. These were floated out across reservoirs and lochs, then secured across the direction of the prevailing wind.

The skills of the Wehrmacht in the art of disguise became legendary, as did their ruthlessness. Scottish Command briefings asserted that agents were to be employed in the invasion of Scotland, 'to guide troops and aircraft, to increase panic among civilians and to interfere with defensive measures. They will also be used for sabotage, to spread defeatism among our troops and even to fire on them.'

Home Guardsmen were informed that 'a large proportion of German troops employed in France had a good knowledge of English and French.' It was said that this allowed them to pose as British soldiers, obtain supplies, direct refugees and indulge in a little spying. Their multilingual abilities would apparently allow enemy troops to pose as Dutch, Polish, Norwegian and Czech soldiers. When responsibility for the defence of Scotland rested with troops of precisely these nationalities, this was a particularly foolish, and wholly untrue, assertion to make to Home Guardsmen flushed with excitement at having just received their first rifles.

Typical of the sort of nonsense which gained currency at this time was the story that the Luftwaffe were dropping balloons filled with poison gas on Glasgow. On investigation, these turned out to be weather balloons.

The Public Health and Housing Departments in Glasgow were daily expecting groups of enemy agents to seize their vehicles, and it was widely believed that saboteurs were about to poison Glasgow's water supply. A strong military response to parachute landings around Loch Katrine was prepared and a survey of 16 wells in the city was undertaken. Many, like those at the former Brisbane's Dairy in Shawhill Road and at Parkhead Forge, were discovered to be hopelessly polluted. Cleanest and most productive, at 5,000 gallons per hour, was the well at the Zenith Paper Mills in Thornliebank. Had the Loch Katrine supply been lost, and even if all 16 wells, including the most polluted, had been brought into use, continuous pumping for 24 hours would have yielded one-third of a gallon per head of population.

Plans for the defence of Glasgow were based on the hopelessly optimistic assumption that the population would resolutely 'stay put' in the unlikely event of invasion. Feeding schemes were expected to operate with half the city overrun. It appears not to have occurred to anyone that the issue would have been decided long before the German Army reached Scotland. The alarums and excursions of the previous summer had largely died down by mid-1941 when, following the German invasion of the Soviet Union, it became obvious to all but a few that a simultaneous invasion of Britain was impossible. Nevertheless, both the military and the civil defence authorities attempted to keep the threat alive. In February 1942, more than two months after Pearl Harbor, a lecture on the danger of invasion was given to civil defence personnel in the west of Scotland. Heavy-handed, boring and patronising, it suggested that Britain remained Hitler's only real obstacle on the road to world domination and that he would risk all to conquer the country.

Determined to keep the population on a warlike footing, in 1942 the Government instituted the Invasion Committees. By September that year there were approximately 150 of these committees busy counting shovels and digging useless slit trenches in towns and villages throughout the west of Scotland. Both the military and the civil service complained bitterly of the excessive administrative load caused by self-important committees generating reams of meaningless, trivial correspondence.

Measures to meet the non-existent threat continued until the end of 1944 when, to the regret of a few, the Home Guard and Invasion Committees were stood down. For a brief but vital period in the summer of 1940, the fear of invasion had served to rally a nation deeply shaken by defeat in Belgium and France. Notions of the technical superiority and unscrupulousness of the enemy had provided the means whereby that defeat might be rationalised.

Chapter Three

With the Greatest Fortitude

PARACHUTISTS IN THE PINKSTON AREA

The sirens sounded over Glasgow at 0039 hours on 26 June 1940 when enemy aircraft were detected approaching the Forth Estuary. At 0201 hours wardens reported 'Parachutists in the Pinkston area'. These advance parties of Hitler's invasion armada turned out to be parts of a barrage balloon which had come apart in mid air. A lone Heinkel did reach the west coast after passing over Beith, Ardeer and Glasgow, where it was picked up in the beam of a searchlight. Owing to thick cloud, it was unable to find its target – the ICI explosives plant at Ardeer – and it returned eastwards only to run into both Spitfires and anti-aircraft fire over Edinburgh. It was brought down into the North Sea off Dunbar at 0204 hours.

The first bombs on the west of Scotland were dropped across the southeast corner of Mull at midnight on Tuesday, 11 July 1940. Two fell near Salen and two near Torosay; none did any damage. The bomber had flown across the North Sea in low cloud and heavy rain, crossed the east coast over Leuchars and on to Helensburgh and Dunoon where it was heard overhead at 2336 hours before going north to Mull. Having dropped its bombs, it then strafed a trawler between Mull and Tiree.

The sirens sounded at 0007 hours on 13 July. Three minutes later a policeman at the door of Maryhill Police Station reported hearing an aircraft passing westwards to the south of the city. Another aircraft was heard over Govan at 0025 hours. The first bombs in the Clyde Valley were dropped on Boylestone Quarry and Fereneze Golf Course at Barrhead. Others were dropped shortly afterwards on Easter Yonderton Farm next to Abbotsinch airfield, on Enelly Farm at Bridge of Weir, on Amochrie Farm (now Foxbar housing estate), and at Gleniffer Braes.

The aircraft which passed over Govan went on to scatter 50kg bombs between Kilmacolm and Inverkip. In Greenock these fell at the east end of Weir Street, in a front garden in Quarrier Street, in Ladyburn Street and Leitch Street. Two people were killed and one injured.

At 1603 hours on 17 July a Heinkel 111 of Kampfgeschwader 26 based in Norway passed south-west over Ballater and Helensburgh towards Ayrshire. It strafed the streets of Stevenston and dropped six bombs on the ICI plant at Ardeer. One destroyed a detonator packing house, killing two and injuring six. Four additional 3.7" anti-aircraft guns were mounted at Ardeer within 48 hours.

The first raid on Glasgow took place in blustery, showery conditions at 1020 hours on the morning of 19 July 1940. One bomber appeared over the city from the north-west and dropped four 250kg bombs beside Dumbarton Road. The first exploded in the garden at the rear of 34 Langholm Street, where it demolished a newly built air-raid shelter and seriously damaged the adjacent tenement. The second fell two feet from the end gable of 26 Blawarthill Street. The end of the tenement was completely demolished. The other two bombs fell into a chicken run and close to Blawarthill Farm but did no serious structural damage. Three people were killed including the mother of two-year-old Eleanor Dick. She was dressing her daughter at the time of the blast. Eighteen people were injured.

This bomber dropped its remaining four bombs at Tinto Park football ground in Govan. There, 13 people were injured, including eight in the nearby Ordnance factory. An air-raid shelter was demolished, a newsagent's shop wrecked and 21 families made homeless. Despite the fact that the bomber had been tracked since it crossed the Scottish coast near Peterhead, no alert had been sounded. This was fortuitous as it meant that neither of the demolished shelters was occupied.

Four bombs and 40 incendiaries were dropped on the new Hillington industrial estate at 0635 hours on 24 July. Eighteen people were injured, a printing works suffered a direct hit and other buildings were slightly damaged including the Rolls-Royce factory where roofs were damaged and office windows blown in. Dykebarhill battery fired six rounds at the bomber which they identified as a Junkers 88.

An enemy reconnaissance aircraft appeared over the Clyde in fine summer weather the following evening. Three RAF Defiants exercising over Greenock could not be contacted in time to intercept.

Two aircraft dropped 14 bombs in Lunderston Bay and next to Ardgowan House near Inverkip at 0012 hours on 8 August and, at 0130 hours on the following morning, an HE111 bomber on a mission to lay mines in Belfast

Lough flew into Eastman's Cairn at Cairnsmore of Fleet in Wigtonshire. All on board were killed. Another aircraft on a mission to Belfast dropped two mines which exploded at Inch, Wigtonshire, at 0105 hours on 13 August 1940.

The first serious attack on Glasgow began at 0106 hours on the morning of Wednesday, 18 September 1940, when a lone HE111 came in low from the north-east and dropped a bomb in a rhubarb field at Westthorn Farm on London Road. It dropped a further two bombs and incendiaries on sidings south of Dalmarnock railway bridge. More incendiaries fell in Dalmarnock Gas-works and on Fintry Drive, Ardmay Crescent, Millport Avenue and Aikenhead Road in King's Park. No major damage was done.

The alert had sounded, as was so often the case, two minutes after the attack commenced. It was still in force when a barrage balloon broke loose and dragged its cable across the city, tearing down telephone and power lines on its way. The cable broke windows at Cardonald signal box and the operator, a somewhat agitated Charles Murphy, told police that his box had been machine-gunned.

The all-clear sounded at 0145 hours only for the alert to wail out again at 0210 hours, three minutes after incendiaries began falling over Partick and a high-explosive bomb dropped into Yorkhill Dock, damaging the quay wall and transit sheds.

A further raid, again just one aircraft, appeared west of Glasgow at 0308 hours. Aiming for the fires started in the earlier raid, its first bomb exploded immediately over the Underground tunnels next to Merkland Street Station, causing a crater 30 feet wide by 20 feet deep and blocking the line. The next bomb burst a water main on the quay wall beside the River Kelvin at Henderson's shipyard. The last bomb was a direct hit on the 8"-gun cruiser HMS *Sussex* lying at berth 8, Yorkhill Dock. An oil bomb fell at the corner of Crow Road and Laurel Street, and a number of incendiaries caused minor fires in, for example, the top flat at 11 Walker Street.

HMS *Sussex* was due to complete a refit on 21 September and had her full complement of fuel and ammunition aboard. Fortunately, many of her crew, including her captain, were on final leave. The bomb sliced through a whaler and fell through an open hatch on her starboard side, just aft of amidships. It cut through three decks before exploding in the bowels of the ship, immediately over her oil tanks. The explosion in the confined space of the engine-room had a devastating effect and a fierce fire started immediately. Two sailors trapped in the gyro compartment were burned alive. A further 14 died and 29 were injured.

When Firemaster Martin Chadwick arrived, he discovered that the fire had gained a considerable hold. Burning oil was flowing through the ship's lower compartments, thick black smoke and flames were pouring from her superstructure and the ship's electrical supply had failed completely. In complete darkness, firemen and sailors wearing breathing apparatus crawled into smoke-filled compartments to fight the flames.

Torpedoes and depth-charges lined the cruiser's decks and it was discovered that, owing to pumps having been damaged, it was impossible to flood her main magazine. The danger of a huge explosion led to the evacuation of everyone within half a mile on both sides of the river. Around 400 people were taken to Govan Town Hall in Summertown Road and 300 to the Lesser Town Hall in Langlands Road. The Sick Children's Hospital was hurriedly cleared, and an Incident Room set up by the police in Yorkhill Drill Hall was moved after being deemed vulnerable. Fortunately, and with the help of pumps mounted on the Govan ferry, *Sussex* was able to partially scuttle herself. All but a total wreck, she was out of action for two years. The evacuees were allowed home later that morning.

Operations to save HMS *Sussex* had hardly got under way when the next enemy aircraft appeared over the city. It dropped an oil bomb which damaged St David's School beside Cathedral Street, and four 250kg bombs in a line from the north-east to the south-west at 116 John Street in the city centre, at the Lyon Club in North Frederick Street, beside an air-raid shelter in George Square and into Arthur's Warehouse at the junction of Ingram Street and Queen Street. The bomber turned south of the river and scattered a trail of incendiaries from Hospital Street, over Adelphi Street, the Albion Bridge, the High Court (where a fire started in the roof), the fruitmarket in Candleriggs (where 1,200lbs of tomatoes were reported to have been destroyed by fire), Albion Street and Castle Street. All these fires were quickly extinguished.

According to a report in the *Daily Record*, these raids served to reduce complacency in the city about the risk of air attack. Certainly, when a lone raider returned to the city less than 24 hours later, wardens were pleased to report that most people took to the shelters on hearing the sirens. On this occasion, at 0055 hours on 19 September, a single JU88 was caught in searchlights and assailed by anti-aircraft fire as it crossed the city. It dropped two bombs on to Ralston Golf Course beside Paisley Road West and four bombs and incendiaries on open ground 400 yards west of Duart Street in Maryhill, before making off to the north-east.

For the Luftwaffe High Command, both the Ordnance factory at Bishopton and the new Rolls-Royce factory at Hillington were targets too tempting to ignore. Four 250kg bombs and two oil bombs were dropped at Bishopton at 0138 hours on 2 October. None of them exploded and the only damage to the Ordnance factory was from an anti-aircraft shell which fell through the roof. A similar bomb load was dropped in Renfrew at 0625 hours on 14 October. Bungalows, a masonic hall in Queen Street and a dairy were damaged. Two bombs again failed to explode after falling in Glebe Street and Haining Road. The last unexploded bomb (UXB) was not removed from the

Vehicular Ferry No. 4, better known as the Govan ferry, was pressed into service as a fire float to fight the fires raging aboard HMS Sussex *at Yorkshill on the morning of 18 September 1940. As Firemaster Martin Chadwick wrote later that day, "Three heavy mobile pumps were placed on this vessel and, with the assistance of a Royal Navy crew from HMS* Sussex, *she was manoeuvred alongside the port side of the burning vessel. We managed to get 16 one-inch jets from these pumps and they did very valuable and excellent work in cooling and keeping the fire in check on the port side.'*
(COPYRIGHT UNKNOWN)

town until 5 December. Its extraction had proved particularly difficult for the Royal Engineers as it was found some way down in quicksand. It was demolished at the bomb sterilisation site at Barr Meadow, Lochwinnoch.

The Chain Home radar station at Douglas Wood, north of Dundee, first detected a group of 13 raiders approaching the east coast near Montrose at 0150 hours on Thursday, 24 October 1940. After crossing Scotland to Loch Lomond they began scattering bombs and mines over a wide area. Of these 12 exploded between Luss and Arden on Loch Lomond itself, ten between Renton and Cardross, 14 between Rhu, Shandon and Glen Fruin, eight around Roseneath, two behind Kilcreggan, three in the sea at Cove Bay and four on the hills at Kilchrenan west of Loch Awe. Two unexploded bombs were found at Garelochhead and Shandon. Meanwhile, the Clyde anti-aircraft guns had come into action, Garscadden Mains battery at Drumchapel being the first to open fire at 0236 hours, Langbank battery following with 29 rounds at 0244 hours.

South of the river, two bombs exploded in Graham Street, Johnstone – one at number 50 and one at Trinity Church Manse. Nine people were injured. The same aircraft dropped one UXB at Milliken Sawmill, Kilbarchan, along with a further UXB and an unexploded parachute mine at North Mains Farm, Houston. The UXB at Milliken Park was found to be of the 1,000kg variety and was removed by 91 BDS on 7 November.

Six bombs were dropped on Gourock and a further 14 fell in the Kilmacolm area. Three seriously damaged houses in Gourock's Glen Avenue and others exploded on tenements in Cardwell Road, Caledonia Crescent and Shore Street. Seven people died and ten were injured, including 14-year-old Jack Barbour and his younger brother Nicol, both of whom were trapped in bed. Nicol was released first and Jack was rescued 30 minutes later only to die on the way to hospital. Both the boys' parents were among the dead.

A mine exploded while still suspended on its parachute over Ayr Harbour at 2320 hours on 26 October. Two bombs fell near Kilsyth that night during which enemy activity was mainly concentrated on the east coast.

At 1930 hours on 4 November one of six raids operating over the Glasgow area dropped four bombs on Greenlees Farm above Cambuslang and four 250kg bombs on Glenburn Avenue and Calderwood Road in Burnside. The alert had sounded at 1926 hours and there were no casualties, although it was said at the time that there had been a number of narrow escapes. About 25 minutes later, a number of bombs were scattered across farmland east of the city and into Stirlingshire as the raid spread across central Scotland from Fife and the Lothians. An unexploded bomb was found at Easterhouse Station. The line was closed and the stationmaster's house evacuated.

The streets of Campbeltown were busy with cinema-goers just after 1800 hours on Wednesday, 6 November 1940. Suddenly, a single raider roared over the harbour from the south and, coming down to 500 feet, dropped a number of flares then four bombs at the pierhead. It carried on to the west, dropped four bombs at Parkfergus on the southern fringe of Machrihanish airfield, then returned over the town to strafe the streets.

Six people were killed when one side of the Royal Hotel fell into the street. Around a hundred residents and staff escaped serious injury, though one woman was trapped up to her neck in debris. The bomber was last seen over Inveraray at 1835 hours as it made its way back to Stavanger. Another lone raider dropped bombs and incendiaries over New Cumnock and Kirkconnel in Dumfriesshire. One woman was injured by flying masonry.

An HE111 came up the Irish Sea, passed over Prestwick and Kilmacolm, and circled the city for 25 minutes until 2050 hours on 20 December 1940. It dropped bombs at Edmund Street and Eveline Street in Dennistoun. Two people trapped in 88 Eveline Street were released and found to be suffering from shock. A further four bombs fell in Carntyne, one which failed to explode in the garden of 288 Warriston Street and three which did explode in Gartcraig Road and at 30 and 31 Warriston Street. Gas, electricity and water supplies were cut off in the Carntyne area. The Heinkel was briefly illuminated by a searchlight battery near Rutherglen and fired at by a nearby gun battery as it made off to the south.

Another raider appeared over Hillington at 0100 hours the next morning. Clearly looking for the Rolls-Royce factory, it did not tarry when the battery at Dykebarhill opened fire. At 0115 hours it reappeared from the north-east and dropped a parachute mine and a bomb in Garscadden, neither of which exploded, and a bomb next to Yoker Power Station which did.

A single JU88 appeared 500 yards west of the British Aluminium works at Corpach near Fort William at 0850 hours on 22 December. Coming in at 100 feet it dropped two 500kg bombs, both of which failed to explode. One fell apart after hitting a powerhouse, the other landed 30 yards away. Sergeant McAdams and a party from 91 Bomb Disposal Section were despatched by road to Fort William and had made both bombs safe by the early hours of the following morning.

TO GIVE SUCCOUR TO THE WOUNDED

Decoded German signals traffic during the early weeks of 1941 convinced Intelligence analysts that an attack on Clydeside was imminent. This was confirmed when Luftwaffe radio navigation beams and weather reconnaissance flights were detected over central Scotland on the morning of Thursday, 13 March 1941.

The first action of the day came as a complete surprise. Oberleutnant Fidorra's JU88 roared across the central Highlands to attack the British Aluminium factory at Fort William at 1435 hours. Understandably unwilling to loiter over enemy territory in daylight, Fidorra dropped his bombs in some haste and they exploded in the hills some four miles from Fort William.

Civil defence control rooms in central Scotland were fully manned by 2107 hours that night. Fighters from Drem and Prestwick were patrolling the clear, moonlit sky over Glasgow and anti-aircraft gun positions around the city were on full alert. Sirens sounded along the east coast at that moment and were followed three minutes later by those in Glasgow. For the previous three hours a fleet of almost 250 bombers had been taking off from airfields in occupied Europe, then forming up for the long trip to Clydeside.

At the Leckie Hall in Govan, as elsewhere in the city, volunteer wardens for the area were dispersing after their weekly training night. They had been given no advance warning of what was about to happen. In Dalmuir, the first waves of aircraft approaching up the river could be heard as soon as sirens ceased their wailing. Ambulance-driver Hugh Campbell was returning his vehicle to its lean-to garage at Dalmuir School when an incendiary bomb landed at his feet. He kicked it away and ran to phone the ARP control centre in the basement of Clydebank Public Library.

A practice alert had been due to be sounded in Clydebank at 2120 hours so that the blackout at John Brown's shipyard, long thought inadequate, could be assessed. When the bombs began to fall Chief Constable McIntosh, at Rothesay Dock to view the blackout test, ran to his car and hastened to the control centre.

Almost from the moment the sirens sounded, streams of flares, known as Molotov Chandeliers, began to bathe Clydeside in a greenish glow. Pathfinder units dropped hundreds of incendiaries to mark the target for the main force approaching up the Irish Sea from airfields in northern France. Further waves of bombers from Holland and northern Germany were, at that moment, passing over South Queensferry. Another formation of around 20 bombers from KG26 was on its way from Stavanger Sola airfield in Norway.

Though mainly equipped with flares and incendiaries, these first bombers also carried a small number of high-explosive bombs, mainly designed to drive population and firefighters alike into the shelters. No altruistic motive lay behind this tactic; rather, it was designed to ensure that fires started by the incendiaries could spread unchecked and serve as a beacon for following aircraft.

One of the first bombs to fall was a direct hit on 11 Queen Victoria Drive in Scotstoun which killed 16 people. This was followed, at 2123 hours, by the first bombs in Clydebank which fell into Beardmore's Diesel works at Dalmuir. Sent there with his ambulance, Hugh Campbell was passing a pub at the corner of Beardmore Street and Dumbarton Road when the building suffered a direct hit. Collecting some of the injured from Beardmore's, Campbell was taking them to hospital when another bomb exploded close to his ambulance, sending a manhole cover crashing through its roof and killing two of the injured men inside. Campbell ran back to the depot through what had become a hail of high explosive and incendiary bombs, got another ambulance, returned to the disabled vehicle and got his casualties to safety. Campbell, who had experienced a Zeppelin raid on Edinburgh in April 1916, would remain on duty for the next four days and nights without sleep, eventually setting up a dressing station in Clydebank Town Hall. His dedication and courage were recognised with the award of the OBE.

The main enemy force arrived over Clydeside just after 2130 hours and, eight minutes later, bombs dropped near the Sick Children's Hospital in Garscadden Road. Nurses had placed heavy sheets over the infants' cots on the alert and, despite flying glass from broken windows, none were injured. These were followed almost immediately by a series of explosions which rocked Knightswood and Drumchapel. Bombs exploded in Trinley Road, in Cowdenhill Avenue, at Friarscourt Avenue and Baldwin Avenue, in Fereneze Crescent and Fulwood Avenue. A bomb in Friars Place set fire to 73 Friarscourt Avenue from where a number of people had to be rescued. North of Great Western Road, 44 houses were wrecked, 80 were badly damaged and a further 441 slightly damaged. Bombs also fell in Eastcote Avenue in Scotstoun, at the corner of Crow Road and Sackville Street and in the Barclay Curle recreation ground opposite. Among those killed in Crow Road was Special Constable John Gray.

Parachute mines fell on Fulwood Avenue and in Caldwell Avenue, in the latter case on the west wing of Bankhead School, then in use as a first-aid and Auxiliary Fire Service depot. A rescue party and a bus ambulance left Esk Street depot in under four minutes and at 2235 hours Main Control received a message from the Superintendent of Knightscliffe AFS depot stating that 'I have received message per runner Bankhead Depot wiped out by landmine. They request all assistance I can give'.

Fifteen-year-old Neil Leitch of 21 Hayburn Crescent was one of the many messengers who braved the bombs that night. Four of them were killed. He was carrying a message from Bankhead School to Partick Fire Station when he was blown from his bicycle by a bomb and suffered both bruising and shock. Recovering his senses, he continued on his journey, delivered the message and was given first-aid before setting out to return to Bankhead School. On his way there an oil bomb landed close to him, blasting off his clothes and causing him severe burns. He died soon afterwards and the *Glasgow Herald* reported that he bore his sufferings 'with the greatest fortitude'.

Some 46 people died at Bankhead School including the school janitor, Alex Fraser, and his family, 20 officers and men of the Auxiliary Fire Service and a number of first-aid personnel. A further 80 people were injured. Fires at the school burned well into the following day and grisly remains, including severed limbs, teeth, heads, and a crushed tin helmet containing a piece of skull, were still being found in the wreckage over six weeks later.

As the thunder of the Forth guns continued, wardens at South Queensferry were still recording incoming waves of bombers every ten minutes. As the twelve JU88s of 1/KG54 appeared over Clydebank, a parachute mine drifted down over Kilbowie Hill and on to Second Avenue. The front wall of the tenement was blown clean off and thrown across the street. Among the 88 killed in this one explosion, whole families were wiped out including ten members of the Diver family at number 76 and eight of the McSherry family at number 161. Some of the incendiaries dropped by the pathfinder aircraft had fallen into a huge store of timber in Singer's. This burned readily and was soon a roaring mass of flame. Along with the flames from Radnor Park School, another early casualty, this provided an unmissable beacon for incoming aircraft. Wardens threw dustbin lids, sand and earth over incendiaries in a desperate effort to stop more fires taking hold.

Mary Haldane, a 21-year-old cashier and volunteer ambulance attendant at Radnor Park first-aid post, was sent to Livingstone Street to collect casualties. She had just arrived when a bomb blew her vehicle on its side. Another ambulance nearby was destroyed, killing and further injuring its occupants. Mary Haldane went immediately to their rescue and stayed in the burning hell of Livingstone Street until dawn. She was awarded the OBE for gallantry.

Also in Livingstone Street that night was William Smillie, a sub-officer with Clydebank Fire Brigade. He recalled later that the area was very popular with lodgers and was heavily overcrowded with war-workers. Almost every room had its own coal fire and the blast of high-explosive bombs, five of which fell between Victoria Street and Gordon Street, blew embers out of the grates on to the floor. When he arrived, the whole street was alight. One of the bombs was a direct hit on 69 Livingstone Street. A 19-year-old girl was blown under the sink where she remained trapped for 14 hours. At the time of the blast she had been holding her neighbour's baby. The child did not survive.

Earlier, Smillie had been throwing earth over incendiaries in Second Avenue when he heard a voice shouting, 'For God's sake, help us!' He found some men holding up the roof of a collapsed shelter on their backs. As he and his men got the people out of the shelter, a leaking gas main nearby caused vomiting and four firemen collapsed.

Smillie and his men were tackling a burning building at the corner of Montrose Street and Kilbowie Road when a bomb landed close by and blew him over a wall. Coming to, he found a massive crater in Kilbowie Road out of which were sticking the broken ends of a 15" water main. Firemen's hoses fell limp in their hands.

Sandwiched between the fires at Singer's and Old Kirkpatrick, Dalmuir suffered grievously. Telephones, electricity and water had all been cut off by 2145 hours. Two bombs exploded in Jellicoe Street, one on the canal bank and one on tenements opposite; 31 people were killed at number 78. Patrick Rocks was at work and not until the next morning did he discover that his entire family of 15 had been wiped out. Only his two married daughters, who lived elsewhere, survived. His mother-in-law, his wife Annie, their six sons and one daughter, their daughter-in-law Bessie and five grandchildren, all aged six or under, were dead.

Tenements in Glasgow Road, Yoker, ablaze in the early hours of Friday, 14 March 1941. The smaller building (centre) is Yoker Pavilion, and the embankment of the west coast main railway line is marked by the telegraph poles (right).
(CLYDEBANK DISTRICT LIBRARIES AND MUSEUMS DEPARTMENT)

A further 14 people were killed just after midnight in a direct hit on 12 Pattison Street. They had taken shelter in the ground-floor flat. A shelter in the back court of 5 Pattison Street was hit just minutes later and all of its occupants killed.

In Knightswood, a bomb fell on the pavement outside 77/79 Boreland Drive at 2155 hours. The house at 81 Boreland Drive collapsed, trapping all eight of the Hastie family. They were rescued by 16-year-old schoolboy Gerard McMahon and wardens Alex Hamilton and Alex Glennie. After they had used a car to pull off the remains of the roof, Glennie burrowed into the wreckage with his bare hands. The scene was lit by flames leaping 20 feet into the air from the ruptured gas main in the street. Shrapnel from anti-aircraft shells dropped around the rescuers as they worked.

Having toiled at the scene for over four hours, Gerard McMahon went home to 103 Boreland Drive to check that his parents were safe in their Anderson shelter before returning to the rescue. All the Hasties were brought out alive and Mrs Hastie gave birth to a son in Stobhill Hospital just after 0800 hours the following morning. Alex Hamilton continued patrolling after the rescue and, in the blackout in Commore Drive, tripped over fellow warden David Black who was lying in the street having been knocked unconscious by the blast.

A mine exploded on a tenement in Lime Street off Victoria Park Drive South at 2215 hours killing nine and injuring five. At almost the same moment a parachute mine fell at the corner of Blackburn Street and Craigiehall Street in Govan. One of the first on the scene was Senior Warden William McQueen. He was followed almost immediately by Sergeant Williams and a team from Plantation Police Station, a first-aid party under Superintendent Manson and an Auxiliary Fire Service team which quickly dealt with a small fire.

Mrs Elizabeth McGeachan had gone downstairs on the alert to take shelter in her sister Mrs Ross's flat on the ground floor. Having gone out to phone relatives, Mr Ross and his son returned to discover their home wrecked. Mrs Ross and their three other children were dead along with Mr McGeachan and his baby daughter. Five days after the raid, low moans were heard coming from the wreckage. Rescuers dug a tunnel into which crawled Serbian-born Dr Stevan George of Paisley Road West. One witness described how, 'with his bare hands he burrowed like a rabbit until he was within a few feet of the woman'. He tied a rope round a large boulder which lay between him and Mrs McGeachan. Crawling back into the ruins he packed blankets and hot water bottles around her and remained there until she was released at 0810 hours on 19 March. She died in hospital some hours later.

This attack had left 36 dead and 38 injured, including a full-time warden. The same aircraft dropped another mine into Princes Dock which exploded at 0715 hours on 16 March, bringing down an overhead crane and causing serious damage to the steam lighter *Pibroch*.

Aircraft in the same wave dropped two parachute mines into Fairfield's Shipyard – one of which failed to explode and was made safe two days later – another mine into Stephen's yard at Linthouse and bombs which fell at Shieldhall Wharf and Sewage Works.

North of the river, in Scotstoun, a mine exploded on a shelter in the back court between 148 Earl Street and 1571 Dumbarton Road. Tenements were wrecked and fires started by incendiaries soon took hold. In all, three shelters were demolished, 66 people died and 60 were injured. A bomb also damaged the Clyde Structural Engineering plant in South Street.

The 12 HE111s of Kampfgruppe 100 were due over Clydeside between 2154 hours and 2225 hours. This unit had, for some months, operated in the pathfinder role equipped with the 'X Gerat' radio beam navigational system.

The role of lead pathfinder unit had passed, in January 1941, to III/KG26 commanded by Major Victor von Lossberg, when their Heinkels were fitted with the more sophisticated and longer range 'Y' beam system. Both systems had been identified, and countermeasures taken, by the end of February 1941. Their beams compromised, the Luftwaffe had turned its attention to ports which, being on the coastline, were easily found. Hull, Belfast, Merseyside and Clydeside were among those attacked.

Pilot Officers Denby and Guest were on patrol over Ayrshire in their 600 (City of London) Squadron Blenheim. Denby's Blenheim was operating with the new Ground-Controlled Interception radar station at St Quivox. GCI guided the nightfighter to within 1,000 yards of its target when its own Airborne Interception radar took over.

At 2151 hours Denby and Guest made a successful interception of one of KGr100's Heinkels on its way to the target. They attacked twice and shot it down to crash at Drumshang Farm near Dunure at 2220 hours. The four crew survived, three of them injured. Two other bombers involved in the Clydeside raids that night were shot down. The four-man crew of a JU88 of 3/Kfg 106 were killed when it was shot down into the North Sea off Amble at 2225 hours by Flight-Lieutenant Desmond Sheen of 72 Squadron. The other bomber was shot down at Bramdean in Hampshire by a Beaufighter of 219 Squadron. Two of its crew were killed and two were taken prisoner. Among the 30 fighters on patrol over Glasgow that night were four Spitfires of 602 (City of Glasgow) Squadron. Fighter Command was experimenting with a new method of combined operations against night raiders called, simply, a 'Fighter Night'. Up to 12,000 feet the anti-aircraft guns would have full access to the enemy without having to worry about hitting RAF fighters which were to be stacked up in layers above 14,000 feet. Unable to leave their allocated height band between 19,500 and 20,000 feet, the Glasgow Squadron pilots looked on in horror and frustration as large areas of their city were set alight. Only one, Flying Officer O. V. 'Pedro' Hanbury, managed a short burst at a bomber silhouetted against the flames and searchlights after he deliberately disobeyed orders and left the height band at 2330 hours.

As another wave of bombers passed over, at 2242 hours, a mine demolished tenements in Govan Road between Moss Road and Burghead Road. Blast damage was caused almost 400 yards away. The aircraft responsible also dropped bombs near King George V Dock and around Sheildhall Farm, which broke windows in the Southern General Hospital; 37 people died including James Campbell, a driver with the rescue service, who was killed when another bomb exploded near his van. Former nurse and part-time warden, Ann Campbell, whose own home had been demolished by the mine, went repeatedly into the wreckage to comfort one of her trapped neighbours.

The fires still blazing in Knightswood from the first attacks served to attract further bombs which came down outside 394 Alderman Road, in Kestrel Road and Baldric Road.

Shortly after 2300 hours high explosive and incendiary bombs fell around the junction of Radnor Street, Overnewton Street and Argyle Street. Police reported damage to Miss Cook's Dairy at 13 Radnor Street, but no serious injuries. Two exploded in Kelvingrove Park, one on the bank of the Kelvin 30 yards west of the bridge at Kelvin Way. This broke hundreds of panes of glass on the north side of the Art Galleries and at the Kelvin Hall. Another stick of bombs was dropped over Finnieston, one of which extensively damaged Lowrie's bonded store in Hydepark Street.

Cloberhill Public School and the adjacent United Free Church in Great Western Road suffered severe damage at 2320 hours when a mine exploded at the junction of Turret Road and Blairdardie Road. Three people were injured, ten houses were demolished, 24 were rendered uninhabitable and 309 were damaged. A canister of incendiaries was dropped by the same aircraft, some of which started a fire at 66 Glanderston Drive, and two people were trapped when railway cottages at Drumchapel were all but demolished.

The first-aid post at Boquhanran School in Clydebank was hit by incendiaries and high explosives early in the raid. As the top floor blazed, casualties were carried out to the playground shelters. Owing to the heat from the burning buildings and the danger of their collapse, they were moved again, at about 0200 hours, to the newly built Janetta Street School (now Clydebank High School). The corridors echoed to the screams of the injured and the dying. Elgin Street School first-aid post was damaged by the blast from a parachute mine. Here again the injured were moved out to the playground shelters. More than 190 casualties, some of them very seriously injured, were treated by the light of hurricane lamps. The hospitals at Blawarthill and Canniesburn were soon filled and the ambulances were diverted to Robroyston and Killearn Hospitals.

Far from these scenes of havoc, in the quiet suburb of Giffnock, an off-duty nurse hitched a lift in an ambulance speeding towards Clydebank through the darkened streets. Arriving at Radnor Park Church Hall at around 0200 hours, she and her driver found 60 casualties had been gathered there but that there was no medical attention available. Getting back into the ambulance, they drove to the Western Infirmary where, as casualties streamed in from incidents throughout the city, they found a group of final-year medical students who volunteered to help.

With scarcely credible bureaucratic small-mindedness and despite the fact that they were within nine days of their finals, Dr McQueen, the Medical Superintendent at the Infirmary, refused to provide the students with any supplies. Ward Sister Isabella MacDonald defied her superior and tied

The clock tower on the huge Singer's factory in Clydebank is just visible through the smoke and flames in this photograph which was taken from the Boulevard on the night of 13/14 March 1941. The fires on Clydeside could be seen clearly by RAF pilots circling the airfield at Dyce, near Aberdeen. The sound of explosions could be heard in Bridge of Allan, north of Stirling.
(CLYDEBANK DISTRICT LIBRARIES AND MUSEUMS DEPARTMENT)

quantities of supplies up in eight bedsheets. There followed an eventful journey back to Clydebank during which they ran into an unexploded parachute mine. At Radnor Park Church, Senior Warden Janet Hyslop, the Revd James McNaught and a small number of volunteers were attempting to cope with an increasingly desperate situation. When the white-coated students walked into the charnel-house atmosphere, the cry went up, 'The doctors have come, the doctors have come!'

All the casualties had been cleared from the hall by dawn, a mobile surgical unit had been set up in Hardgate and a large convoy of ambulances had arrived at Dalmuir from Airdrie. The students set out to walk back to Glasgow, two of them to face exams. Although the identity of neither the young nurse who commandeered the ambulance, nor that of its driver, are known, Alex Jamieson, George Wilson, Sutherland McKechnie, Alex

McLachlan and L. G. McLachlan went on to pass their finals and practise medicine in Glasgow.

The scenes of appalling horror in Clydebank continued through the night. Blasted by bombs, wounded, often grievously, by shrapnel and seared by the flames, rescue parties worked until they dropped. Conditions in the shelters deteriorated as terrified people soiled themselves. ARP workers, not having a ladder, were unable to help a young girl standing at the window of a burning house. The roof caved in and she was gone. One of the early bombs of the raid had fallen on tenements at 57-59 Whitecrook Street killing and injuring a large number. A man who had lost both legs was being carried to an ambulance when another bomb exploded nearby at the end of Stanford Street and blew the ambulance attendant's legs off. Both men lay side by side in the street and bled to death.

At 2327 hours a pair of bombers, possibly two of the 12 Heinkel 111s from 1/KG1, dropped five bombs and a mine across Partick. They fell in Peel Street opposite the West of Scotland Cricket Club, Dumbarton Road, at Hayburn Street, near the fire station in Sandy Road, and in Crow Road. Tenements between 29 and 45 Peel Street were reduced to a pile of smoking rubble; 50 people were killed and eight injured.

Another bomb struck a tenement in Langholm Street near Kelso Street. This aircraft also spread incendiaries along Dumbarton Road and dropped a bomb into Yoker Distillery, immediately starting a huge fire which burned fiercely for many hours. The aroma of whisky spread over a wide area and formed a piquant mixture with the acrid smell of burning buildings. Dumbarton Road remained closed to tram traffic the following day as hoses were still running across the road.

Bombs and mines were also falling on Hyndland. At 2330 hours what Kelvinside's Head Warden George Miller described as a heavy bomb demolished number 3 Queens Gardens and considerably damaged numbers 2 and 4. One person was killed after falling through from number 4 into number 3. Blast damage put the first-aid post at Notre Dame Girls School out of action. A mine struck a detached villa at 26 Turnberry Road. The house was totally destroyed and no trace was ever found of the two occupants, who were simply blown to pieces. Number 25 Turnberry Road was gutted by fire and number 31 had to be demolished some weeks later.

Another mine exploded on tenement property between 8 and 12 Dudley Drive. Three closes of 24 houses at 8, 10 and 12 were totally destroyed; 6, 14 and 7 Dudley Drive were demolished later. It left 36 people dead and 21 injured. Three people were trapped in 5 Airlie Gardens, immediately behind Dudley Drive. The casualty list would have been longer had not many of the residents already taken to the shelters in Hyndland School. Some 500 people were made homeless.

Warden Ian Buchanan had been in Clarence Drive west of the railway bridge when the explosion occurred. He recorded that pieces of slate, shrapnel, masonry and other debris flew through the air for considerable distances. At the scene he was struck by the 'lack of life' and ran to the phone box on the corner of Clarence Drive to summon help. When he returned to the scene he found a civilian who was clearly suffering from shock. Two soldiers then appeared and all went in search of stirrup pumps and buckets of water. A further shower of incendiaries was dropped on the existing fires at 0314 hours.

The incidents in Peel Street and Hyndland were to reveal some of the most serious and avoidable defects in Glasgow's civil defence services. At 1100 hours on 19 March, almost a week after the raid, a demolition squad from Samuel Allison & Co turned up in Peel Street to clear the site. There they found part-time warden Miss Wilson in a state of some distress. She told the squad leader that between 20 and 30 of her neighbours were still trapped in the wreckage and that nothing was being done about it.

Allison's men displayed little sense of urgency, one angry local describing their efforts as being akin to 'scratching on top of the debris like a lot of hens at a farmer's midden'. Miss Wilson told Inspector W. T. Brown that their attitude seemed to be that 'They're all dead now, so what's the use of exerting ourselves'. That evening four bodies were recovered and, on the following morning, the bodies of four-year-old Jean Spence and her parents brought out.

Three days later, Inspector Brown wrote that: 'It is shocking to relate that this morning, Friday 21st March, it is reported that groans were heard emanating from the ruins of 31 to 39 Peel Street. I say without any equivocation *that someone is guilty of criminal negligence.*' [Inspector Brown's italics] At 1330 hours Police War Reserve Constable Fred Clarke was freed from the wreckage, and, at 1915 hours that evening, John Cormack was brought out alive. He had been trapped in bed with a heavy beam only inches from his chest. Fortunately, his blankets had prevented the onset of hypothermia and he made a good recovery. Fred Clarke died in hospital five hours after being rescued. Originally from Kingussie, he had been lodging with the Docherty family in Peel Street, all of whom had been killed.

Residents at Dudley Drive were astonished by the lack of diligence shown by rescue workers. A boy who could be heard speaking from the debris was left buried when rescue workers stopped work and went home on the blackout. They did not restart operations until the following morning. The boy's brother was so incensed that he lodged a formal complaint with the police. Their report states that 'He further alleges that offers from civilians to assist in the work of rescue were absolutely refused. So bitterly does this boy feel in the matter that he is writing to the Master of Works.'

That same night a bomb burst in Anniesland Road at Kingsway killing one man and blocking Anniesland Road with fallen cables. A mine landed without exploding in Kennedy Street. Five minutes later, at 2335 hours, Glen Crescent in Yoker was partly demolished.

Also at 2335 hours, two bombs, one of which failed to explode, fell into a back court at 144 Earl Street in Scotstoun. Moments later a parachute mine exploded on offices at Yarrow's Shipyard. The building collapsed on to a basement where around 200 men were sheltering. The mobile unit from Knightswood Hospital was on its way to the yard within five minutes, and it was they who provided one of the most stirring stories of the rescue in the Clydeside Blitz.

The trapped men were buried under a massive area of wreckage into which Probationer Nurse Joan Anderson and Staff Nurse May Stanley crawled repeatedly to tend the injured. The mobile unit operated from Yarrow's own first-aid post under Dr William Brown of Beechwood Drive. With him were Probationer Nurses Margaret McDermid, Janet Valentine, Agnes Leitch and Elizabeth Will.

At 0131 hours a second parachute mine was seen drifting down into the yard. A Home Guardsman pushed Joan Anderson to the ground and lay on top of her to shield her from the blast which wrecked the Electrical and Paint shops. The Home Guard was injured but Anderson carried on with her duties. According to a report by the Medical Officer of Health, Dr A. S. M. McGregor, Nurses Anderson and Stanley 'were outstanding . . . the two continued to give succour to the wounded under difficult conditions from midnight until the early morning.' At one point Anderson had to be held by the ankles as she fought her way into the wreckage. She was awarded the British Empire Medal.

The death toll at Yarrow's that night came to 67; over 80 were injured, some of whom had to be cut from the wreckage in operations conducted by torchlight.

The worst single incident of the Clydeside raids took place just after the mobile unit was arriving at Yarrow's. At one minute to midnight bombs exploded in McLure and MacIntosh's factory in Florence Street off Ballater Street and in Chapel Lane in the Gorbals. These were followed by two parachute mines on Tradeston. The first exploded in Nelson Street and the second on the stationery and fruit departments at the SCWS warehouse in Morrison Street.

The mine in Nelson Street came down between a tram and a tenement at the corner of Centre Street. The blast was so powerful that it killed three French sailors in the Broomielaw on the other side of the river. Some 110 people died and a further 118 were injured. Eleven of those who died were in the tram from where, despite its complete destruction, 20 people were rescued.

The truly ghastly sights which greeted ARP workers sifting through the still smouldering wreckage left emotional scars which remain more than fifty years later. The shattered, burnt, often unrecognisable bodies of the dead, the anguished appeals of surviving relatives, and the screams of the grievously injured meant that there were some rescue workers who were simply unable to cope. There was always, as the bombs fell, the additional worry over the safety of their own families.
(CLYDEBANK DISTRICT LIBRARIES AND MUSEUMS DEPARTMENT)

Another 40 were trapped at 101 Nelson Street. Buildings collapsed on an underground shelter at 90 Nelson Street trapping 41 people, 36 of whom were brought out alive.

Head Warden E. Jones commented that 'It should, however, be placed on record the splendid manner in which the civilians of Tradeston came forward and put themselves under the charge of wardens and other services, and rendered assistance with total disregard to danger. They were really splendid.'

Local residents were organised into three rescue parties, one each for the tram, 90 Nelson Street and 61 Nelson Street. On 14 March 11 bodies were recovered from the ruins in Centre Street, nine from 101 Nelson Street, four from 92 Nelson Street and four from the back court at 146 Nelson Street. The corpses had begun to decompose by 19 March and urgent requests were sent to Main Control for protective gloves and disinfectant. Two severed female feet were recovered from 120 Nelson Street on 21 March, each still clad in its black lacing shoe. The incident post was not closed until 8 April and Nelson Street was not fully re-opened to traffic until 10 April.

The Nelson Street incident had a sad postscipt later in April when it was re-opened after a Mr Sutherland of 101 Nelson Street alleged that his wife and three children had not been recovered from the ruins of their home. A further two-day search revealed no trace of the family.

Six people were believed to have been trapped in the wreckage of the SCWS warehouse in Morrison Street. They were never found. In an effort to reach two women clinging to jutting masonry on the remains of the third floor, Thomas Denholm used his docker's hook to edge himself along floors hanging at crazy angles. Tying blankets together, he lowered them to the ground. Denholm also rescued a man perched on a narrow ledge. The only ladder he could find was eight feet short, despite which, again using his hook, he managed to reach the man and bring him to safety. Denholm went from there to give assistance in the rescue work at Nelson Street. He was awarded the George Medal.

Bombs were also dropped at Windmillcroft Quay and a fire started in Wordie's Stables in West Street from where all the horses were brought out unharmed.

At 0006 hours a firewatcher reported that MacLachlan's Cold Storage Warehouse at the corner of Kilbride Street and Logan Street had 'burst open'. Constable Archie Walker had been walking home along Polmadie Road when he was thrown to the ground by the blast. He ran to the scene and worked through the night with rescue party foreman James McKenna to release five people trapped in 101 Logan Street. Ignoring unsafe walls and overhanging timbers, they lifted furniture, beams and rubble to get at the trapped.

Another rescue party was digging its way into 200 tons of butter and 300 tons of bacon in MacLachlan's warehouse. They were attempting to release firewatcher John Gray of 27 Castlemilk Crescent who was buried under what one witness described as a 20-foot pile of debris. Ammonia fumes from the cooling plant made continuous work impossible and the rescuers had to work in relays. The deeper into the debris they dug, the stronger the fumes became.

Dr John MacKenzie of 48 Queen Mary Avenue, Crosshill, arrived on the scene at 0245 hours and took charge of the rescue effort. He assisted in the removal of debris, periodically crawling under it to examine Gray and give him morphia. Despite the acrid fumes, he never left his patient's side until Gray was released, alive, at 0730 hours. Later rescue worker John Malone was to say, 'I consider the ammonia fumes must have had an effect on the doctor as later in the day I became dizzy and sick. In my opinion, Dr MacKenzie's conduct and devotion to duty under such trying circumstances are worthy of special praise.' Dr Mackenzie also received a special commendation from Regional Civil Defence Commissioner, Lord Rosebery.

Sadly, and despite repeated appeals from distraught relatives, the body of one victim was not released from 95 Logan Street for another two months.

The raid also spread along the south shore of the Clyde, taking in Renfrew, Paisley and Barrhead. The Scottish Cables works in Renfrew suffered three direct hits and one near miss. Machine tools were destroyed and 90 per cent of the 250,000 square foot roof was damaged. Two bombs damaged the Babcock and Wilcox works, two mines fell at King's Inch, 15 bombs were dropped on Blythswood Golf Course and in the grounds of Blythswood House, and other bombs were scattered across High Street and Queen Street in Renfrew. Reports show that 24 fires were started in the town. Unexploded bombs fell in the carpark at the Rolls-Royce factory and in Hillington Road. Two bombs damaged the India Tyre plant at Inchinnan and others cratered surrounding farmland. Homes and shops were damaged in Barrhead.

Three sticks of bombs fell across Dumbarton between Strathleven Road and the Tidal Basin. Two of these bombs exploded in Stirling Road near its junction with Round Riding Road. Around 50 incendiaries fell between Millerston Police Station and Hogganfield Loch and a bomb exploded in Cumbernauld Road at Riddrie. Two mines floated down over Dalmarnock; one, which came down at Dalmarnock Bridge, failed to explode and the other shattered the roof of Dalmarnock Power Station.

A pair of mines drifted down on to Kelvinside at 0043 hours. The first exploded on Tulloch's garage at 14 Queen Margaret Road at the junction with Queen Margaret Drive. Numbers 9, 10, 11, and 12 Queen Margaret Road were all demolished and the gable end of number 8 collapsed. Two pedestrians at the corner of Queen Margaret Drive and Kelvin Way were killed instantly. Warden's post F22 opposite 14 Queen Margaret Road was flattened. Warden Alex Munro of Rolland Street crawled out of the wreckage with serious injuries. His fellow warden Marian MacDougall, a former pupil of Hillhead High School and a one-time hockey internationalist, died on the way to hospital. Another three people died at 8 Queen Margaret Road, six were injured and 50 trapped. Around 500 houses and shops were damaged including the BBC studios in the former Queen Margaret College and a considerable quantity of glass in the Kibble Palace was broken.

The second mine crashed through the roof of the Aberholme Hotel at 84 Kelvin Drive and came to rest on the landing, fortunately without exploding. More than eight feet long and two and a half feet in diameter, black, and with its green parachute still entangled on the roof, it was made safe by a naval mine disposal party the following morning.

A bomb exploded in Cleveden Road, Kelvindale, at 0115 hours. The same aircraft dropped a parachute mine in the back garden at 16 Chelmsford Drive

The densely packed tenements of the 'Holy City' overlooking Dalmuir were almost totally destroyed.
(CLYDEBANK DISTRICT LIBRARIES AND MUSEUMS DEPARTMENT)

and a bomb which damaged shops in Dorchester Avenue. Eight houses between 10 and 24 Chelmsford Drive and another six houses in Leicester Avenue were destroyed by the mine. A further 150 houses suffered damage including broken windows and fallen ceilings. Men from Maryhill Barracks and the Barrage Balloon detachment in Hughenden Road helped with the rescue effort. Among the seven killed were Edward Catelinet, aged five, and his seven-month-old brother, Marcus.

A lull began at around 0200 hours and continued until 0325 hours when bombs and showers of incendiaries were aimed at existing fires such as those at Yoker Distillery, Blythswood Shipyard and Halley's tweed factory. The last bombs were dropped by a lone, low-flying aircraft at 0535 hours. Six houses in Glenburn Street, Maryhill, were demolished. Six people were killed including the Young family at number 26. The bodies of their daughters Agnes and Margaret were found in the back garden.

As dawn broke, the people of Clydebank emerged from their shelters into scenes of almost unimaginable horror and devastation. A huge pall of smoke from a burning tank in the Admiralty oil depot at Old Kilpatrick hung over the river and mingled with the lighter smoke from burning buildings. The north-easterly breeze carried a strong smell of whisky over the town from the still burning Yoker Distillery. In addition, the colliers *Clermiston* and *Belhaven* had been hit in Rothesay Dock. The *Belhaven* was sunk and the burnt-out wreck of the *Clermiston* was finally towed to Ardrossan two years later.

Everywhere fires burned unchecked, particularly in the upper part of the town, in the timber-yard at Singer's, in the Royal Ordnance factory at Dalmuir, in John Brown's Shipyard, at Rothesay Dock and Turner's Asbestos factory. Three bombs had fallen into Turner's works, two of which exploded in the early hours. Over two weeks later, a party from 91 Bomb Disposal Squad was still attempting to remove the third. Kilbowie Hill was in flames. Burning and blasted houses smouldered in Parkhall, Radnor Park, Kilbowie and along Dumbarton Road. Rubble, slates, broken furniture and glass were everywhere and corpses lay in the streets.

Exhausted firemen had done their best with the limited water supplies available. All of the burgh's 16 fire appliances, half of which were lightweight trailer pumps manned by the Auxiliary Fire Service, had been in action from the outset. One AFS station had been demolished and the other two seriously damaged.

Glasgow Fire Service headquarters had received three calls for assistance from Clydebank between 2237 hours and 2250 hours. As a result, under the Regional Reinforcement Scheme, 32 fire appliances were sent to the town from as far afield as Kirkintilloch, Coatbridge, Motherwell and Helensburgh. By 0350 hours 65 units from other brigades were operating in the town. Those from further afield, being less familiar with the area, were held up when they found the main roads blocked by craters and UXBs.

The most serious problem for fire-fighters remained the failure of the water supply owing to damage to the mains, most particularly at the corner of Kilbowie Road and Montrose Street. While the Forth and Clyde Canal represented a ready supply of water, many pumps were insufficiently powerful to raise water from there up the hill to Radnor Park and much of the higher part of the town had to be left to burn itself out.

There was also a serious shortage of hoses. Fergus Roberts, the Town Clerk of Dumbarton, made his way through the devastation to Clydebank Town Hall, itself a shambles after a bomb had exploded in the ventilation well. He offered what assistance he could to his opposite number, Henry Kelly. A shocked and distressed Kelly was able to show him a letter from Civil Defence headquarters in Edinburgh refusing Clydebank a further supply of fire hoses. These could have been used to replace those hoses lacerated by broken glass and shrapnel which were further reducing water pressure.

Sir Steven Bilsland, the District Civil Defence Commissioner, arrived in

Clydebank with eight of his staff at 0800 hours and set up his headquarters in the billiard room of the police station, one of the few undamaged public buildings. According to Bilsland, the whole machinery of local authority control had broken down.

One of Bilsland's first actions was to order Henry Kelly to supersede the Clydebank Firemaster, Robert Buchanan, with the second officer of the Paisley brigade. In a report written some days later, he writes of Buchanan's lack of competent operational control. This view is supported by Martin Chadwick, the Glasgow Firemaster who was responsible for the regional reinforcement scheme. He wrote that Glasgow and Edinburgh officers despatched with personnel to report to Clydebank Fire Station in Hall Street were unable to contact any officer in a position to redistribute them to the salient points in the area. Firemen were left hanging around in Dumbarton Road while officers tried to contact some competent authority. On two occasions, reinforcement units gave up and were ordered to return to Glasgow. Martin Chadwick eventually took matters into his own hands and redirected other units out of the town to the oil tank fire at Dalnottar.

Later, Bilsland did acknowledge that 'the sheer weight of the attack caused fires to develop so rapidly, that even with a perfect organisation (which Clydebank was far from having), the damage by fire would have been extensive.'

By mid-morning, some of the fire appliances operating in Clydebank were standing idle for want of petrol. Desperate to keep the fire-fighting effort going, and unable to reach Glasgow by telephone, Deputy Town Clerk James Hastings drove to the office of the petroleum department of the Board of Trade in Bothwell Street. He arrived at lunchtime to find it virtually deserted. The office boy and typists there had no authority to respond to his eloquent pleas for help. An official was reached by telephone and Hastings described the situation to him as vividly as he could, but to no avail. After having what he recalled as 'a devilish barney' with this person, he was told that he would just have to come back in the afternoon when the staff returned from lunch. Hastings went straight to the petroleum depot at Port Dundas from where, with commendable resource, the depot manager sent a lorry-load of petrol immediately and without waiting for authorisation.

Around 250 fire appliances were in action in Glasgow, this being half the city's strength. Of these, 28 were at the Yoker Distillery fire. Some 64 serious and potentially serious outbreaks were under control by early morning on 14 March.

One service in Clydebank which collapsed completely was the operation of rest centres for the homeless. Variously described as 'very shaky' and 'a most serious problem', this service was almost wholly dependent on the services of volunteers. Such was the immediate ferocity of the raid that not one of the volunteers turned up for duty. Locally recruited volunteers were always going to be torn between care of the homeless and concern for their own families. The service really only ever worked well when staffed by volunteers drawn from outwith the immediate area under attack. When 40 WVS volunteers were drafted into Clydebank from Glasgow and Giffnock on the Friday, the service began to operate more effectively.

Clydebank had eight full-time and eight part-time first-aid parties based on four depots. Three of these depots were gutted and the other suffered severe damage. A number of casualty service personnel were killed and injured. Seven of the town's 23 ambulances were destroyed and a further 24 casualty service vehicles damaged. As bombs and mines rained down and amid the thunder of anti-aircraft fire, one first-aid party undertook patrols based on a series of strengthened closes designed to serve as shelters. Despite these handicaps, the casualty services performed extraordinary feats with what Bilsland termed 'great fortitude'.

James MacWilliam and George Aitkenhead, respectively assistant engineer and foreman with the Clydebank Water Trust, had made heroic efforts to maintain water pressure. While the raid was at its height, they had gone round the distribution system, shutting valves in an attempt to prevent flooding and maintain supplies for fire-fighting. Arriving for a meeting in the Water Trust office at 0750 hours, MacWilliam was found to have been injured by shrapnel. In addition, he had lost touch with his family.

Daylight revealed a crater 30 feet wide and 12 feet deep in Kilbowie Road, immediately north of its junction with Montrose Street. Two water mains, a gas main and a sewer had been breached and tramway rails lay twisted and broken over the crater. As repair squads from Glasgow and Dumbarton toiled to repair the damage, a delayed action bomb exploded nearby, showering them in debris. They were surrounded by burning buildings, in one of which lay an unexploded bomb. A partial supply, fit only for industrial use, was restored by the mid-afternoon. Domestic needs were to be met by water tankers for some days to come and, given the presence of a breached sewer in the crater, even when domestic supplies were fully restored they required double chlorination and boiling. Further damage was done to water mains on 16 March when a delayed action bomb exploded further down Kilbowie Road.

Retail distribution in Clydebank was at a complete standstill and one of the most urgent tasks was to feed the townspeople. All that remained of two SCWS shops in Second Avenue was a fragment of a wall containing a barred window and a potato bunker; 38 shops owned by the Clydebank Co-operative Society had been destroyed and, in Radnor Park, only one back shop remained almost intact. Some 4,000 meals had been sent into the town by road by 1300 hours on the Friday.

Electricity supplies had been cut. Two tons of candles and 6,000 matches were brought in that Friday afternoon along with 70,000 cigarettes and 15lbs of tobacco.

Aid workers approaching the town were met with an unforgettable sight. All along Dumbarton Road files of shocked and bewildered survivors shambled their way to safety. Their faces were caked with plaster dust and soot and many were still in their night clothes.

The number of homeless at the end of that first night was quite impossible to estimate but ran into many thousands. During the Friday afternoon it was decided to clear the town's rest centres against the possibility of further raiding that night. In addition to those who simply walked away, a shuttle service of buses took 2,500 people to the Vale of Leven and 1,000 each to Helensburgh and Kirkintilloch. Rest centres in the Vale of Leven designed to cope with, at most, around 600 people found themselves having to deal with many times that number; Dunbartonshire County Council were overwhelmed. As James Hastings recalled, 'conditions were terrible for a time'. One of the myriad of problems which arose was a shortage of baby food; another was a desperate lack of sanitary towels.

Some semblance of order was beginning to return to Clydebank by 1430 hours; roads had been partially cleared, rest centres were beginning to function properly and the social services had settled down. Five enemy reconnaissance aircraft were detected over central Scotland during the day, the first over Glasgow at 0815 hours. At 1800 hours the only telephone still functioning, albeit intermittently, of the 16 in the Clydebank Control Room, rang. It was picked up by Goddard, one of Sir Steven Bilsland's staff. Replacing the receiver, he turned to Hastings and said simply, 'Well, they're coming back.' Two hundred bombers were on their way back to Clydeside.

The alert sounded at 2040 hours and the first bombs of the night exploded in Drumchapel just before 2100 hours. Ten minutes later Radnor Park, Kilbowie and Dalmuir were being heavily attacked. The infant department of Dalmuir School was set ablaze and, with commendable phlegm, the Superintendent of the first-aid post there telephoned the Control Centre with the news that 'some very heavy stuff is falling and the room is on fire'. The 5,270-ton steamer *Trevarrack* was hit and sank in Dalmuir Basin.

Warden's post B53 in Drumchapel Post Office was put out of action. Senior warden Alex Farquharson and his team moved their post to a room in 'Mansfield', Garscadden Road. A delayed-action bomb from this attack exploded at Firdon Crescent, next to Drumchapel Station, at 2145 hours. Mines also exploded in Knightswood at Kaystone Road, in Waldemar Road at Chaplet Avenue and in Lincoln Avenue at its junction with Archerhill Road. Six were killed in Lincoln Avenue and six blocks of houses were demolished.

A bomb cratered and blocked Great Western Road at Drumry, an

74

unexploded mine was discovered at the corner of Cowdenhill Road and Great Western Road and incendiaries fell on farmland north of Maryhill. James McLymont, farmer at West Millichen, managed to extinguish one by picking it up on a shovel and throwing it into the midden.

Luftwaffe pilots operating from bases in northern France reported that they could see the fires on Clydeside while still many miles away over the Irish Sea. Particularly noticeable was the blaze at Old Kilpatrick where a fire had raged continuously from the night before. At 2250 hours the tank farm was hit again by heavy bombs and one German pilot spoke of a huge explosion which sent flames leaping 3,000 metres into the clear, moonlit sky. Eleven oil tanks were destroyed before the fires were finally extinguished some days later.

District Nurse Cecilia McGinty was attending a pregnant woman in Bridgeton when, at 2245 hours, a mine destroyed a tenement nearby in Allan Street. She went into the wreckage along with Dr Daniel Millar and Police Surgeon Dr John McLaren Ord to rescue 44-year-old Thomas Sherriff who was trapped with his leg jammed between a kitchen range and a stone staircase. They amputated his right foot by torchlight in less than 40 minutes. Sadly, Sherriff died later in hospital. His rescuers were awarded the MBE.

The mine, which had come down in the middle of Allan Street, a short distance from Dalmarnock Road, caused damage over a wide area and destroyed the Methylating Company's spirit works. The blaze which followed was particularly intense and was remarked on by more than one Luftwaffe pilot. Part of the mine casing, with its parachute still attached, was blown across Dalmarnock Road and came to rest in the Power Station yard. There were a large number of casualties and 600 people were rendered homeless.

The second night's raid consisted mainly of large bombs and mines which, as one observer in Clydebank noted, 'leave little or nothing of the smaller type of houses, and their occupants, which receive a direct hit. In the case of blocks of tenements or larger type houses, they leave only a large heap of rubble.'

One mine came down outside Clydebank's ARP depot in Dumbarton Road, killing four. Another hit the west side of Janetta Street School – fortunately the opposite side from that being used as a first-aid post. A pair of mines which fell in Radnor Street and Crown Avenue added to the considerable damage of the previous night's raid; and a shelter at 2 Castle Street in Dalmuir took a direct hit as did the Parkhall Warden's Post.

A mine exploded on number 5 berth in Denny's Shipyard, Dumbarton, at 2330 hours. The keels of two vessels under construction were damaged. Another mine crashed through the roof of the shipyard canteen without exploding. This was disposed of the following day. Dunbartonshire saw 60 people killed over the two nights, with 217 others seriously injured and 188 suffering minor injuries.

Warden R. Scott was on patrol in Maryhill Road when, at 2348 hours, the first of a pair of mines fell in a ploughed field next to Duncruin Street. The blast caused considerable damage to St Mary's School and blew the second mine into the back of tenements in Kilmun Street. Warden Scott regained consciousness lying in the middle of Maryhill Road and found himself surrounded by packets of Cochrane's Tea. He remembered thinking that, for once, he did not need a ration book.

At St Mary's School, although the red sandstone frontage stood up well, doors and windows were blown in and rooms wrecked. Despite this, personnel manning the AFS post there had what was described as 'a marvellous escape'. Numbers 32 and 36 Kilmun Street were completely demolished as were surrounding properties in Shiskine Street, Kilmun Lane and Kirn Street, and others were set on fire.

On reaching F11 post at the corner of Lennox Street and Maryhill Road, Warden Scott found dozens of people rushing from the scene. He guided many of them to the tramway depot in Celtic Street where, by 0025 hours, more than 100 people were taking cover in the pits. He wrote later that he 'noticed that the homeless would be in the way of any work being done. So I "borrowed" one of the trams and, with one of my wardens, we drove the homeless to the rest centre at Eastpark School, Avenue Park Street. It was quite an interesting journey from Maryhill to Bilsland Drive. At some points I had to get out and remove shrapnel that blocked the rails.'

Just one of the many ghastly sights to greet rescue workers in Kilmun Street was that of a mother clutching her baby to her blood-stained chest. The child had no head.

Returning to Maryhill, and after what he described as 'much scrounging', Scott and his team had enough to set up a small canteen for rescue workers, the homeless and survivors. This was run by Mrs Wilkinson and a group of boy messengers.

Here again, according to Scott, there was 'heavy criticism' of the rescue service. Surprisingly, he noted with regard to first-aid parties that, 'in some cases, those in charge did not put forth the spirit one would look for in such a service'. On the other hand, he also commented on a lack of gratitude shown to staff at the rest centre.

The job of removing the dead from the ruins went on for more than two weeks, the last two bodies being recovered on 28 March. The death toll reached 83, and a further 180 were injured. Among those recovered by the afternoon of 16 March were the bodies of James Simpson (10), Thomas Isbister (11), James Graham (11), Maureen McDonald (3) and her sister 'Blondie' (2), all of 32 Kilmun Street, and Edward Tuthill (5) and his brother Daniel (9 months) of 11 Kirn Street. Eleven bodies were unidentifiable. More than 100 homes were demolished and 250 were uninhabitable. The blast caused glass to be broken over a mile away, and 100 shops were damaged.

Two unexploded mines on either side of Cambuslang's Clydebridge Iron Works were reported by 947 Barrage Balloon Squadron just after midnight. One had fallen in the Lanark County Council sewage works and the other at Westthorn playing fields. A bomb dropped on Sheildhall Wharf a few minutes later was followed by another in Stephen's Shipyard. Sheildhall Power Station was slightly damaged. Further bombs dropped in Knightswood, one in Broadlie Drive next to the ruins of Bankhead School and another, which did not explode, lodged in the back garden of 2 Fereneze Crescent. At 0115 hours two more exploded in Alderman Road at Lochlibo Avenue and Fulwood Avenue. Gas mains were set on fire and two houses completely demolished.

The Observer Corps reported that, at 0210 hours, 'Our table is now clear of enemy aircraft.' Five more bombers appeared shortly after 0300 hours but did little further damage.

During the night's raiding a mine exploded in Blanefield village, killing three and injuring 11. Bombs had fallen around Killearn, Baldernock, Drymen and Fintry. Two mines exploded at Browntod Farm near Hamilton, injuring three. In Renfrewshire, five bombs fell on farms near Eaglesham, one fell on East Renfrewshire Golf Course, four near Newton Mearns, one at Barrhead Station and a mine exploded nearby in Kelburne Street. A number of bombs and mines came down around Neilston and four landed close to the Royal Ordnance factory at Bishopton. The tug *Warrior* was passing the entrance to the River Cart with the steamer *Ferncourt* in tow at 0400 hours when she detonated a mine and had to be beached at Renfrew. Some 27 bombs fell around Erskine Hospital and the adjacent ferry. Incendiaries also started a serious fire at the hospital. A return dated 30 March shows that casualties in Renfrewshire for the two nights' raiding amounted to 12 killed and 78 injured, 15 of whom were seriously hurt. Four bombs were dropped in the hills behind Rothesay and one fell three miles west of Sannox Bay on the Isle of Arran.

'When daylight came on the 15th, it was easy to see that Clydebank had suffered a major disaster.' So wrote Regional Commissioner Lord Rosebery to Home Secretary Herbert Morrison. He continued, 'The first impression one gathers on entering the town is that great harm has been done. Behind the façade of the main street, especially on the north side and beyond the Town Hall, there is widespread havoc. In particular the houses in street after street of the Radnor Park district are completely gutted, with only the gables standing, charred and gaunt, while the Whitecrook, Kilbowie and Mountblow housing estates, though not touched by fire, were heavily damaged by high explosives and parachute mines.'

Dr J. P. Hutchison, the Director of Education for Dunbartonshire, wrote that the wreckage 'made a picture of dreadful and heart-rending tragedy'.

In total 9,276 houses in the town had been to some extent damaged. A further 2,881 had been demolished or were completely beyond repair. Five schools had been demolished and three more had been very seriously damaged. The public library, directly over the Control Room, had taken a direct hit on the first night, leaving the Control Room without power or ventilation. It had continued to function by the light of hurricane lamps.

By the evening of Saturday, 15 March, official figures show that over 40,000 people had left the town, of whom less than 15,000 had been officially evacuated. Organised parties were taken as far afield as Stirling, Kirkintilloch and Hamilton. Around 5,500 had arrived in the Vale of Leven, multiplying the County Council's already considerable problems with feeding, clothing and finding billets. Others had made their own way to Dunoon, Rothesay and Dumfries. Some were even to be found spending the night on Parkhall Golf Course despite the fact that it was dotted with bomb craters, including one on the 18th tee.

Repairs to damaged properties were an urgent necessity, not least because of the need to restart vital war production. John Brown's Shipyard alone was desperate for the return of its 10,000 workforce, more than two-thirds of whom had been scattered across Scotland. A drift back to the town began almost immediately, partly because of the overcrowding in the Vale of Leven rest centres. Families worked to make at least one room in their shattered homes habitable and did their cooking out of doors. Whitecrook School was opened as a hostel for 'blitz bachelors'.

A massive effort resulted in 2,095 homes being fully repaired within two weeks. Over 1,000 extra workmen were drafted into the town and salvaged material from destroyed buildings was used to repair others less seriously damaged.

In Glasgow, 647 people had died and 1,680 had been injured; 803 had been admitted to the city's hospitals, 267 of them to the Western Infirmary. Some 6,835 houses suffered major damage, of which 312 had been totally demolished and 361 had been wrecked beyond repair. Something approaching 25,000 houses had suffered minor damage such as broken windows. Over 10,000 people had been made homeless. Around 2,000 were still living in Glasgow's rest centres at the beginning of the following week. On 1 April people were found to be living in basement shelters in Bridge Street and Warwick Street.

Clydebank's Sanitary Inspector, William Cunningham, was presented with a set of quite insuperable problems, not least because the Town Council had expected him also to fulfil the roles of Ambulance Officer and Chief Billeting Officer. By the Sunday he had been on his feet for over three days and urgently needed rest. A. M. McConnell, his opposite number in Kilmarnock, arrived in the town that morning and took over. He had the primary task of preventing the spread of disease, and, with squads brought in from Ayr,

Paisley, Glasgow and Motherwell, they set about clearing sewers, getting chemical toilets into shelters where many homeless people had by then taken up residence, restoring a pure water supply and searching for animal and human corpses. Lean-faced and starving dogs and cats foraged among the ruined closes where the bodies of both humans and their pets had begun to decompose and give off the most appalling smell. Hundreds of dogs and cats were destroyed on Clydeside in the days following the raids.

The funeral of the unidentified dead at Dalnottar Cemetery, Clydebank, in the early evening of Monday, 18 March 1941. Standing on the left, with his head bowed, is Secretary of State Tom Johnston. The diminutive figure facing the camera immediately behind the clergyman is Sir Steven Bilsland, the Western District Civil Defence Commissioner.
Although not advertised as such, reprisal raids were mounted against German cities under the code-name 'Operation Abigail'. Targets included Mannheim, Bremen and Dusseldorf and, according to the operational instruction, they had the object of causing 'widespread uncontrollable fires. Suggest that the first ten sorties carry incendiary bombs only'.
(HERALD AND EVENING TIMES)

Fire-fighting was still continuing on that Sunday afternoon, with personnel having been brought in from as far afield as Dundee and Ayrshire. At peak periods during and after the second night's raiding, 400 appliances and over 4,000 personnel had been in action in Glasgow, Dalnottar, Old Kilpatrick and Clydebank alone. Even the Newcastle and St Andrews brigades had been warned to stand by, though they were not called on.

The most pressing problem facing Clydebank was the burial of its dead. Dealing with hundreds of bodies was quite beyond the capabilities of the local authority and the matter was handed over to the Scottish Home and Health Department. One of their officials, J. McRobbie, arrived in Clydebank on the Sunday afternoon. Almost 170 bodies were found lying, just as they had been brought in, among broken glass and plaster on the floor of the makeshift mortuary in St James's Church Hall in Dumbarton Road. Another 33 bodies were found at Janetta Street School and a further 21 in sheds at Kilbowie Cemetery. There were no coffins and no preparation facilities. There were nowhere near enough undertakers. There was no water to wash the bodies and there were no vehicles to transport them. Above all there was the awful sight of anxious and distressed relatives picking their way through the bodies, attempting to identify their loved ones. Owing to shortage of space, some bodies had to be prepared in the open at Kilbowie.

Some time before the raids, a trench had been dug at Dalnottar Cemetery and back-filled with loose earth. This was opened up to serve as a mass grave for the unidentified dead. McRobbie's desperate pleas to Glasgow and Edinburgh brought, from Glasgow, 12 gravediggers and 150 shrouds. From Edinburgh came a mortuary superintendent and eight assistants, although a request for Union Jacks to serve as palls was denied as Edinburgh Corporation disapproved of using the national flag at funerals conducted by a local authority. These were eventually supplied by the Navy.

A mass funeral for the unidentified dead was arranged for 1600 hours on the Monday. That morning police arrived to photograph such bodies as were likely to be identifiable. As the day wore on there was considerable difficulty in meeting legal requirements as regards death certificates. A family which had lost its breadwinner desperately needed a death certificate to claim on an insurance policy. Distraught relatives were so anxious to know where their dead were buried, even when the victim had perished in the flames, that they would claim a totally unrecognisable corpse. Many bodies had been thrown out of the ambulances to make way for the living. Further confusion was caused by these having been found some distance from where they had been picked up.

Somehow, McRobbie managed to secure the use of six large vans as hearses and, with the clerical tasks only completed at 1530 hours, loading began. Just then, a father arrived at St James's looking for the body of his three-year-old child. It was eventually found in one of the vans, though not before four other children's bodies had had to be examined.

The cortège was over an hour late leaving for Dalnottar Cemetery, where an official party including Secretary of State Tom Johnston witnessed the somewhat unceremonious lowering of the first few bodies, wrapped only in linen shrouds, into the grave. An inter-denominational service was held against the background of more explosions as Royal Engineers dynamited dangerous buildings and filled craters. A bulldozer had arrived from Inveraray that afternoon and was being used to clear blocked roads.

By 25 March 281 bodies had been disposed of in Clydebank, 116 of which were unidentifiable; 561 bodies had been dealt with in Glasgow. More would surface in the ensuing days as rubble was cleared.

On Sunday, 16 March, refugees still caked with plaster dust and ash had packed into a church in Bonhill to sing the 124th psalm:

> Had not the Lord been on our side,
> May Israel now say;
> Had not the Lord been on our side,
> when men rose us to slay;
> They had us swallow'd quick,
> when as their wrath 'gainst us did flame

ENEMY PLANES FLYING DOWN THE GARELOCH IN LARGE NUMBERS

The blackout began in Glasgow at 2036 hours on Monday, 7 April 1941. The sirens at 2155 hours came as something of an irritation to those looking forward to *The Billy Cotton Band Show*, due on the Forces Network five minutes later. On the Home Service at the same time, Jessie Matthews was in *Journey Across the Water, a Musical Adventure*.

Probably due to poor visibility, some time elapsed between the arrival of the first bombers over the city and the first bombs which came down in Aikenhead Road not far from the Locomotive Depot at Polmadie at 2310 hours. Two bombs fell on the south side of Great Western Road, one of which blocked the carriageway 200 yards west of Garscadden Road. The other breached the banks of the Forth and Clyde Canal at lock 35. A deluge of water poured into the Yoker Burn which overflowed as a result, blocking Dumbarton Road.

Frank Kastelle, Chief Engineer on the Dutch freighter *Der Gerling* lying at Yorkhill Quay, watched as, at around 2330 hours, three bombs whistled over his head. One fell in the river next to the Govan ferry terminal, the other two exploded in Water Row, Govan. A travelling crane and other plant in the west platers' shed at Harland and Wolff's Shipyard were seriously damaged. Tenements in Govan Road and cottages in Water Row were also damaged, and a dangerous gable-end in Water Row led to the closure of the Govan ferry. Five people were injured in Govan Road, debris landed on the roof of Govan Station and one large piece of shrapnel was found on the roof of SCWS shops in Helen Street.

Mines exploded in Bourtrees Woods near Largs, Glenville Nursing Home and nearby houses in Greenock were damaged by another mine and 12 bombs fell on Inchbeam and Midton Farms near Riccarton. One bomber passed low over Gretna scattering a trail of 50kg bombs which killed 28 and injured 19 when they destroyed a masonic hall.

Bombs in Gelston Street, Shettleston, caused many casualties and were followed five minutes later by two more next to a former chemical works across Springburn Road from the St Rollox locomotive works. Shortly afterwards, janitor Charles Buchan found a 500kg unexploded bomb six feet under the floor of a classroom on the ground floor of Possilpark School in Allander Street.

The next bombs fell on the LMS Clydesdale branch near West Street Station and opposite the junction of St Andrew's Road and Kenmure Street where many houses were damaged. Around 120 people rendered homeless arrived at the rest centre at Pollokshields Primary School only to find their way barred by the janitor who resolutely refused to let them in without instructions from the Welfare Department. The same aircraft dropped another bomb which destroyed much of the two-storey brick-built cooperage of Slater, Rogers & Co in Seaward Street. This bomb also started a chimney fire in a tenement at 249 Seaward Street.

Another railway target suffered just minutes afterwards when, at 2357 hours, bombs were scattered around the High Street and College Street Goods Stations; 65 wagons were damaged to varying degrees, rails were torn up and one bomb in Kent Street off London Road killed 16. Two bombs fell in Charlotte Street near its junction with Greendyke Street. Other bombs and mines exploded in Soho Street, Bell Street and in Bellfield Street beside Bellgrove Junction. Incendiaries were scattered between Glasgow Green and Lancefield Street where two burned out on the roof of the Harland and Wolff plant, already damaged in the heavy raids in March. Two high-explosive bombs also fell in the ICI yard at Lancefield Street and another fell into Queens Dock without doing any serious damage.

One aircraft dropped four bombs on the Hutcheson's Academy playing fields, Thornliebank, and four between Arden Drive in Orchard Park and Percy Drive in Giffnock, all just after midnight. Bomb disposal officers were called out the following day to a house in Thornliebank after a suspicious hole

GB 83 25 b c

Nur für den Dienstgebrauch

Bild Nr. 596 L 101

Aufnahme vom 2. 10. 39

Glasgow-Govan

Schiffsmaschinengießerei „Harland & Wolff Ltd."

Länge (westl. Greenw.): 4° 19′ 00″   Breite: 55° 51′ 25″

Mißweisung: – 13° 27′ (Mitte 1941)   Zielhöhe über NN 10 m

Maßstab etwa 1 : 16 500

Genst. 5. Abt.   September 1941

Karte 1 : 100 000

GB/S 26

1. Werkstatt- und Fabrikationshalle, massiv, mehrstöckig
   Satteldach mit aufgesetzten Reitern, kleine Schornsteine   etwa 36 300 qm
2. Betriebs- und Nebengebäude, massiv, Satteldächer etwa   2 400 qm
3. Materiallagerplätze

   Gleisanschluß vorhanden

Bebaute Fläche   etwa 38 700 qm
Gesamtausdehnung etwa 93 600 qm

GB 45 42 Princess Dock
GB 45 43 Queens Dock

GB 50 11 Kraftwerk
GB 58 76 Getreidespeicher
GB 82 77 Lüftungsanlagen auf Kriegsschiffen
GB 83 19 Harland & Wolff, Schiffsmotorenbau
GB 83 20 Schiffswerft Henderson
GB 83 44 Werft von Curle, Barclay & Co.
GD 03 47 Werft von Stephens & Sons
GB 83 48 Werft von Fairfield
GB 83 49 Werft von Harland & Wolff
GB 83 50 3 Trockendocks und Werkstätten

was discovered in the front garden. This turned out to have been left by a
gardener transplanting roses.

Bombs also exploded in Pollok Estate, Linn Park and near Eaglesham
House. Eight exploded on Cathkin Braes and one failed to explode when it
came down at Mid Netherton Farm, Carmunnock.

A further 37 bombs exploded and five failed to explode around Strathaven
and East Kilbride. Bombs and mines were also scattered around Paisley,
Neilston, Patterton, Bishopton, Inchinnan and Abbotsinch airfield, three
dropping on the airfield itself. A huge 1,000kg 'Hermann' remained buried on

the south side of Renfrew airfield until 1946. It is now on display at the Royal Air Force Explosive Ordnance Disposal Flight HQ at RAF Wittering.

At 0015 hours a somewhat agitated caller from a telephone box on Great Western Road informed Glasgow Main Control that there was an unexploded bomb in the front garden of Redlands Hospital. Three further bombs from the same stick had exploded in Westbourne Gardens at the corner of Westbourne Road and in Hyndland Road. Senior Warden Lt-Col Mears set up roadblocks at Kirklee Road and Hyndland Road to divert traffic. To his considerable chagrin, some vehicles chose to ignore the roadblocks and simply drove straight past – one car he noticed going by at 'quite 30 miles an hour'. Boy Scout stretcher-bearers assisted with the somewhat hurried evacuation of Redlands Hospital, the patients being taken to Cleland Hospital in Lanarkshire. The bomb, which had displaced the terrace walls onto the pavement, was made safe the following day by Lieutenant Gerhold of 91 Bomb Disposal Squad.

Meanwhile, bodies were being recovered from Westbourne Gardens and Westbourne Road. A collie dog was discovered searching for its dead owner in the wreckage, and a strong smell of gas was emanating from 48 Westbourne Gardens. A delayed action bomb, which had fallen into the basement of 49 Polwarth Gardens, exploded at 1010 hours that morning.

The worst incident of the raid took place at 0105 hours when a single large bomb and a number of incendiaries were dropped at the corner of James Gray Street and Deanston Drive in Shawlands. Wardens running to the scene from Shawlands Cross found that 33 Deanston Drive had collapsed, numbers 31 and 35 were partly demolished and tenements in James Gray Street seriously damaged. Ten people were trapped in a back-green shelter in Afton Street. Rubble had also been strewn across shelters in the rear of James Gray Street.

One of the first on the scene was Pollokshaws Ambulance Depot Superintendent, Harry Pike. Pike, a Great War veteran, climbed into the burning tenements to search for survivors only to be ordered out as the building began to collapse around him. Pike was back on the scene two days later when moaning was heard coming from the wreckage. He crawled through a gap not much more than two feet square and into a cavity where he found two women, one seated in a chair and the other lying at her feet. Both died shortly afterwards, bringing the death toll at the incident to 18.

Mines and bombs fell in Mechan's Ironworks, damaging plant, and Connell's Shipyard where a ship under construction was badly damaged. Eight were injured at 0300 hours when a mine fell on vacant ground in Springfield Road, Dalmarnock, opposite the end of Bogside Street. James Young & Co's soapworks was wrecked. The last bombs of the raid fell on open ground between Muirhead and Easterhouse.

The bombing had been scattered across central and western Scotland. Some 122 were dropped in Lanarkshire, 60 in Renfrewshire, 50 in Glasgow, 49 in Dunbartonshire, 30 in Morar, 11 in Paisley, four near the torpedo range at the head of Loch Long, two at the head of Loch Fyne and two on Jura. Two enemy aircraft were shot down while returning from Clydeside; an HE111 was brought down off Worthing and a JU88 near Southport.

In all, 29 people were killed, 71 seriously injured and 253 slightly injured. Around 4,000 people were made homeless in Glasgow, though most for only a short period.

At 0345 hours on 16 April 1941 a lone raider, having strayed from a particularly devastating raid on Belfast, dropped two 250kg bombs at 1 Wallace Street and 1 Thom Street in Greenock, killing eight and injuring a number of others.

The rural peace of the Devon countryside was disturbed just after midnight on Tuesday, 6 May, by the roar of aircraft engines and machine-gun fire. Flying Officer Joll and Sergeant Dalton in a 604 (County of Middlesex) Squadron Beaufighter shot down Junkers 88 B3+BM of 4/KG54 which crashed in Hiddon's Wood near the village of Chawleigh, mid-way between Exeter and Barnstaple. It was one of 183 enemy bombers which had been sent to attack targets between Rutherglen and Dalmuir on the north bank of the Clyde, and Greenock on the south.

The alert had sounded from Oban to Stranraer at 0003 hours and enemy bombers were already over Glasgow when Joll and Dalton scored their victory. The first stick of bombs landed in Maryhill at 0025 hours. One exploded in Maryhill Road at Dawsholm Road, then an oil bomb in the sidings at Maryhill East Goods Station set fire to two LNER wagons and three bombs straddled number 3 Falcon Terrace. Although they had fallen in both the front and back garden, and in the house itself, no one was injured. In fact, as Head Warden Scott wrote, 'From the few stones that remained standing, two elderly ladies came back from the dead.'

Rescue operations had only just begun when more bombs arrived, one of which clipped the chimney-tops before exploding in the back court at 21 Crosbie Street. The blast partially destroyed the tenement. It also demolished a wash-house being used as a shelter, though it must be said that the only security this would have provided was a sense of togetherness. Constable William Crookston and local residents immediately set about releasing the 13 people trapped. Six were seriously injured and three – namely Mrs Muir, Mrs Cowie and Mrs Steel, all of 21 Crosbie Street were brought out dead.

The second bomb of this attack tore a large crater out of the front lawn of the manse at 2022 Maryhill Road, throwing earth across the roadway as far as the tramway terminus. Despite the damage to his home, Revd Gray of Maryhill Old Parish Church took in many of the injured from Crosbie Street.

Another oil bomb fell between the boundary wall and the lodge house of Sir Charles Clelland's estate. It demolished a coalhouse and started a small fire which was quickly dealt with by stationmaster Mr Oldham, and Home Guard personnel.

Yet another bomb was heard to 'flutter' down shortly afterwards. It buried itself, without exploding, seven feet under the kerb on the south side of Rosedale Gardens, 25 yards from Caldercuilt Road. According to Sergeant William Melville of Maryhill Police, 'The cratur (sic) was examined by Sergeant Greenwood and nearby houses evacuated.' Bomb disposal personnel had considerable difficulty with this one and it was not removed until 16 May.

At 0035 hours, just as the bomb fell in Rosedale Gardens and large numbers of enemy aircraft were reported passing westwards at 15,000 feet through searchlights and anti-aircraft fire over the Forth, a single bomb caused a water-filled crater in the front garden at 11 Midlothian Drive in Shawlands. Others fell south-east of Hopeman Street, Kennishead, and on farmland between there and Nitshill Road.

Two mines and a bomb exploded in a field beside the Forth and Clyde Canal and Blairdardie Road, Drumchapel, at 0110 hours. Blast damage spread out as far as the Sick Children's Hospital annexe, and beyond. Bombs and mines fell on the west side of Paisley three minutes later. The first mine exploded in a yard adjoining 34 Newton Street, between St Mary's Church and the West School. The blast set fire to both the trailer pump and towing vehicle of an Auxiliary Fire Service patrol, three of whom were killed, and two injured. The second was a direct hit on a first-aid post at Woodside House in William Street. Rescue workers toiled through the night to release the dead and injured trapped in the wreckage. Among the 92 who died were Malcolm Mitchell, Senior Warden at the West End ARP Post, members of the Paisley Co-operative Wholesale Society ambulance section of the St Andrew's Ambulance Association, along with Dr Gibson, the section doctor, and many other ARP and first-aid personnel. Another 22 people were seriously injured. Fires were also started in Bridge of Weir. From Paisley, the raid spread westwards towards Port Glasgow and Greenock. A bomb in Queen Street, Renfrew, killed two and injured six.

Bombs at the east end of Port Glasgow did considerable damage across Woodhall between the railway and Pleasantside Avenue. A 250kg bomb struck a shelter in Woodhall Terrace and brought down part of a nearby tenement. More than 30 people were killed. Tenements in Belville Street, Greenock, were struck, causing a large number of casualties and setting a gas main on fire. Shortly after the arrival of the fire brigade, another bomb destroyed both the water mains and a 5,000-gallon steel coffer dam provided as an alternative source of supply. Water had then to be relayed from Victoria Harbour, a distance of almost half a mile.

Greenock police were, according to one report, apprehensive that looting would follow and asked for a military guard to be placed on the damaged properties. To the considerable relief of Colonel Norman Campbell, the officer commanding Clyde sub-area, this was refused in favour of police reinforcements.

An unexploded bomb caused some damage when it hit the Power House at Rothesay Dock, Clydebank, at 0123 hours. It was made safe by 91 Bomb Disposal Squad the following day. A mine exploded nearby, igniting a gas main. Two other mines fell in Yoker, both of which failed, at first, to explode. One did explode later, damaging railway property. The other was defused. Bombs at Dalmuir Station damaged the LNER up line to Glasgow.

Another unexploded bomb was found less than 100 yards from the railway at Howgate between Renton and Dumbarton. Another two 250kg UXBs were found between 200 and 400 yards from the line which was closed. Two bombs fell on the Earnock Colliery branch line near Burnbank Road, Hamilton, and another hit the LNER line just west of Garscadden Road bridge, Drumchapel.

At 0129 hours Air Force personnel at RAF Rhu reported 'enemy planes flying down the Gareloch in large numbers'. Having used Loch Lomond as a landmark, these aircraft flew south to the river before turning eastwards, up the Clyde, to drop their bombs. A stick of four bombs fell in Knightswood, roughly parallel to Kestrel Road, at 0145 hours. The first demolished houses in Baldric Road, opposite its junction with Thane Road. The second fell into 153/155 Kestrel Road which, fortunately, was unoccupied. ARP personnel were unaware of its presence until it exploded, demolishing the building, at 0215 hours. The third bomb completely demolished a house at the south-west corner of the junction of Kestrel Road and Pikeman Road. It also made a crater in the road and set a gas main on fire which Sergeant John Tinch first attempted to extinguish by throwing earth over it. The leak was finally plugged by a repair party at 0235 hours.

The fourth bomb also failed to explode and was found in the roadway outside 142 Kestrel Road by Constable Henry Tyrie. As local residents were all found to be safely in their Anderson shelters, they were left there until the all-clear at 0357 hours. It finally exploded at 0808 hours, again breaching a gas main which burned fiercely.

Four people died at 0151 hours in Culzean Crescent, Kilmarnock, when a lone bomber passed over the town from the north, scattering a mixed load of 50kg and 250kg bombs as it went. Most of the bombs fell on Southdean Farm and the adjacent cemetery. Two heavy bombs also exploded shortly afterwards at Sandilands Farm, Stewarton.

In Dumbarton two 50kg bombs, one of which exploded, fell on the east side of Castle Road in the Blackburn aircraft factory. Four bombs landed in the grounds of Dumbarton Castle and two mines, neither of which exploded, were found on the bank of the Clyde opposite the Castle. Other high explosive bombs and incendiaries in the town started fires and blocked roads.

Sixty-three bombs exploded in and around Cardross village. An unexploded mine found in a field next to the station self-exploded later in the day. Helensburgh's electricity supply was cut off until 1300 hours.

Although this seemed like a pointless and vicious attack in which the village was severely damaged, it was a direct result of the proximity, in the hills immediately behind the village, of a decoy fires or 'Starfish' site. These sites, originally called 'Crashdeck', were developed by the Army with the assistance of technicians and designers from the film industry. Different types of fires could be simulated: burning coal sprayed every so often with paraffin were known as 'repeaters', baskets filled with wood were called 'cribs'. Oil fires were created using drums filled with creosote. Paraffin was pumped out to flare baskets on the hillside and ignited electrically.

It was not unknown for large areas of hillside to be accidentally set on fire. On one occasion it proved impossible to bring the sites into action as the handle had come off the generator used to power the telephones, and Starfish Control could not contact any of the sites. 'Starfish' remained operational until July 1944.

During the first heavy raids on Clydeside in March 1941, the sites north of the Boulevard around Loch Humphrey and Cochno Loch, and on Auchenreoch Muir, deflected a considerable proportion of the attack from Clydebank and Dumbarton. 205 bombs and six mines were dropped on the sites between Renton and Cardross during the May raids. A further 196 bombs and eight mines fell on the sites on the north of Clydebank.

Other sites were established at Loch Thom behind Greenock, on Gleniffer Braes near Paisley, at Edinbarnet and Douglas Muir west of Milngavie, at Craigend near Blanefield, around Lennoxtown in the Kilsyth Hills and near Cumbernauld. Later developments included the replication of street layouts and even the simulation of flashes from tramcar pick-up arms. Dummy airfields, or 'Q' sites, were constructed where car headlamps were pulled along wires to simulate aircraft landing lights.

Five cottages in Southinch Avenue at Tweedvale Avenue in Yoker were destroyed at 0215 hours. Accommodation for 130 homeless people was found in the Spiers of Elderslie Hall. The coming of daylight brought the somewhat alarming sight of two unexploded mines lying between electricity pylons in Kelso Park, 100 yards west of Kelso Street in Yoker. Work in nearby factories was stopped and the railway was closed until they were made safe by a Naval disposal party at 1500 hours.

The Admiralty tank farm at Old Kilpatrick was the target for later bombers. The first bombs fell in the area at 0240 hours, blowing out most of the windows in Milton School. Five minutes later, a large number of incendiaries were scattered in the vicinity of Dumbuck and just west of the underground petrol storage tanks at Milton. They burned for over an hour. At 0318 hours and to the accompaniment of heavy anti-aircraft fire, heavy bombs were dropped on the hillside above Milton. More incendiaries were dropped on Milton village at 0338 hours, the only damage being caused to a house occupied by the manager of a piggery behind the village. All other fires were quickly put out by fire-fighting squads from the 13th Argyll and Sutherland Highlanders. Privates Flynn, Roberts and Simpson of 'A' Company were commended for their gallantry in extinguishing incendiaries in a pump house at Milton petrol depot which had threatened to cause a massive explosion and destroy the entire installation.

Other bombs fell around East Kilbride, Thorntonhall, Busby, Bishopbriggs, Bothwell, Lesmahagow and at the north end of Little Cumbrae but did little damage.

The following night 155 aircraft of Luftflotten 2 and 3 returned bearing 174 tonnes of high explosive and 38,750 incendiaries on what was destined to be their last visit, in force, to Clydeside.

The attack began with a particularly vicious assault on the ICI explosives plant at Ardeer in Ayrshire. The first bombs were somewhat wide of the mark, falling at Meadowhead and Auchingate Camp, Dundonald, at 0030 hours. Ardeer, sited as it is on a spit of land in Irvine Bay, was easily identified, even in the rather cloudy conditions that night. The plant was hit by a total of two oil bombs, 64 bombs which exploded and nine which did not. Twenty buildings were destroyed and serious fires started which required the attention of 34 fire appliances. Despite this, the major explosion hoped for by the Luftwaffe did not occur. Three bodies were found in the factory, one of which could not be positively identified, and 11 workers suffered burns.

Eight bombs fell in Irvine, one fell on the foreshore and 21 fell around Bogside Racecourse. Two blocks of houses were demolished. Three people, including two wardens, were killed, and six injured.

Three hundred incendiaries were dropped over Kilwinning, 13 bombs and two mines exploded in and around Stewarton, and others were recorded around Largs and Loudon. Incendiaries were seen falling near Langbank at 0045 hours. The main weight of the attack was destined to fall on Greenock, however, and among the first bombs of the raid were those which started a major fire in Ardgowan Distillery. Three million gallons of spirit went up in flames and the blaze was so intense that the bomber crews were convinced that they had struck Greenock Gas-works. Burning whisky flowed down the gutters in Baker Street. It ran into the drains and flames sprouted from manhole covers further down the hill. The flames leaping hundreds of feet into the night sky provided a beacon for approaching bombers and illuminated surrounding buildings which were systematically destroyed.

Hundreds of incendiaries and 51 bombs caused massive destruction along either side of Baker Street. Dellingburn Power Station was struck by three 250kg bombs, and a parachute mine; a further 50kg bomb and a large number of incendiaries fell between it and Dellingburn Street.

The Westburn Sugar Refinery was hit by a mine, a large bomb and many incendiaries. Workmen were trapped under the wreckage of masonry and machinery and several were killed. Rescue parties arriving at the scene found their way barred by streams of boiling syrup cascading through the wreckage from the broken sugar pans. By 0230 hours the fires in Greenock were clearly visible to troops stationed near Clydebank.

The possibility of an attack of this intensity on Greenock had long been viewed with considerable apprehension by military and civil defence authorities alike. Road communications were virtually confined to the main

Bomb damage in Rue End Street, Greenock, opposite Victoria Harbour. Ironically, this site is now occupied by Greenock Fire Station.
(INVERCLYDE DISTRICT LIBRARIES)

road along the foreshore to Port Glasgow and the Kilmacolm Road. These could easily be blocked denying access for fire-fighting and civil defence reinforcements. The destruction and fires in Dellingburn and Baker Streets, the fire which swept through Ingleston Street and further destruction in Belville Street effectively blocked access by Kilmacolm Road. Fortunately, Port Glasgow Road remained clear although traffic in the harbour area was seriously delayed by the fire hoses stretching across the roadway.

Four people were killed when a tenement in Antigua Street collapsed. Four aircraft – a Sunderland, two Catalinas and a Swordfish – were destroyed by a direct hit on a hangar in the Aircraft Assembly Unit operated by Scottish Aviation at RAF Greenock. St Lawrence Catholic Church in Dellingburn Street, the United Free Church in Carnock Street, St Andrew's Square and Newton Street were all deluged with incendiaries.

Peter Brown led a group out of a basement shelter under a burning tenement opposite the Town Hall and organised them into a fire-fighting party. Cathcart Street, Terrace Road, Mearns Street, Shaw Place and Duff Street were all well alight when, just before 0300 hours, the Town Hall itself was struck by a bomb and many incendiaries. The top three floors were soon on fire. Civilians, naval ratings, Maintenance and Control Room staff from the fire station in the basement helped to contain the blaze until reinforcements arrived.

A spectacular fire was started at Beaton's Stables in Dalrymple Street. A large number of horses were safely brought out of the collapsing building.

Opposite Victoria Harbour, in Rue End Street, a tenement collapsed after suffering a direct hit; 30 people trapped in the basement shelter were released after rescue workers tunnelled in from an adjoining basement. First through the tunnel was a doctor who gave first-aid to the injured. In another basement shelter under a burning tenement near Cathcart Square, Robert Thomson recalled that '. . . we only became aware of it when smoke and dust began to penetrate through the shelter. We rushed into the open. We were not a moment too soon as the roof of the building collapsed just as we reached the adjoining church.'

A family of ten were killed instantly when their shelter was hit. Daylight revealed only a large smoking crater, odd pieces of torn clothing, a bank book and a purse.

Two parachute mines destroyed much of the hutted camp at the Clyde Fixed Defences gunsite at Cloch Point although, fortunately, all personnel attached to the site had been 'stood-to' and there were no injuries.

At Sheildhall, two mines fell in the river just to the east of King George V Dock at 0135 hours, but failed to explode. One was exploded during minesweeping operations by the Navy at 0710 hours the following morning. The other self-exploded at 0800 hours.

At 0145 hours, 60-year-old NAAFI canteen attendant James Tripney was asleep in his Nissen hut in the army camp on Pollok Estate when a piece of anti-aircraft shrapnel came through the roof and struck him in the face. At almost the same moment another piece of shrapnel injured 78-year-old John Toole of 25 Jordan Street, Whiteinch. Overhead, a Defiant of 141 Squadron was chasing a JU88 bomber across the city towards the north-east.

A reincarnation of the First World War Bristol Fighter, the Defiant was a design failure, being overweight and under-armed. On 19 July 1940, during the Battle of Britain, a hitherto untried 141 Squadron arrived with their Defiants at RAF Hawkinge. Nine of their number were scrambled early that afternoon only to fall easy prey to a formation of ME 109s which shot down five of the Defiants without loss to themselves. Having lost half its strength in under an hour, the remnant of the Squadron was hurriedly despatched north to recuperate, not least because their continued presence would have damaged the morale of other units.

With its power-operated turret, the Defiant did have some limited value as a night-fighter, and it was in this role that 141 Squadron found themselves operating from RAF Ayr in 1941.

Squadron-Leader Wolfe and Sergeant Ashcroft, both survivors of the July 1940 massacre, chased their victim north from Ayrshire, where he had been attempting to bomb Ardeer. At Blackhill Farm north of Maryhill, John Findlay heard sharp bursts of machine-gun fire and watched the bomber pass overhead streaming flames. The 3rd Battalion, Dunbartonshire Home Guard, reported that it crashed and exploded on high ground at Newlands, south of Lennox Castle Hospital at 0202 hours.

Hauptman Hansmann, Staffelkapitan of Kfg 2/106, a unit more usually employed on maritime reconnaissance and mine-laying, died in the wreck of his aircraft along with Oberleutnant Coenen. Oberfeldwebel Langanki and Feldwebel Muller baled out and landed at Balmore, near Torrance. One of them was taken into custody by Home Guard Tom Miller who found him lying on a golf course, nursing a sprained ankle.

A total of six victims were claimed that night by 141 Squadron, although the only other confirmed victory was scored by Flying Officer R. L. F. Day who destroyed a 5/KG30 Heinkel 111 coded 4D+EN which made a forced landing on the north side of Holy Island on the Northumberland coast. Further north, off St Abbs Head, Squadron-Leader Tom Dalton-Morgan of 43 Squadron downed a JU88 at 0153 hours.

Bombs and mines were meanwhile falling across Knightswood and Drumchapel. Two mines fell into John Brown's Shipyard in Clydebank at 0247 hours, damaging a wharf and storehouses, and injuring ten. A number of bombs and incendiaries fell in Dumbarton, one of which struck the Child

Welfare Clinic in Strathleven Road, another destroying a nearby gasometer. Bombs also fell around Helensburgh and Balloch.

Two women and three children were killed and seven injured when a stick of 250kg bombs exploded in Rutherglen. The first demolished the annexe at the rear of Stonelaw Academy in Parkhall Drive. Others fell in the back garden of 131 Stonelaw Road and on a nearby bowling-green. Five houses were demolished and 100 damaged by blast.

Constable Peter Barclay watched as four bombs were dropped immediately behind Knightswood Bus Garage, between Knightsbridge Road and Anniesland Road, at 0300 hours. The first two, one of which had landed in the back garden of 28 Knightsbridge Street, did not explode and were removed by bomb disposal personnel the following morning. One of those which fell on the football pitches behind the bus garage exploded on contact, the other at 0830 hours. Local residents were evacuated to Temple School rest centre while bomb disposal operations were under way and 'DANGER UXB' boards blocked the surrounding streets.

Relations between the police and wardens in Knightswood appear to have become somewhat strained. Head Warden Crawford Roger was less than pleased to discover that police officers at the incident seemed to be less interested in the UXBs than the fact that Roger's car, which had been damaged in the previous night's raid, was being driven without lights Relations were not improved by allegations that police were seen drinking tea in the engineer's room at Knightswood Hospital when they were meant to be searching the grounds for a suspected UXB. Chief Constable Percy Sillitoe ordered a discreet enquiry into the matter and it proved that the allegations were groundless.

Some 246 people died in Greenock during the two nights' raiding and 626 were injured, 290 of them seriously. A further 52 were listed as 'missing, believed killed' in the town. Ninety-five died in Paisley, mainly at the William Street first-aid post. All but five of the 77 who died in Renfrewshire were from Port Glasgow. Some 169 were injured in the county. A total of 455 died in the west of Scotland, with 434 people suffering severe injuries, and 563 being slightly injured.

The intensity of the raid was such that Greenock's civil defence services were shattered. According to Major Small of the 14th Argyll and Sutherland Highlanders, 'The civilian services were not good. Naval ratings from ships at the Tail o' the Bank gave invaluable help to Greenock and undoubtedly steadied the people of that town.' Although carefully excised from later official reports, the contemporary accounts of Scottish Office officials refer to a frightened and angry mob of townsfolk desperately trying to board buses taking them out of town in anticipation of a second night's raiding.

Unlike Clydebank Town Council, Greenock Corporation was allowed, if only in name, to remain in effective control in the immediate aftermath of the raids. The reality was, however, that many of those on whom the efficient running of the town depended had been among the first to leave. The District Commissioner's staff had to conduct operations using the Corporation Emergency Committee chaired by Baillie Scott as a front. Greenock was almost twice the size of Clydebank, the raid was less severe and much valuable experience had been gained from the earlier raids.

The raid and subsequent bomb disposal and demolition work accounted for 24 serious breaches in the town's water mains. Repair parties from Paisley and from Glasgow Water Department under foreman James Wilson worked long hours to restore supplies. Meanwhile, water carts were catering for domestic needs. Many gas mains had been breached but, again with help from outside the town, supplies were almost all restored by 12 May.

By far the most serious damage to utilities was that done to Dellingburn Power Station. At first it appeared that the power station had been completely demolished and all its equipment wrecked. A more detailed examination on 9 May revealed that 80 per cent of the switch gear was still in working order. Using transformers and other gear drawn from a central pool held by the Central Electricity Generating Board, supply was restored to much of the town's industrial undertakings by 13 May and to domestic consumers by 15 May.

Almost half of the 18,000 houses in Greenock were damaged to a greater or lesser extent, 1,800 of which had been or would require to be demolished. Five thousand houses were given priority first-aid repairs in order to get war production workers back in the town. Surveyors were supplied by Robert Urquhart, the Town Clerk of Renfrew, and repair squads were brought in from Glasgow.

As one Greenock headmaster said at the time, 'My school was opened as a rest centre. When I got there, I found some hundreds of people in the hall. We had no instructions except that they were to remain there until they were told where to go.' After waiting several hours for food to arrive, he was forced to commandeer mobile canteens from the streets nearby.

Again, it was the volunteers of the WVS who brought some order to the chaos. A register of the homeless was established, billeting arrangements were put in hand and thousands of meals were provided by local caterers and Glasgow Education Department.

Both the Navy and the RAF assisted with the feeding of the homeless, not least because, as in Clydebank, the rest centre service broke down completely at the outset of the raid, and never fully recovered.

The lack of water and electricity supplies added considerably to the difficulties of feeding. Almost 12,000 people were made homeless, some being forced to squat in derelict and condemned property in Tobago Street and

Cathcart Square, Greenock, seen from Cathcart Street shortly after midday on
Wednesday, 7 May 1941. The raid was particularly intense in this area and the gutted
and blasted buildings are still smouldering in this photograph.
(INVERCLYDE DISTRICT LIBRARIES)

Drumfochar Road. As had happened following the earlier raids, hundreds
simply packed what they could carry and walked out of the town. Drivers of
military lorries took pity on those they came across walking dazedly towards
Largs and Glasgow. Those officially evacuated to the Ayrshire coast found
themselves increasingly unpopular as boarding house proprietors became
anxious about the disruption to their summer trade.

Initially the demolition of unsafe properties and the clearance of debris
was carried out by a section from 421 Field Company, Royal Engineers and
200 men of the Pioneer Corps. Considerable difficulty was experienced by the
sappers dealing with the overhead passageway which connected the north and
south portions of the Westburn Sugar Refinery. This had collapsed across
Drumfochar Road and attempts to clear it using explosives failed. It had to be
cut into sections using acetylene torches. Meanwhile, naval ratings were

salvaging furniture from damaged houses and arranging it in piles in the streets.

Forty police reinforcements were made available by Glasgow Constabulary to cope with the flood of sightseers which descended on the town on Sunday, 11 May. As hundreds of the morbidly curious gawped at the damage that Sunday afternoon, rescue parties from Glasgow, Lanark and Greenock were still working amid the smouldering debris. Thirty bodies had been recovered from the Westburn Sugar Refinery and almost 400 tons of debris remained to be moved before the incident could be closed.

The refinery was one of four incidents still outstanding on 15 May. Another was that at Ingleston Street where hundreds of tons of debris, including large blocks of masonry, had fallen on top of three shelters. In Terrace Road, a number of bodies remained to be recovered from the ruins of the gutted mortuary.

After every heavy raid the target area was littered with unexploded ordnance and the work of the Bomb Disposal Squads began. Mines were generally dealt with by naval DTM parties as they had particular skills in dealing with that type of weapon. On 8 May 91 Bomb Disposal Squad, Royal Engineers, were called to a UXB at Arthur Street railway sidings in Greenock and, on the following day, they removed a 50kg bomb from Cartsdyke Station. On 10 May they worked with a naval party on a new type of mine discoverd in Dumbarton, and on 11 May they demolished a 250kg bomb at Cardross Station.

A UXB at Paisley Ropeworks was dealt with on 14 May and, in the ensuing days, bombs and unexploded anti-aircraft shells were dealt with in Knightswood, Bowling, Cardross and Eaglesham. Lieutenant Gerhold and Corporal Marshall were summoned to a 250kg UXB in John Brown's Shipyard at Clydebank on 22 May. The bomb detonated while it was being sterilised, killing Corporal Marshall. Bomb and mine clearance from the May raids went on until August when a landmine was disposed of in Renfrew.

At 0230 hours on 8 May, a single JU88 dive-bombed the SCWS hosiery factory at Sheildhall. A huge fire gutted the buildings in under two hours. One of the two bombs dropped failed to explode and was discovered in Bogmoor Road, and 84 people were evacuated while it was made safe.

In attacking Clydeside, the Luftwaffe had two primary purposes. First was the need to divert attention from preparations for the invasion of the Soviet Union set to commence just over a month later in June 1941. Second was a desire to cause the maximum disruption to industrial production and distribution.

Following the heavy raids in March, damage to the vitally important John Brown's Shipyard in Clydebank amounted to the destruction of two timber stores and a pattern store. The experimental tank, funnel shed, shafting shop, machine shop, tool room and other buildings were all damaged, some seriously. Yet, by 1 April, Brown's were able to report that all but 650 of their 10,000 workforce were back at work and that production was almost normal.

The Royal Ordnance factory in Clydebank was described as having suffered 'severe damage'. Rapid progress was being made with repairs completed by 1 April 1941, and production was returning to normal. War production at the giant Singer's plant was at 50 per cent by the end of March, despite heavy damage. Ironically, it was the non-essential production of sewing-machines which was ended by the raid. Despite direct hits by two bombs and a large number of incendiaries, Drysdale Pumps in Yoker were producing normally by the end of March. The Scottish Cables factory in Renfrew, despite three direct hits, a near miss and the loss of over 90 per cent of its roof, was back to normal production by mid-April. Even at Yarrow's Scotstoun West yard, where so much havoc had been wreaked, 50 per cent production had been resumed by 1 April. The yard was not fully restored until the end of the year. Also on 1 April, Mechan's Scotstoun Ironworks reported 60 per cent production and Stephen's Shipyard at Linthouse was producing normally.

The picture was much the same following the raids in May. In Greenock the most severe damage had been done to the Power Station, Ardgowan Distillery, Rankine and Blackmore's marine engineering plant, Lamont's and Scott's Shipyards. Despite the massive fire at Ardgowan Distillery, much of the plant was found to be serviceable and it was possible to restart limited production as early as 1 June. Rankine and Blackmore's had been almost totally destroyed by fire. Despite this, all plant and machinery was found to be virtually intact. Urgently carried-out repairs meant that the boiler shop, smithy and one machine shop were able to restart production as early as 26 May. The Blackburn Aircraft factory in Dumbarton, despite two direct hits, stated that the effect on production was negligible.

Two heavy bombs had exploded in Lamont's Shipyard causing severe damage to buildings and plant. One fell into the engine-room of the coaster *Blue Stone,* at the time lying in Lamont's dry dock, and blew her apart. The Admiralty drifter *Gowan Hill,* also in the dry dock, was thrown against the dock-side and smashed to pieces. At Scott's, the main offices and drawing offices had been destroyed by fire as had part of the boiler shop. Over 200,000 square feet of walls and roofs had suffered blast damage. Production both here and at Lamont's took rather longer to get back to pre-raid levels.

Black's of Greenock, having lost their main factory and offices to fire, simply transferred their production, along with salvaged plant, to other premises. At the Westburn Sugar refinery it was discovered that many parts of the works remained unaffected by the damage and some production had been restored by mid-summer. The most severe attack had been on the ICI explosives plant at Ardeer where 20 buildings had been destroyed and over 100 damaged. By the end of May, production was almost back to normal and it was forecast that most of the repairs would have been completed by the end of June.

It is surprising to note that the resilience of industry to heavy raiding appears to have escaped the notice of RAF commanders at that time planning the destruction of German productive capacity.

The Luftwaffe continued with occasional daylight intrusions by single aircraft to the west of Scotland during the remainder of 1941, although much of this effort was directed against maritime targets.

The last raid on the west of Scotland took place in the early hours of 25 April 1943. Coming as it did after many months of enemy inactivity, it was a complete surprise. At 0005 hours 12 explosive incendiaries fell around Kirkpatrick and Annan in Dumfriesshire. That the raid was ill-directed is confirmed by the fact that the next bombs exploded 20 minutes later at the north end of Loch Sloy and on Ben Vorlich. Thirteen explosive incendiaries fell over Neilston and Barrhead as, at 0030 hours, enemy aircraft approached Glasgow.

At 0045 hours a container of incendiaries was dropped over Crosshill and Strathbungo. Panes of glass over the platform at Queen's Park railway station were shattered and a number of small fires started in Craigie Street, Regent Park Square and Glencairn Drive, most of which did little damage. The most serious casualty was the fine 'Greek' Thomson church in Langside Road which was gutted in a huge blaze which could be clearly seen from Drumchapel.

Incendiaries also fell on Govan and into the river, bombs fell on farmland near Strathaven and New Cumnock and a considerable number of unexploded anti-aircraft shells were found across the south side of the city and in Knightswood. One was discovered lying in the playground of Haghill Girls School.

Three enemy aircraft were shot down by anti-aircraft fire over Edinburgh. A Dornier 217 of 7/KG2 crashed onto Craigingillan Hill, Carsphairn, at 0025 hours as a result of engine failure. It had previously strafed a beacon site at RAF Dumfries and jettisoned its bomb load over open countryside before crashing. Three of the crew managed to bail out and were found wandering the moors by a police sergeant who took them into custody.

Chapter Four

Serious Injury to the Enemy

German forces overran Denmark on the morning of 9 April 1940. They also mounted a simultaneous invasion of Norway and the military débâcle which followed remains a terrible indictment of both the Chamberlain administration and Allied High Command at the time.

The British and French had for some months been agonising over 'Operation Wilfred', a planned small-scale mining of Norwegian territorial waters. This was intended to cut off German supplies of iron ore which were being routed, from Sweden, through the ice-free port of Narvik and Norwegian coastal waters to Germany. Hitler, no less aware of the strategic importance of Norway, both with regard to the supplies of iron ore and as a base for naval operations in the North Atlantic, planned his own invasion. By coincidence, both sides went into action on Tuesday, 9 April.

Though some sort of German response to 'Wilfred' was foreseen, preparations to meet this threat were hopelessly inadequate. A flood of intelligence had been reaching the War Cabinet about German intentions towards Norway. Even the *Daily Telegraph* carried reports of troop concentrations in several German ports. Despite this, the Allies dithered and the Norwegian government remained supine.

The first troop convoy sailed from the Clyde on 11 April bound for Trondheim and Narvik. Regular army units included the Irish Guards aboard the *Monarch of Bermuda* and the First Battalion of the Scots Guards in the Polish liner *Batory*. Most of the troops were territorials, however, at best partially trained and hopelessly ill-equipped for a campaign in Scandinavia. The 1/4 Battalion Yorkshire Light Infantry and the 1/5 Battalion of the Leicester Regiment were put aboard the *Empress of Australia* without stores or equipment – in fact, with little more than they stood up in. The uneven quality of this mixed force soon showed itself under fire.

An Anglo-French convoy left the Clyde on 20 April and carried its troops straight into a disaster in the making. The only maps available to General Paget, who was ordered to carry out a half-baked plan for an attack on Trondheim, were tourist guides and pages torn out of school geography books.

The French destroyer *Maille Breze* had come north to provide escort cover for FS2, an Anglo-French convoy which left the Clyde for Norway on 25 April. Having completed her mission, she was back at anchor off Princes Pier, Greenock, on 30 April. Suddenly, during maintenance, one of her starboard torpedoes exploded accidentally. The blast could be heard ten miles away.

Lieutenant-Commander William Fenwick took the boom defence vessel *Barfield* alongside the blazing destroyer and passed over fire hoses to two French sailors. Almost immediately, the destroyer was rocked by another explosion and the hoses snaked back towards *Barfield* with pieces of flesh still adhering to the nozzles. Thirty men were trapped behind buckled hatches in the foc'sle and were being roasted alive. As, one after the other, screaming men pushed their arms out through a porthole, a doctor from the carrier *Furious* gave each one an injection to ease his terrible death.

Convoy FP3A sailed that same day with troops for the investment of Narvik. Although this force succeeded in achieving its immediate objective, it was a costly and complete waste of time given that the War Cabinet had already begun to face the inevitable: that defeat in Norway was a *fait accompli*. The campaign staggered on for another month, although, following the German invasion of France and the Low Countries, it was relegated to the status of a side-show. Its failure did, however, ensure the downfall of Chamberlain's inadequate administration.

The final evacuation of Narvik began on 2 June 1940. Churchill hoped that as many as possible of the British, French and Polish troops there could be brought out to regroup in the Clyde area for the defence of Paris. The first large evacuation convoy of six liners arrived in the Clyde, escorted by six destroyers, on 9 June. By this time the situation in France was also well beyond redemption.

Shortly after 1600 hours on 8 June, the old battleship *Valiant,* one of the escorts for that day's evacuation convoy, received an incomplete signal from the carrier HMS *Glorious* reporting a force of enemy surface ships.

Glorious had anchored off Greenock at the beginning of May 1940 and taken on board the Hurricane fighters of 46 Squadron. These had been flown into Abbotsinch and were put aboard lighters in the River Cart before being towed to the Tail o' the Bank and winched aboard the carrier. When 46 Squadron flew off the carrier to land in Norway, they were one of just two fighter squadrons in the entire theatre, the other being 263 Squadron with their obsolescent Gloucester Gladiator biplanes. Despite this and myriad other problems, both squadrons acquitted themselves well, tying down Luftwaffe units which would otherwise have been able to wreak havoc among the evacuation convoys.

On 8 June, with the evacuation all but over, 263 Squadron were ordered to fly their eight surviving Gladiators aboard *Glorious;* 46 Squadron were ordered to destroy their Hurricanes and their stores, and evacuate personnel by sea. It was believed that the higher landing speed of Hurricanes not fitted with arrester hooks precluded landing aboard a carrier. Squadron-Leader Kenneth Cross was determined that the valuable fighters should not be left behind and, with sandbags tied to their tails, ten Hurricanes managed to land safely on the crowded flight deck. This was a considerable feat, especially considering that none of the pilots had previously attempted a deck landing.

Glorious was short of fuel and able only to steam at reduced speed. In addition, her escort consisted of just two destroyers, *Ardent* and *Acasta*. Incomprehensibly, Captain D'Oyly Hughes did not fly off aircraft to seek out enemy ships ahead of the carrier. Had he done so, he could have avoided blundering into the German battle-cruisers *Scharnhorst* and *Gneisenau*.

Ardent was quickly sunk. *Glorious* was hit by the *Scharnhorst's* second salvo, and repeatedly thereafter. On fire, she rolled over and sank. *Acasta* charged the German ship and hit her stern with a torpedo before she too was sunk. Just two sailors survived from *Ardent* and one, Leading Seaman Carter, from *Acasta*. A total of 1,474 sailors went down in *Glorious*. Of the RAF pilots, only two survived: Squadron-Leader Cross and Flight-Lieutenant Jameson of 46 Squadron. Both were badly frostbitten.

The comprehensive and tragic failure in Scandinavia highlighted the need for an integrated command structure, able to generate active co-operation between the armed forces. This led directly to the development of Combined Operations. Specially trained troops such as the French *Chasseurs Alpins*, and the British Independent Companies under Brigadier Colin Gubbins, had shown great potential in Norway and led to the establishment of the Commandos.

The term 'Kommando' was first used to refer to small, highly mobile groups of lightly armed Boers during the South African war of 1899 to 1902. On 17 July 1940 Admiral Sir Roger Keyes, the naval hero who had led the raid on Zeebrugge in 1918, was recalled from retirement to the post of Director of Combined Operations. His task was to organise raids of between 5,000 and 10,000 men against the coast of occupied Europe.

Keyes' appointment was greeted with dismay by the service establishment as he was known to be both tactless and notoriously immodest. Combined Operations was also seen as an empire in the making, run by Churchill and

The spire of Greenock Town Hall looks down on the wreckage.
(INVERCLYDE DISTRICT LIBRARIES)

Keyes personally. It would thus be in direct competition with, and not in any way answerable to, the Chiefs of Staff. In addition, Keyes was Churchill's man. The Prime Minister, in those desperate summer months of 1940, fell completely under the spell of the Admiral's resolutely offensive spirit.

The first proper Commando raid of the war was thought up in January 1941, by Hugh Dalton, the Labour Minister of Economic Warfare in Churchill's coalition cabinet. Dalton proposed a landing on the Norwegian Lofoten Islands with the main object of destroying fish-oil plants. These were an important source for the Germans of vitamins A and D. Churchill was enthusiastic and 'Operation Claymore' became a reality.

The landing force was composed of 500 men of 3 and 4 Commando, demolition parties from the Royal Engineers and Free Norwegian guides and interpreters. It sailed from Scapa Flow on 1 March 1941 in two converted Dutch ferries, *Prinses Beatrix* and *Queen Emma*, escorted by five destroyers. The landings took place, unopposed, on the morning of 4 March. A total of 18 factories, including four fish-oil plants, were destroyed along with seven oil

Winston Churchill watching a landing exercise near St Catherine's on the shores of Loch Fyne on 27 June 1941 during a visit to the Combined Operations Training Centre at Inveraray. Peering over the Prime Minister's right shoulder is Admiral Sir Robert Keyes. This was the last occasion on which Churchill and Keyes saw eye to eye. The Prime Minister very much enjoyed his visit to Inveraray. That evening he fired off a lengthy minute, requiring progress on the development of equipment for amphibious landings.

Five days earlier, on Sunday, 22 June, Hitler invaded the Soviet Union, and Britain gained a powerful new ally. Now, at last, there could be some realistic hope of eventual victory. Stalin's paranoid suspicions concerning the reasons for Rudolf Hess's flight to Scotland the previous month were allayed, at least in part, by a broadcast made that night by Churchill who promised unconditional support for the Soviet Union.

Churchill realised that he must draw a veil over the truly awful nature of Stalin and his régime if there was to be any chance of victory. Propaganda about 'Uncle Joe' and the Soviets found a receptive working-class audience and played a major part in shaping the immediate post-war political scene.

tanks containing 800,000 gallons of oil. Eleven ships were sunk and 225 prisoners, including ten quislings, were taken. Some 315 volunteers returned with the raiding force to join the Free Norwegian forces, among them eight women who wished to enrol in the Norwegian Red Cross. The Commandos re-embarked after only six hours ashore.

Rear Admiral Lord Louis Mountbatten, as Commodore Combined Operations, inspects naval personnel in training at Inveraray in February 1942. Later that month these men took part in Operation Biting, the raid on the German radar station at Bruneval on the coast of occupied France.
Mountbatten's reputation as a dashing destroyer captain made a considerable impression on the Prime Minister and resulted in his appointment to Combined Operations as Keyes' successor. That he soon fell out of favour was due in no small measure to his outspoken support, while still a serving officer, for the Labour Party.
(TRUSTEES OF THE IMPERIAL WAR MUSEUM, LONDON)

While escorting a section of the raiding force into the port of Stramsund, the destroyer HMS *Somali* had been fired on by the German armed trawler *Krebbs*. Quickly reduced to a smoking wreck by *Somali*'s guns, the *Krebbs* ran aground and was boarded by men from the destroyer. Among the items they brought back were two spare rotors for the German naval 'Enigma' coding machine which were found in a locked drawer in the captain's cabin. Given the importance of this find, it is little wonder that Churchill signalled to Admiral Tovey, the C-in-C Home Fleet, 'I am so glad you were able to find the means of executing "Claymore". This admirable raid has done serious

Members of Dundee Home Guard battalions get in some practice in the art of silent killing during a specially laid-on course at the Commando Training Centre, Achnacarry, in 1944.
(TRUSTEES OF THE IMPERIAL WAR MUSEUM, LONDON)

105

injury to the enemy and has given an immense amount of innocent pleasure at home.'

The Prime Minister's pleasure at the success of 'Claymore' conceals a growing distancing between himself and his Director of Combined Operations. Keyes had become an insufferable bore, constantly harping on about ill-considered schemes for the assault and capture of unimportant islands in the Mediterranean. He gave little or no consideration to the problems of, for example, over-extended lines of supply that this success would pose.

'Exercise Leapfrog' was mounted in mid-1941 as a dress-rehearsal for the seizure of the Canary Islands proposed in anticipation of a German invasion of Spain. Commandos were loaded into assault ships on the Clyde and sailed to mount a practice landing at Scapa Flow. The exercise was a shambles beset by recurring mistakes which had not been rectified despite having been a feature of earlier exercises. Churchill was forced to sack Keyes after the friction between the Admiral and the Chiefs of Staff boiled over into a flaming row. His replacement was Captain the Lord Louis Mountbatten.

The first truly combined operation, 'Operation Archery', involved a return to the Lofoten Islands on 26 December 1941. This raid was to coincide with another taking place further south at Vaagso and Maaloy. The Lofoten Islands part of the raid, carried out by 12 Commando and 150 Free Norwegian troops, was again unopposed.

The landing at Vaagso was carried out by 3 Commando, two troops of 2 Commando, an RAMC detachment and 600 Norwegian soldiers, all of whom were carried in two former Belgian cross-Channel ferries. Naval support was provided by four destroyers and the whole operation was under the command of Rear-Admiral Harold Burrough. Despite stiff initial opposition, factories were destroyed, nine ships sunk and 102 prisoners taken before the commandos retired after six hours ashore.

The Irregular Warfare Special Training Centre first opened at Inverailort Castle in 1940 and was soon dubbed 'Hell's Glen'. By the beginning of 1941, the volunteers of 4 Commando were learning to swim, carrying full kit, in the open-air swimming pool at Troon. Troops from 12 Commando were to be seen wading across the River Doon at Ayr prior to setting off on forced marches in the Carrick Hills. The Special Canoe Section of 6 Commando, later to become 101 Troop, was perfecting its skills on Arran and the Ayrshire coast, and the first mountaineering courses were being held at Braemar and Glencoe. Assault-craft crews were practising opposed landings at Inverkip and a Combined Training Centre, HMS *Quebec*, was opened at Inveraray in October 1940 under the command of Vice-Admiral Theodore Hallet. One of the more colourful figures to be seen leading exercises in Loch Fyne was

Major Jack Churchill. He would storm ashore, crossbow strapped to his back, holding a pistol with one hand and brandishing a claymore with the other. During Operation Archery he stood on the beach, bristling with weaponry, and piped his men ashore with 'The March of the Cameron Men'. One squaddie is said to have remarked: 'Look at that. If Robin 'ood were alive today, 'ed be fucking blushing.'

Among those training at Inveraray in early 1942 were Major J. D. 'Johnny' Frost and 'C' company of the 2nd Battalion, the Parachute Regiment. They were preparing for 'Operation Biting', the seizure of German radar equipment from an installation at Bruneval near Le Havre. The paras were dropped behind the radar station on the night of 27-28 February and, under heavy fire, a small party of engineers ripped out parts of the radar set which were then carried down steep gullies to the beach.

A naval force under Commander F. N. Cook then rushed the beach with assault landing craft and took the paras off. The raid was a complete success. As Professor R. V. Jones – the Air Ministry scientist who first suggested it – wrote, there was one particularly helpful and unforseen side effect to the raid. The Germans were forced to surround all their radar installations with substantial barbed-wire entanglements, under which the grass grew unchecked and in which all sorts of rubbish became caught. This made the sites highly visible to aerial reconnaissance and soon the positions of all the radar sites on the north coast of France were known. Johnny Frost and 2 Para gained a place in military history for their courageous stand on the bridge over the Rhine at Arnhem in September 1944.

The rigours of the regime at the Commando Basic Training Centre at Achnacarry Castle, the ancestral home of Cameron of Locheil near Fort William, has become the stuff of legend. Achnacarry was opened by Lieutenant-Colonel Charles Vaughan in 1942, after which every Commando recruit went there for a 12-week induction course. The régime was tough both physically and mentally. Trainees arrived at Spean Bridge railway station and were met by trucks – the last transport they would see until the completion of the course.

Everything was done at the double; there were hurdles placed along the paths between the huts, speed marches, night exercises on mountains in the dead of winter, fieldcraft, physical training, assault training, weapons training, street fighting, unarmed combat and knife fighting.

All training was done using live ammunition and accidents of one sort or another were common. A 2 per cent death rate and 10 per cent injury rate was deemed acceptable with no questions asked. Epitaphs such as 'He ran in front of the Bren' and 'He showed himself on the skyline' on a line of dummy graves inside the castle gate were a salutory reminder to the potentially careless.

As the awesome reputation of Achnacarry spread through the army, it was dubbed the 'Slaughterhouse'. Colonel Vaughan became known as the 'Wolf of Badenoch' and the 'Rommel of the North'. His instructors were spoken of in hushed tones. Those who failed to last the pace suffered the ignominy of being returned to their units. Among those RTU'd was the Prime Minister's son, Randolph Churchill, who was remembered as having been unnecessarily rude to an instructor.

The relentless pressure culminated in the 15-mile pass-out speed march to Spean Bridge and back, in full kit. It was never enough just to complete an exercise; a Commando had to be both smiling and ready to do it all again, if so ordered. Having the right attitude was of vital importance.

The Highland Fieldcraft Centre in Glen Feshie, near Kingussie, taught men to live off the land in the most extreme conditions. Sabotage training was undertaken at a special school at Lochailort. From here, 11 (Scottish) Commando were engaged in demolition exercises using the West Highland Railway. One of those to pass through Inverailort was a young actor called David Niven.

One of the most successful recruiters for the Commandos was Lieutenant-Colonel Charles Newman V.C., affectionately known as 'Colonel Charles' by his men. Newman led the landing forces in 'Operation Chariot', the raid on the Normandie Dock at St Nazaire in March 1942. Part of 5 Commando's initial training for this operation involved them in practice demolitions of harbour installations at Burntisland in Fife.

3 Commando under Lieutenant-Colonel John Durnford-Slater, and 5 Commando under Lieutenant-Colonel the Lord Lovat, were landed to cover the flanks of the main landing during the disastrously costly Dieppe assault in August 1942.

Any landing on enemy-held territory is at its most vulnerable while the assault force is still trying to get off the beach. One of the major shortcomings shown up by the Dieppe landings in 1942 was the lack of properly trained Naval Beach Commandos able to secure this vital initial phase of operations. A specialist school, the quaintly named HMS *Armadillo*, was set up at Ardentinny on Loch Long to remedy this deficiency. Exercises for the Beach Party trainees included swimming across Loch Long to Coulport in full kit, supported by a log. They were then made to march round Loch Long, Loch Goil and back to camp. Live Bren gun rounds tore into the surface of Loch Long as the Beach Commandos practised opposed landings. The Assistant Training Officer at Ardentinny was Lieutenant Roger 'Hereward' Wake whose deceptively friendly smile led to him being described by one of his trainees as 'an amiable assassin'.

Beach Masters, whose job it was to control shipping in the beach head, were being trained at Inveraray. According to Vice-Admiral Hallet, they had to be tough, resourceful, assertive and able to live in the open for periods of a week or more. Scrambling nets were fixed to the cliff-face behind the camp in order to simulate the side of an assault ship.

The Western Highlands were by no means the sole province of the Commandos. Arisaig House was at the centre of a network of Special Operations Executive Paramilitary Training Schools. Here agents were trained to operate behind enemy lines, carrying out espionage, sabotage and assassinations.

Small arms training involved being able to strip, reassemble and load any weapon in total darkness. Among the instructors were William 'Dan' Fairbairn, formerly an Assistant Shanghai Police Commissioner, and Eric 'Bill' Sykes who had commanded the Shanghai Police snipers unit. Fairbairn and Sykes trained SOE recruits to drop the traditional duelling pistol stance when using a hand gun. They taught them to shoot two-handed, from the waist, with the knees bent, and always to fire two rounds. This method, known as the 'double tap', is still in use today. They also taught trainees how to break free from a man holding a pistol in their back, at the same time breaking his finger in the trigger guard.

The two men are best known for their invention of the 'Fairbairn-Sykes Fighting Knife', better known as the Commando Knife. Wilkinson Sword manufactured 250,000 of these weapons during the war years. Fairbairn specialised in teaching the art of silent killing. Agents were trained to creep up on sentries, hook the left hand around their victim's chin, pull his head sideways and plunge the knife into his neck. The subclavian artery having been severed, the victim would be unconscious in two seconds and dead, having drowned in his own blood, in less than four seconds.

Other SOE training at Arisaig included map reading, house storming, the setting of ambushes, moving ghostlike through open country, canoeing and small boat work. Instructors included Gavin Maxwell, the naturalist, and John Hunt who was later to lead the expedition which conquered Everest in 1953.

Men and women of many nationalities passed through the SOE schools around Morar, Knoydart and Aviemore. Jan Kubis and Josef Gabcik were two of ten Czech volunteers put through a particularly rigorous course at Camusdarroch House early in 1942. At 1035 hours on 27 May 1942, Gabcik stepped out into a street in Prague. He raised his sten gun towards an open-topped Mercedes but the gun jammed whereupon Kubis threw a hand grenade. Reinhard Heydrich, the notorious Riechsprotektor of Czechoslovakia, staggered from the car and fell dying to the ground.

Kubis and Gabcik were betrayed, for money, by one of their own countrymen. They were discovered in the crypt of a church in the university quarter of the city and shot themselves, rather than be captured, after a prolonged gun battle. Following Heydrich's assassination, the Germans unleashed an orgy of revenge killing. Around 5,000 died, including all the adult population of the villages of Lidice and Lezaky.

Training of a very different kind, designed to help win the Battle of the Atlantic, was taking place in harbours and lochs up and down the west coast. Commodore Gilbert Stephenson was called back from retirement to open

Churchill watches a landing craft containing a light tank being launched from an assault ship during his visit to the Combined Operations Training Centre at Inveraray in June 1941.
(TRUSTEES OF THE IMPERIAL WAR MUSEUM, LONDON)

HMS *Western Isles*, the Royal Navy's first specialist school for convoy escorts, at Tobermory in July 1940.

Stephenson, despite his diminutive stature, quickly acquired a larger-than-life reputation. On boarding one newly arrived corvette, he threw his cap to the deck, turned to the sailors manning the side and shouted, 'That's a live bomb! What are you going to do about it?' One of the astonished sailors showed considerable initiative by smartly kicking the cap over the side. Stephenson, whose energetic approach earned him the nickname 'Monkey', rounded on the unfortunate rating, pointed at the floating cap and yelled, 'That's a survivor, he's drowning. Jump over the side and rescue him!'

HMS *Western Isles* ran intensive 15-day courses designed to work up newly commissioned fleet mine-sweepers, Bay-class frigates, Castle-class corvettes and Western Approaches destroyers. The course included instruction in radar, gunnery, signalling, general seamanship, boatwork and ship's administration. ML 453 was used to simulate a U-boat running on the surface during night encounter exercises west of Mull. Submarines, also working up off the west coast, were used to provide Asdic targets.

HMS *Clover*, a Flower-class corvette, completed her working-up period and sailed from Tobermory at 2200 hours on 20 October 1944. Two days later, the First Lord of the Admiralty, A. V. Alexander, signalled, 'My congratulations on the 1,000th vessel worked up. You and your staff have every reason to be proud of the fruits of your labours.' Another congratulatory signal from the Admiralty read, 'Congratulations on the magnificent record achieved at Tobermory. Your name has become famous in all quarters of the globe, and U-boats are not the only ones who quail at its mention. Your splendid efforts continue to inspire all those who go down to the sea in escort vessels.'

The syllabus used at Tobermory was so successful that it was used at the second escort school opened in Bermuda at the end of 1942. A further school, HMS *Mentor*, was opened at Stornoway on 14 December 1943. The sound of automatic gunfire echoed across the Minch as corvettes exercised their close range anti-aircraft gunnery against kites towed by launches. Fast gunboats were used to simulate attacks by E-boats, smoke floats burned and Verey lights soared into the night sky.

HMS *St Christopher* at Fort William provided preliminary training for the smaller craft of Coastal Forces. Fairmile-class motor launches worked up at HMS *Sea Hawk* at Ardrishaig on Loch Fyne.

Following the successful completion of her acceptance trials, HM submarine *Vandal* arrived alongside HMS *Forth*, the depot ship of the 3rd Flotilla in the Holy Loch, on 21 February 1943. She sailed the following day to carry out a three-day independent working-up exercise, under operational conditions, in the Clyde. Having spent the night at anchor off Lochranza,

Vandal was seen putting to sea on the morning of 24 February. Nothing more was seen of Lieutenant John Bridger and his crew. Five submarines and the Free French sloop *La Capricieuse* swept the trial area without success. Reports from other boats exercising in the area indicate that she lies in deep water off Inchmarnock.

Another brand new submarine, HM S/M *Untamed*, arrived to work up in the Clyde on 29 May 1943. She sailed from Campbeltown the following morning to exercise with the anti-submarine training yacht *Shemara*. *Untamed* dived for the second time that day at 1348 hours. *Shemara* detected the first signs of possible trouble at 1418 hours when a smoke candle from the submarine was unexpectedly sighted on the surface.

Around 160 feet below the surface, in the submarine, a petty officer had been carrying out routine maintenance on the sub's electro-mechanical log. The Ottway log used a small impeller protruding from the boat's hull to measure her speed through the water. This could be withdrawn into the boat after shutting off a sluice to maintain watertight integrity. It would appear that this operation was not carried out correctly and the outer sluice valve was only partially closed when the log was withdrawn.

By 1602 hours Commander Buckle in *Shemara* was convinced that something was seriously wrong with *Untamed* and sent a signal to that effect to the Naval Officer in Charge, Campbeltown. *Shemara's* trainee hydrophone operators could hear the sound of motors being run and tanks being blown as the trapped crew of the submarine desperately attempted to bring their partially flooded boat to the surface. The last sounds from *Untamed* were heard at 1745 hours.

Divers found the submarine lying upright, on an even keel, on the morning of 1 June. The Admiralty were determined to get to the bottom of what was still a mysterious accident, particularly as there had recently been rumours of sabotage. The Liverpool and Glasgow Salvage Company were contracted to raise the submarine and Lieutenant-Commander Arthur Pitt DSO, the commander of the submarine *Taku*, then refitting at Troon, was appointed Admiralty representative.

Four nine-inch steel wires were passed under *Untamed* and secured to a salvage vessel specially built after the *Thetis* disaster in Liverpool Bay in 1939. The submarine was raised 16 feet with each tide and moved to shallower water. The operation should, in theory, have been completed in five days. In the event, it became a grim 11-day battle against severe gales during which, on one occasion, the flooded submarine had to be allowed to fall back to the sea-bed.

Pitt had the unenviable task of being first into *Untamed* when she was pumped out. He found that her fore ends had flooded up to the Control Room bulkhead, thus sealing her fate. This was believed to have been due to her inexperienced crew having panicked and neglected to close a watertight door which allowed the crew space to flood up. Her ship's log showed that the crew had struggled to raise her for seven hours before realising their position was hopeless.

The two men working on the Ottway log had been trapped in the fore ends as they flooded and were already dead. The remaining 34 crew members crowded into the engine-room which they attempted to flood in order to equalise pressure, enabling them to open the escape hatch. Their efforts were in vain. Fourteen sets of escape apparatus had, in the initial panic, been left in flooded compartments and the valve designed to allow rapid flooding of the engine-room had been wrongly assembled. Additionally, the men were in the final stages of carbon monoxide poisoning. Their watches were stopped by the rising water at 2020 hours, 12 hours after they became trapped. *Untamed* was refitted and went to war as HM S/M *Vitality*.

A small number of Italian frogmen carried out a successful 'human torpedo' raid on Alexandria harbour in December 1941. The battleships *Queen Elizabeth* and *Valiant* were left crippled and sitting on the sea bottom after limpet mines were attached to their hulls. This exploit led Churchill to press the Royal Navy to develop a similar 'human torpedo' capability.

The submarine depot ship HMS *Titania*, 'Tites' to all who knew her, served as depot ship for the 3rd Flotilla in the Holy Loch until January 1942, when she was replaced by HMS *Forth*. Sailing then to Loch Erisort, she was to carry out early trials with the Royal Navy's version of the manned torpedo, known as the 'chariot'.

The base at Loch Erisort closed after only a few months and operations were transferred to Port HHZ, a larger establishment in Loch Cairnbawn, south of Cape Wrath. Seven two-man chariot crews had been trained during the summer at Loch Erisort and they were immediately put to the test when the new battleship HMS *Howe* steamed in to provide them with a target for dummy attacks. To the considerable chagrin of the battleship's crew, the charioteers managed time and again to 'sink' her. One pair even managed to place their dummy mine, unseen, on the underside of the starboard accommodation ladder, right under the noses of both the officer of the watch and the quartermaster. Further dummy attacks were carried out on the battleship HMS *Rodney* off Loch Broom.

Two chariots were suspended under *Arthur*, a Norwegian fishing boat which had escaped to Scotland and which was one of a number operating on the 'Shetland Bus' run taking agents and supplies into occupied Norway. After all the training attacks on battleships, there could only be one target: the huge new German battleship *Tirpitz*. From her lair in a Norwegian fjord near Trondheim, the *Tirpitz* represented a considerable threat to the North Atlantic and Russian convoys.

The first attempt on the *Tirpitz*, launched at the end of October 1942, had to be abandoned almost within sight of the target after the chariots broke away during a storm. The four charioteers and *Arthur's* crew set out to walk across the mountains to neutral Sweden. During the march, Able Seaman Bob Evans was shot and injured by a German police patrol. Nursed back to health by the Germans, he was interrogated then shot as a spy. The rest of the party reached the safety of neutral Sweden and returned by air to RAF Leuchars.

HMS *Varbel*, the shore base of the Experimental Submarine Flotilla, opened in August 1942 under the command of Commander David Ingram DSC. It comprised the Kyles of Bute Hydropathic Hotel overlooking the village of Port Bannatyne and Ardtaraig House, a shooting-lodge at the head of Loch Striven. Loch Striven was reserved as a submarine exercise area closed to all traffic not under the control of *Varbel*.

The real reason for *Varbel's* existence became apparent on 31 August when *X3*, the first of the flotilla's midget submarines, arrived by rail at Faslane. More 'X' craft arrived from the builders and, early in 1943, one of them became the only submarine to penetrate the Clyde defences undetected. It is said that a Home Guardsman on coast watch at Cloch Point spotted the little craft but thought it was 'a wee man in a rowin' boat wi' nae oars. Didnae think it was worth mentioning'.

While initial training of new crews continued in Loch Striven, a base for advanced training was again established in Loch Cairbawn, this time around HMS *Bonaventure*, a former Clan Line steamer converted to the role of depot ship.

Six 'X' craft left Loch Cairnbawn under the tow of parent submarines on 11 September 1943. *X5*, *X6* and *X7* were to attack the *Tirpitz* by laying charges of amatol, carried in pods attached to their sides, under the battleship's keel. *X9* and *X10* were to attack the 26,000-ton battle-cruiser *Scharnhorst*, and *X8* was to make an attempt on the cruiser *Lutzow*. They were to be towed to a point off the Norwegian coast and would then be released to continue up Altenfjord under their own power. They would have to penetrate formidable anti-submarine defences before laying their charges.

The tow-rope securing *X8* to her parent submarine, *Seanymph*, broke early on the fifth day of the tow. *X8* was adrift for 37 hours before *Seanymph* could recover her. She was subsequently jettisoned after the flooding of her side charges made her uncontrollable. *X9* simply disappeared during the tow and was never seen again. Lieutenant Godfrey Place had to kick a mine away from *X7* after it became entangled in the tow-rope securing her to HM S/M *Stubborn*.

At 0715 hours on 22 September, despite a flooded periscope, Lieutenant Donald Cameron in *X6* succeeded in penetrating the nets around the *Tirpitz* and released his charges directly under the battleship's 'B' turret. Cameron and his crew of three were forced to scuttle X6 after coming under fire and were picked up by *Tirpitz's* picket boat. Meanwhile, Godfrey Place had overcome a faulty gyro-compass to lay his charges exactly on target. At 0812 hours, as *Tirpitz's* crew desperately tried to get her under way, eight tons of amatol exploded on the sea-bed beneath her. The huge 45,000-ton ship was heaved fully five feet in the air, all three main engines were damaged, the electrical supply failed, and her port rudder was rendered inoperable. Much other equipment was damaged and the battleship was put out of action for many months.

X7 became entangled in the nets around the battleship and was damaged by gunfire and depth-charges. Lieutenant Place decided there was no alternative but to abandon ship and brought the midget to the surface. He had got over the side when X7 suddenly sank beneath him, taking the other three crew members with her. Only Sub-Lieutenant Bob Aitken succeeded in escaping from the sunken submarine. X5 was sunk by either depth-charges or gunfire from *Tirpitz*. X10 developed a long list of mechanical faults on the way in to the target area and had to abort her part of the mission. Both Place and Cameron were awarded the Victoria Cross.

X24 undertook two missions to Bergen harbour in the summer of 1944. On the second, in September, she destroyed a large floating dock. These missions should have been undertaken by the unlucky X22, which had been rammed and sunk by her parent submarine, HM S/M *Syrtis*, during a towing exercise in a strong gale when *Syrtis* turned suddenly to rescue her Officer of the Watch who had been washed overboard.

Two weeks after this unfortunate incident, *Syrtis* and Arthur Pitt's *Taku* sailed from the Holy Loch on a patrol to penetrate the Skaggerak and sink German ships supplying their garrison in Norway. At the forward base at the Alexander Wharf, Lerwick, they were joined by *Satyr* commanded by Lieutenant Toby Weston. *Satyr* had come north from the 9th Flotilla base at Dundee.

Lieutenant Michael Jupp of *Syrtis*, Arthur Pitt, Toby Weston and Lieutenant-Commander Goosens of the Dutch submarine *Zwardfisch*, were entertained to dinner by the Senior Officer (Submarines) at Lerwick, Lieutenant-Commander H. C. 'Hairy' Browne and his wife Nesta. Dinner over, Michael Jupp was about to play his harmonica when the phone rang. Intelligence had been received from agents in Norway that the *Tirpitz* had finally made good most of the damage inflicted the previous year by the midget submarines. She was reported to be about to make a dash for dockyard facilities in the south. Every available submarine, including those in training, was to be sent north as soon as possible.

Taku, Syrtis and *Satyr* put to sea within the hour. *Taku* encountered a 10,000-ton tanker escorted by a destroyer and Pitt fired a salvo of six torpedoes, one of which hit the tanker. The destroyer escort turned on *Taku* and dropped depth-charges, the first of which exploded close to the submarine's stern. As the boat whipped throughout her length, the crew were thrown off their feet, lights went out and the air was filled with dust. An electrical fire in the engine-room was swiftly dealt with, though the electric motor which drove one of the pumps had burnt out. *Taku* was in a headlong dive and, despite having her planes set hard to rise and blowing tanks, it seemed that nothing would stop her before she reached her crushing depth. Finally, at 280 feet, she stopped her dizzy descent and began to rise. Fortunately, the destroyer had left to escort the damaged tanker into port.

Satyr also suffered serious damage on this patrol and *Syrtis* never returned from her billet off Bodo. It is thought that she may have struck a mine. In the event, the *Tirpitz* did not put to sea.

Taku undertook the planned patrol to the Skaggerak the following month. On the morning of 13 April, while running submerged, she detonated a mine. Such was the violence of the explosion that the hull visibly compressed twice. All the lights went out, a fire started among the batteries, high-power switches in the engine-room started arcing, and a loading rail strong enough to take the weight of two 1.5-ton torpedoes was ripped from its sockets. One periscope had jammed and the other was badly damaged and all but useless. Shafts had been knocked out of alignment causing bearings to run hot and one sailor risked electrocution when he crawled into the space behind the main switchboard and used an oilskin to divert water away from vital switchgear.

Once the dazed crew had regained their senses they set course for home. *Taku's* incredible escape was celebrated by a piece of twisted and flattened bridge voice-pipe which formed the centrepiece of her wardroom ashtray and bore the inscription 'Mined your own business'.

On 20 March 1944, while *Taku, Satyr* and *Syrtis* were engaged on their abortive search for the *Tirpitz* an unusual-looking submarine went ashore and was wrecked on the rocky west coast of Islay. She was HM S/M *Graph,* formerly the German type VIIC U-boat *U570*. Kapitanleutnant Hans Joachim Rahmlow had taken *U570* to sea in August 1941. It was her first patrol and he had a notably inexperienced crew. On 28 August the U-boat was spotted on the surface south of Iceland by Squadron-Leader Thompson in a Hudson of 269 Squadron. Thompson dropped four depth-charges set to explode at minimum depth and the U-boat crew indicated their desire to surrender by waving Rahmlow's dress-shirt.

Lieutenant-Commander George Colvin brought *U570* back to the Clyde and she was assigned to the 3rd Flotilla in the Holy Loch as an experimental boat. Her capture was a gift to the Royal Navy, providing as it did an up-to-date assessment of German submarine technology. British sailors and technical experts were deeply impressed by the quality of her construction and equipment, even if they did find her interior somewhat cramped. It was discovered that her hull could easily withstand water pressures of up to 15 atmospheres, as experienced at a depth of 150 metres. Royal Navy depth-charges were redesigned as a result. Her experimental role resulted in *U570* being commissioned into the Royal Navy as HMS *Graph*.

Lieutenant-Commander Peter Marriot took *Graph* on operational patrol from the Holy Loch on 8 October 1942. On the afternoon of 21 October, Marriot fired a salvo of torpedoes at a similar type VIIC north of Cape Ortegal in the Bay of Biscay. His target was *U333* commanded by Kapitanleutnant Peter Cremer, which was returning to Lorient with serious damage sustained in an encounter with the corvette HMS *Crocus*. Part of the *Crocus*'s hull draped around *U333*'s conning tower caused strange hydrophone noises which Marriot described as sounding like the rattling of biscuit tins. Alert watchkeepers in *U333* spotted the approaching torpedo tracks and took successful avoiding action.

Graph was 35 miles west of Colonsay and under tow of the tug *Empire John* in a severe gale at 0310 hours on 18 March 1944 when the tow parted. The rescue tug *Allegiance* sailed from Campbeltown to assist. *Graph* was being towed as a bare boat with her hatches battened down and, as there was no crew aboard her, it proved impossible to resecure the tow. Efforts to save the submarine had to be abandoned when the *Empire John* broke a steering rod and was herself taken in tow by *Allegiance*. The wreckage of *Graph* was removed from Islay by the Liverpool and Glasgow Salvage Company.

A small flotilla of American submarines, Submarine Squadron 50, including USS *Barb*, USS *Gunnel* and USS *Blackfish*, were operating from USS *Beaver*, their depot ship at Roseneath, by the end of 1942. Work on US Navy shore facilities in the Clyde had begun amid great secrecy some months before the United States' entry into the war in December 1941. Royal Navy officers inspecting the 180 huts completed by October 1941 were most impressed by the standard of accommodation. Work was then well advanced on piers and pen berths.

The siege of Malta was at its height in April 1942 and it was vital that air reinforcements should be got to the beleaguered island as quickly as possible. 'Operation Calendar', a larger-scale version of the movement of fighters to Norway in April 1940, was planned.

The original intention was to load the fighters on to barges in the River Cart and take them to Greenock where they would be loaded on to the American carrier USS *Wasp*. Nobody appears to have considered the fact that the Cart is a tidal river and thus only navigable for two hours with each tide. It was then decided that the carrier should come upriver to King George V Dock. The first four Spitfires were flown into Abbotsinch on 7 April by pilots of the Air Transport Auxiliary (ATA). As more Spitfires arrived at Abbots-inch, landings at the waterlogged grass airfield became decidedly hazardous. In addition, it became apparent that moving large numbers of aircraft through the streets of Paisley would be quite impossible.

The only alternative was to ferry the Spitfires into Renfrew. Renfrew aerodrome was widely held to be too small for Spitfires but, on 10 April, the ATA pilots made 23 successful landings. USS *Wasp* had by then arrived in the Clyde and the Spitfires were taken along Renfrew Road on trailers specially constructed to ensure the aircraft did not foul obstructions such as tramway power lines, lamp-posts and gates.

Forty-seven Spitfires were loaded aboard the *Wasp* and the American ship sailed from the Tail o' the Bank on 14 April. Her formidable escort included the battleship *Renown*, and four Royal Navy and two American destroyers. The Spitfires flew into Malta only for two of their number to be destroyed and a further 17 damaged in an air-raid. Only then was it discovered that nobody had bothered to synchronise the guns before they left Scotland. In addition, the planes' radios were faulty. Just 17 of the Spitfires remained undamaged after 48 hours on the island.

USS *Wasp* returned to the Clyde on 30 April to carry out 'Operation Bowery', the second Spitfire delivery to Malta. By this time, ground crews had reached a peak of efficiency such that they could drain a fighter's fuel tanks, remove its wingtips, place it on a trailer, move it to the docks and load it aboard the carrier all within an hour of the Spitfire's arrival at Renfrew. When they sailed on 3 May, USS *Wasp* and the Royal Navy carrier HMS *Eagle* delivered a total of 62 Spitfires to Malta.

Both Renfrew and Abbotsinch were considerably expanded during the war, the old grass airstrips giving way to extended, surfaced runways, aprons and perimeter tracks. Both Lockheed Overseas and Airwork Ltd at Renfrew prepared hundreds of aircraft either flown across from America or brought to King George V Dock as deck cargo.

Abbotsinch was formally transferred to the Navy in August 1943 although their maintenance yard there was already well established as HMS *Sanderling*. Both Abbotsinch and its sister station, HMS *Landrail* at Machrihanish, were busy with torpedo and deck-landing training for carrier-borne squadrons.

The escort carrier HMS *Dasher* was exercising her Sea Hurricane and Swordfish aircraft in the Clyde on the afternoon of Saturday, 27 March 1943. *Dasher* was a converted American merchant vessel, formerly the *Rio de Janeiro*, fitted with a flight deck and supplied under 'Lend-Lease' agreement. Considerably smaller than a conventional carrier, she provided fighter cover for convoys beyond the range of land-based aircraft.

Off Ardrossan, at 1645 hours, Motor Launch 528 was just one and a half cables astern of *Dasher* when her horrified crew watched as the carrier's after

A busy winter morning, early in 1942, at the 3rd Submarine Flotilla base in the Holy Loch. Furthest from the camera is Unbroken, *commanded by Newfoundlander, Lieutenant Alistair Mars.* Unbroken *torpedoed and damaged two Italian cruisers, the* Bolzano *and the* Attendolo, *on 13 August 1942 during operations in the Mediterranean in which she sank or seriously damaged over 30,000 tons of enemy shipping. On one occasion Mars surfaced his boat close inshore and shelled a train on the Italian coastal railway, completely wrecking it.* Unbroken *was one of a number of Royal Navy vessels, including the battleship* Royal Sovereign, *handed over to the Soviet Navy in May 1944. In the centre, carrying the pennant number N46, is the captured U570, renamed* Graph *for her service with the Royal Navy. Outboard boat alongside the depot ship HMS* Forth, *from where the photograph was taken, is* Sturgeon. *One of the first 'S'-class boats built at Chatham in the early 1930s,* Sturgeon *was transferred to the Free Dutch Navy in 1943, becoming* Zeehond *and operating with the 9th Flotilla out of Dundee. Seven boats of various classes were based at the Holy Loch with the 3rd Flotilla in January 1942. By May 1944, 26 boats were operating with the flotilla and another 15 boats were attached to the 7th Flotilla at Rothesay. A further 12 boats comprised the 9th Flotilla at Dundee in 1944.*

end was ripped apart by a violent explosion. She sank in just four minutes and, of her crew of 527 men, just 149 survived, many of them terribly burned. As the cause of the explosion was not immediately apparent, the area was swept for both mines and possible U-boats, though without result. A Court of Enquiry concluded that the blast had been the result of a chain reaction started when a dropped cigarette end exploded trapped vapour in the petrol control department.

The storage of high-octane aviation fuel in carriers was always risky and required careful handling. The drifter *Honeydew* had just gone alongside the carrier *Indomitable* off Greenock late on 10 October 1941 when she caught fire after being deluged in petrol from the carrier. Two of her crew were badly burned before the fire was put out.

The rather primitive airfield at Annan in Dumfriesshire became the home of 55 Operational Training Unit in April 1942. Here, partially trained fighter-pilots were brought up to operational standard prior to being posted to squadrons. By 1942 Fighter Command was mounting low-level sweeps, called 'Rhubarbs', over occupied France. Hurricane pilots at Annan trained for this role by mounting cine-gun attacks at zero feet on 'targets' in Cumberland and the Isle of Man, the Solway Firth doubling as the English Channel. The combination of old, often battle-weary aircraft and partially trained pilots resulted in frequent crashes.

RAF Annan occupied a particularly ill-chosen site, perched on the top of a hill and subject to notably unpredictable weather. The wind could – and often did – change direction from one end of the runway to the other. This made take-offs and landings by inexperienced pilots a somewhat hazardous affair.

Scottish Aviation Ltd opened a flying boat maintenance base on the site of the former Caird's Shipyard at Greenock in the summer of 1940. This they operated on behalf of the Ministry of Aircraft Production. Large numbers of Catalina flying boats, newly arrived from the United States, were to be seen on the moorings in Cardwell Bay awaiting preparation for RAF service. The RAF's marine craft maintenance was also undertaken here until McAllister's Shipyard at the mouth of the River Leven was requisitioned as 62 Maintenance Unit. The Marine Aircraft Experimental Unit opened at Rhu in 1939 and tested many new types including captured German aircraft brought back from Norway in 1940.

Unquestionably the most important single air terminal in Britain during the Second World War was that at Prestwick. Opened as a grass field in 1936, it had relatively humble pre-war beginnings as 12 Elementary Flying Training School attached to Scottish Aviation. Within the space of just nine years it had become the eastern terminal of the Atlantic 'bridge' which supplied vital aircraft and men for both the Battle of the Atlantic and the bombing offensive over occupied Europe.

After a flight of lasting more than 14 hours, American delivery pilot Captain Bob Perlick
signs over the 19th Liberator bomber he had delivered to Prestwick for the RAF.
(TRUSTEES OF THE IMPERIAL WAR MUSEUM, LONDON)

Early flights from Canada to Prestwick, beginning in January 1940, brought mainly Lockheed Hudsons and could take anything from eight to 15 hours, depending on weather conditions. One of the very first arrivals was described thus: 'We kept pretty good contact with the machine all the way in, considering the tackle we had to work with. At somewhere around 11.30 I saw him coming in towards the field and I set off for the aerodrome, arriving there as he landed . . . There was no elaborate reception committee. We had not spread the news around and there wasn't a newspaper man, nor a photographer; not even a couple of chaps with kilts and bagpipes. Just the CO and myself, and the Customs man from Ayr docks, who at the time constituted the Customs, Immigration and Security Police.'

The Atlantic Ferry Organisation was originally administered by the British Overseas Airways Corporation (BOAC) and flown by their civilian crews, many of them American volunteers. In 1941 it became RAF Ferry Command and subsequently, in 1943, Transport Command.

B24 Liberators, desperately needed for long-range convoy patrols by Coastal Command, followed the Hudsons. The United States entered the war in December 1941 and, on 1 July 1942, the first B17 Flying Fortress for the 8th Air Force transitted through Prestwick. In August 1944, two months after

Beach landing training, Loch Fyne, 1942.
(TRUSTEES OF THE IMPERIAL WAR MUSEUM, LONDON)

General Montgomery inspecting Free French paratroops training for the invasion of Europe at Galston, Ayrshire, in April 1944. Looking on, fifth from the left, is Brigadier Gerald Lathbury who commanded the British First Parachute Brigade during the ill-fated Arnhem operation in September 1944. Lathbury was wounded and captured but managed to escape from hospital. After spending some time working with the Dutch resistance, he was one of a group of approximately 120 escapees who reached American units south of the Rhine on 22 October 1944.
(TRUSTEES OF THE IMPERIAL WAR MUSEUM, LONDON)

D-day, 7,847 aircraft movements were recorded. Many of these flights were taking GIs home after being injured in the fighting in France.

From mid-1942, conclusive proof, if it were needed, that the war in the west was becoming essentially an American affair was arriving fortnightly in the Clyde. The two great Cunarders, *Queen Mary* and *Queen Elizabeth*, were running a shuttle service from North America carrying as many as 15,000 GIs on each trip. Able to make 28.5 knots, the liners could cross largely unescorted, secure in the knowledge that they were too fast for any U-boat to catch. On one winter crossing, while she had 10,000 troops aboard, the *Queen Mary* was struck broadside by a huge wave which rolled her over on to her beam ends.

On 2 October 1942, Captain Gordon Illingworth was bringing the *Queen Mary* into the North Channel and had just made his rendezvous with the inshore escort out of Londonderry. Six destroyers undertook an Asdic sweep ahead of the liner and the old converted 'C'-class cruiser *Curacao* provided anti-aircraft cover. *Curacao* could barely keep up with the *Queen Mary* even when cutting across her zig-zag course. With two vessels in such close proximity and on repeatedly converging courses, a moment's indecision could have fatal consequences, and the *Queen Mary* rammed *Curacao* at a fine angle near 'X' turret, about 114 feet from the cruiser's stern, rolled her over and cut her in two.

Of *Curacao*'s crew of 432, only Captain John Boutwood, one other officer and 99 sailors survived to be picked up by the destroyers *Bramham* and *Cowdray*. Both the survivors, and the 11,000 American servicemen aboard the *Queen Mary* were sworn to secrecy about the collision. Despite some bodies being washed ashore, secrecy was maintained until the end of the war.

The Admiralty sued Cunard for £1,200,000 in compensation for the loss of *Curacao* and her crew. They lost their case and both Cunard and the *Queen Mary* were cleared of any blame for the incident.

In the autumn of 1942, as the great liners were disgorging thousands of American troops into tenders which took most of them on to Northern Ireland, the Clyde Anchorages began to fill up with assault craft. Two large Combined Operations exercises, code-named 'Flaxman' and 'Mosstrooper', were held in the first two weeks of October. These involved beach-landing exercises in the Clyde, the Gareloch, Rothesay, Loch Fyne and Loch Linnhe and marked the final preparations for the eastern element of 'Operation Torch', the invasion of Vichy French-held North Africa.

Both Roosevelt and Churchill were aware of the need to take pressure off the Soviet army, then reeling under relentless German pressure. Roosevelt also had domestic reasons for wanting a victory for American arms.

The proposed invasion of Vichy territory in North Africa was to be a largely American affair, partly because Roosevelt believed, rightly, that the Vichy French still harboured considerable hatred for the British. This was a result of the sinking, by the Royal Navy, of a large part of the French fleet following that country's armistice with Germany in 1940. Naïvely, the Americans believed that they would be welcomed as liberators provided that any British involvement in the operation could be concealed. At one point, Churchill even considered dressing the British troops taking part in American uniforms.

As the huge invasion armada assembled in the Clyde, American demolition teams used Ardhallow Battery to train in the destruction of coastal gun emplacements. American LCI(L) – Landing Craft Infantry (Large) – crews worked up at Inveraray. Both American Rangers and British Commandos were finalising their preparations at Achnacarry Castle.

Security was intense. Colonel 'Con' Boddington, an anti-sabotage expert, was among a number of MI5 officers sent north. The Port Security and Travel Control Office in the requisitioned Ferry Cafe at Gourock became a hive of activity, as did the Observation Post of Captain Tancred, the Clyde Extended Defence Officer, above the Cloch Light.

274 merchantmen and troop transports were formed up, with their escorts, into convoys for two task forces. The Central Task Force, under Commodore Thomas Troubridge, carried 39,000 GIs for a landing at Oran. The Eastern Task Force under Admiral Harold Burrough was to land 33,000 American and British soldiers to capture Algiers.

As the Greenock war diary records at the end of October: 'During the past fortnight, the port facilities at Greenock have been severely strained. At times all berths, including those in Loch Long and the Gareloch, have been occupied, and both HM ships and merchantmen have had to be diverted elsewhere. Ships of KMF1, which were Combined Operations ships, had to remain in their exercise areas until the sailing of KMS1 [on 22 October] made berths available inside the boom. The subsequent servicing of KMF1, in order to get them ready to sail for an operation in the short time available, put a heavy strain on the services of the Clyde, particularly on water boats and the boats of the boat pool.' KMF1 sailed for the Straits of Gibraltar on 26 October.

In Egypt, the Battle of El Alamein had opened on 23 October and, by the time the Torch landings took place on 7 November, Rommel's Africa Corps was in full retreat. Despite this, Vichy forces at first resisted strongly and American landings at Casablanca, launched directly from the United States, came close to failure.

Operations in North Africa and the Mediterranean continued until 1945. Around 13,000 PoWs, mainly German but including a number of Italians, arrived in Glasgow Docks between 6 and 9 June 1943. The majority were placed aboard otherwise empty troop-ships returning to North America before being sent on to prisoner-of-war camps in Canada.

Between 11 May 1942 and 31 December 1944, 339 troop-ships arrived in the Clyde from the United States. They brought with them 1,319,089 GIs. Activity around the west coast reached a new peak in the spring of 1944, as D-Day approached. A number of convoys for the invasion of France left from the Clyde, among them the 10th Cruiser Squadron led by HMS *Belfast*.

With the war in Europe drawing to a successful conclusion, planners turned their attention towards the defeat of Japan. The old battleship *Malaya* steamed up the Kyles of Bute and was moored in Loch Striven. There she acted as a practice target for 'Operation Golfball', the dropping of aerial mines against Japanese naval vessels. The 'Golfball' weapon was based on the

'Highball' anti-shipping mine from which Barnes Wallis developed the famous 'Upkeep' bouncing bomb which was used against the German dams in 1943. They were to be dropped from the specially adapted carrier-based Mosquitoes of 618 Squadron.

In the event, in August 1945, before the Mosquitoes could reach the Far East, the cities of Hiroshima and Nagasaki were reduced to ashes.

Chapter Five

North Western Approaches

It was the U-boat which came nearest to bringing Britain to her knees in the First World War. By the end of March 1917, the Kriegsmarine had 138 U-boats, of which 105 were operational at any one time. Between November 1916 and January 1917 they sank almost a million tons of British shipping, and in March that year a further 564,000 tons. The convoy system had not yet been introduced, largely due to a series of extraordinary miscalculations by the Admiralty. By April 1917 Britain was reduced to having an estimated six weeks' supply of essential raw materials, and merchant ships were being lost at the rate of ten every day. Defeat was more than just a real possibility. Two decisions saved the day: one was the declaration of war by the United States on 6 April, and the other was the introduction of the convoy system.

Britain in 1939 was still dependent for survival on her merchant navy. Around 2,500 merchant vessels were at sea under the red ensign at any one time and more than 190,000 seamen of various nationalities were employed. The British economy relied on the import of 55 million tons of goods, including all of its oil, most of its raw materials and half of its food.

The size of the Royal Navy has always been conditional on the need to protect Britain's vital sea lanes, as is clearly shown by its steady contraction since 1945, in parallel with the shrinkage of the merchant fleet. In the 20 years following the end of the First World War the Navy had been the victim of benign neglect and was thus ill-prepared to meet the challenge of another war of attrition in the North Atlantic.

Parliament, seemingly incapable of comprehending the danger, severely restricted the building of modern vessels suitable for convoy escort duty. Scarce resources were diverted into the, at best, partially effective rebuilding of elderly First World War battleships and the requirement for adequate anti-aircraft armament was largely ignored. Naval aviation had undergone a period of acute decline and the Fleet Air Arm, wrested from the clutches of the RAF but two years prior to the outbreak of war, was short of 100 pilots. RAF Coastal Command was also desperately under-strength and equipped with obsolete and hopelessly inadequate aircraft.

In September 1939 the Navy possessed just 220 vessels equipped with Asdic, the ranging sonar equipment which could detect and track submerged submarines. Of these, 165 were destroyers, the rest being smaller vessels such as trawlers and sloops. Much of the destroyer fleet was required to screen the movements of the Navy's capital ships. Asdic had many limitations, not the least of which was the fact that it was useless against surfaced U-boats, and marine radar was still in its infancy. Too many of the lessons of the First World War were going to have to be relearned at a considerable cost to lives and ships.

The first weeks of the war were disastrous for the Royal Navy. Following the narrow escape of *Ark Royal* and the loss of the carrier *Courageous* (see Chapter One), the battleship *Royal Oak* was torpedoed by Kapitanleutnant Gunther Prien in Scapa Flow at 0116 hours on 14 October 1939. Winston Churchill was one of the many who were aware of the vulnerability of the Home Fleet's main anchorage at Scapa. In an Admiralty memorandum dated 12 October he wrote, 'These next few days are full of danger.'

The Home Fleet had put to sea, leaving *Royal Oak* behind – but not, as in the accepted version of events, to provide anti-aircraft cover. *Royal Oak* possessed strictly limited anti-aircraft armament and there was only one other ship within range of any cover she could provide – the old seaplane tender *Pegasus*. The reality was that *Royal Oak* was too old and slow to keep up with the rest of the fleet and was thus an effective liability.

Prien brought *U47* in through a narrow gap in Kirk Sound on the east side of the Flow and fired a total of seven torpedoes, four of which hit *Royal Oak*. The battleship caught fire, rolled over and sank in around nine minutes, taking 833 of her crew with her. Decades later there were still those, unable to come to terms with the relative ease with which Prien was able to sink this ship, who advanced the theory that her loss had been due to a bomb placed aboard by saboteurs.

The immediate effect of the sinking was the dispersal of the Home Fleet away from Scapa Flow. The vulnerability of Rosyth to air attack was demonstrated just two days after the sinking when 12 Junkers 88 bombers damaged the cruiser *Southampton* and the destroyer *Mohawk*. (For a fuller description of these events, see *This Present Emergency* by the same author.) A further German air attack was mounted against Scapa Flow the following day, 17 October.

Loch Ewe and the Clyde were obvious choices as safer havens, though it was felt by many that this would leave the east coast dangerously exposed. Winston Churchill had other objections to such a deployment. He wrote: 'There are plenty of Irish traitors in the Glasgow area; telephone communication with Ireland is, I believe, unrestricted; there is a German Ambassador in Dublin. I should expect that within a few hours of the arrival of these ships, it would be known in Berlin that the British heavy ships were out of the North Sea and could not return for 60 hours.' There were still those, Churchill included, who believed that the naval war would take the form of a First World War-style face-off across the North Sea in which Britain would be able to shelter behind her fleet.

While outbound from Scapa Flow to Trinidad on 11 February 1940 the tanker Imperial Transport *was torpedoed by U53 west of the Hebrides and broke in two. Brought into the Clyde by the rescue tug* Buccaneer, *she was fitted with a new bow section. Kapitanleutnant Grosse's U53 was sunk by the destroyer HMS* Gurkha *in the Pentland Firth on 23 February while returning from this mission.*
Imperial Transport *was torpedoed for a second time off Iceland by U94 on 25 March 1942 and again survived. After the war she was operated by Norwegian owners.*
(RALSTON COLLECTION, STRATHCLYDE REGIONAL ARCHIVES)

As the homeless Home Fleet sailed on a fruitless chase of the German battle-cruisers *Scharnhorst* and *Gneisenau,* another disaster was averted thanks only to the faulty design of German torpedoes. The Navy's only three modern capital ships, *Rodney, Nelson* and *Hood,* were passing 45 miles to the north of Cape Wrath on 30 October when Kapitanleutnant Wilhelm Zahn in *U56* fired three torpedoes, two of which struck *Nelson* but failed to explode.

The Fleetwood steam trawler *Cresswell* was fired on and sunk by a surfaced U-boat 18 miles north-west of the Flannan Islands on 12 November. Six of her crew were killed. The U-boat captain handed the survivors over to another Fleetwood trawler and told them he had earlier sunk a tanker. This was confirmed when a flying boat of 209 Squadron Coastal Command sighted the remains of the Norwegian tanker *Arne Kjode* west of Lewis. Five of her crew died. Another 26 people died when the Dutch tanker *Sleidrecht* was sunk south of Rockall on 16 November and three more Fleetwood trawlers were sunk north of Ireland four days later. Eleven of the crew of the *Delphine* died.

The armed merchant cruiser *Rawalpindi,* a hastily converted P&O liner, sailed from the Clyde for the northern patrol on 13 November. Ten days later, south of Iceland, she sighted *Scharnhorst* and *Gniesenau.* Having signalled their presence Captain Edward Kennedy and his crew gallantly turned to give action. *Scharnhorst's* battery of nine 11" guns battered *Rawalpindi* into a smoking ruin in just 14 minutes, providing ample evidence, if it were needed, of the folly of sending such ill-equipped vessels out on their own. The British ship managed to score one hit on *Scharnhorst* with her old 6" guns. *Scharnhorst* picked up 21 survivors and the British AMC *Chitral* another 11.

Four U-boats were sent to the north and west coasts of Scotland in mid-November 1939; *U31* and *U48* to the Orkneys, *U35* to the Pentland Firth and Gunther Prien in *U47* to the Minch and North Channel. Prien sank two Fleetwood trawlers, the *Sulby* and the *William Humphries,* in surface gun action 75 miles north-west of Rathlin Island at 1130 hours on 21 November. Five of *Sulby's* crew died.

HMS *Nelson,* at 33,950 tons and with nine 16" guns as her main armament, was one of the most powerful warships in the world. Returning from an abortive sweep of the North Atlantic, she and her screen of four destroyers were approaching Loch Ewe on 4 December 1939. At 0754 hours she was less than a mile from the entrance when a mine exploded under her starboard bow. Badly holed, with a list of three degrees and almost eight feet down by the bow, it took the big battleship almost four hours to struggle to her anchorage in the lee of Ewe Island. One officer and 50 ratings had been injured.

The Kriegsmarine had not been slow to realise that the Royal Navy would fall back on the Clyde and Loch Ewe following the sinking of *Royal Oak* and the subsequent air attacks at Rosyth and Scapa. Kapitanleutnant Johannes Hackebosch in *U31* had attempted to get into the loch on 27 October. Coming up against the anti-submarine nets, he was forced to lay his pattern of 18 mines just off the entrance. It was one of these which exploded under HMS *Nelson*. Others destroyed the Admiralty drifters *Glen Albyn* and *Promotive* on 23 December. On his next mission Hackebosch laid mines in the Firth of Forth, one of which broke the back of the new cruiser HMS *Belfast* on 21 November.

HMS *Nelson* was trapped in Loch Ewe until the fairway could be swept, and did not complete repairs until August 1940. The War Cabinet, on Churchill's advice, kept the news of the damage to the ship under a blanket of secrecy; not even the Dominion Prime Ministers were told.

Nelson was not the only battleship in trouble on the west coast of Scotland that month. Amid thick fog in the early hours of 12 December, the destroyer HMS *Duchess* was lost after colliding with the 27,500-ton *Barham*: 120 men were lost.

Barham's troubles were only beginning. On 28 December 1939, when she was 50 miles from the Butt of Lewis covering a troop convoy on its way to the Clyde from Canada, she was struck by a torpedo fired by Fritz-Julius Lemp in *U30*. A and B shell magazines were flooded and the forward bulkhead of the 6" magazine was leaking. Despite the damage, her pumps were well able to cope and she could still make 11 knots for the Clyde. She was under repair for four months. Some 862 of *Barham*'s crew died when she was torpedoed and sunk in the Mediterranean in November 1941.

At 0230 hours, shortly before torpedoing the *Barham*, Lemp had sunk the trawler *Barbara Robertson* by gunfire. One of her crew was killed and the destroyer *Isis* picked up survivors before embarking on an anti-submarine sweep.

U51 torpedoed the neutral Swedish motor ship *Gothia* 45 miles north-west of St Kilda during a snowstorm on the morning of 18 January 1940. Nine men were reported adrift in a lifeboat near the Flannan Islands on 25 January, though a search by a Coastal Command Anson revealed nothing. An empty raft was found off Norway at the end of May 1940.

The tanker *Imperial Transport*, outbound for Trinidad, was torpedoed by *U53* on 11 February. Her crew managed to reach the stern section before the bow broke away. The rescue tug *Buccaneer* sailed from the Clyde and took the stern half in tow at daylight five days later. Arriving in the Clyde on 26 February, she was beached in Kilchattan Bay while a new forward section was fabricated. *U53* was sunk in the Pentland Firth by the destroyer *Gurkha* on 23 February, five days after Kapitanleutnant Grosse had sunk the destroyer *Daring* off Duncansby Head with the loss of 157 men.

U-boats continued to be employed in laying mines in Scottish coastal waters during January and February 1940. Otto Kretschmer, soon to become an ace, laid mines in the Moray Firth. Both *U32* and *U33* were sent to mine the Clyde; missions their crews thought, with some justification, to be suicidal.

In the early hours of 12 February HMS *Gleaner*, a Halcyon-class fleet mine-sweeper, was on anti-submarine patrol south of Arran when she heard hydrophone noise. Lieutenant-Commander Hugh Price ordered the searchlight deployed on the hydrophone bearing and a U-boat was seen on the surface, making 14 knots on a course which would take her upriver. In *U33*, Kapitanleutnant Hans von Dresky ordered a crash dive to 150 feet, but *Gleaner*'s first pattern of depth-charges pounded her into the sea-bed. Price dropped his third pattern deliberately and at slow speed right across the U-boat. The blast effect from depth-charges exploding so close to *Gleaner*'s hull was sufficient to damage her Asdic and dislodge the carbons in her searchlight. *U33* surfaced at 0522 hours and *Gleaner* fired five rounds at the submarine from her 4" gun. At 0530 hours she signalled that the U-boat had surrendered and scuttled herself three miles south-east of Pladda Light.

Gleaner's boats picked up one officer and eight ratings, while the trawler *Bohemian Girl* rescued two officers and seven men, two of whom died before reaching Lamlash; additionally, Jim Farquhar in the Fleetwood drifter *Floradora* picked up an officer, and the Admiralty trawler *Kingston* recovered 20 bodies and two survivors. One of those who died was Kapitanleutnant von Dresky. Max Schiller, one of those picked up by the *Bohemian Girl*, had the unnerving experience of looking at his own tombstone in Greenock. Following a case of mistaken identity, his name had been added to the list of the dead. After the war he married a Scot and settled in Dumfriesshire.

While ordering his crew to abandon, von Dresky had distributed rotors for the 'Enigma' coding machine among them with orders that they were to be ditched in the sea. When one of the submarine's engineers was picked up, two rotors were found still in his pocket.

The German victories in Scandinavia and France fundamentally altered the strategic position in the North Atlantic. The Kriegsmarine gained new bases on the Atlantic seaboard in Norway and Brittany and the British were forced to re-route convoys through the North Channel, away from enemy-held territory.

The evacuation from Dunkirk had hardly concluded when, on 5 June 1940, the coaster *Stancourt* became the first ship to be sunk in the North Western Approaches since the start of the Norway campaign. She was fired on by a surfaced U-boat at 2215 hours, 50 miles north of the Butt of Lewis. Two boats containing survivors reached Stornoway a couple of days later. The SS *Frances Massey*, bound for Glasgow carrying iron ore, was torpedoed by *U25* while she was 60 miles west of Islay on 6 June. Thirty-five of her crew died, leaving her master as the only survivor. The rescue tugs *Brigand* and *Marauder* sailed from the Clyde later that afternoon escorted by the destroyers *Wren* and *Volunteer* and the mine-sweeper *Gleaner*. They were on their way to assist the AMC *Carinthia* which had also been torpedoed by *U25*. *Marauder* reported that *Carinthia* sank while under tow for the Clyde.

Gleaner and the rescue tug *Bandit* were diverted from the *Carinthia* on 7 June to go to the aid of the SS *Eros*, another of *U25*'s victims. The *Eros* was beached on Tory Island and HMS *Gleaner* stood by the wreck as there were fears that her cargo would be looted.

A U-boat was sighted off the coast of Northern Ireland on 12 June and, on the following day, the AMC *Scotstoun*, formerly the *Caledonia* of the Anchor Line, outbound from the Clyde for the northern patrol, was struck by two torpedoes fired by *U25*. The first torpedo shattered the steering gear and propeller and brought down the radio aerial. The guns were immediately manned but all that could be seen were occasional glimpses of a periscope. Meanwhile the radio operator had rigged a jury aerial and managed to send a distress signal. The second torpedo then struck the ship and she began to keel over and sink. Six of her 350 crew were lost including Reginald Jones, a regular Anchor Line catering employee who, according to First Lieutenant Cookson, served a boat deck gun 'as if he had been doing it all his life'.

The first large Anzac troop convoy arrived off Greenock on 16 June. It included the liners *Queen Mary*, *Aquitania*, *Mauretania*, *Andes*, *Empress of Britain* and *Empress of Canada*. The powerful escort was led by the battleship HMS *Hood* and the cruisers *Cumberland* and *Shropshire*.

The rescue tug *Amsterdam* escorted by the destroyer *Atherstone* sailed from the Clyde on the morning of 20 June in response to reports of a ship torpedoed and sinking 40 miles west of Iona. The SS *Empire Conveyor*, inbound for Manchester with grain, had sunk by the time they arrived.

On 19 June, the day France surrendered, the War Cabinet reluctantly agreed to go ahead with a scheme code-named 'Hedgehog' whereby children aged under 16 could be evacuated to the Dominions. The announcement of the scheme in the House of Commons that afternoon led to the London office of the tactfully entitled Children's Overseas Reception Board being besieged by a crowd of over 3,000 anxious parents. An announcement from the American embassy five days later that they were willing to allow British children to enter the United States brought similar scenes. Within two weeks the British scheme alone had received over 210,000 applications. Foreseeing that an overwhelming response to the scheme would not only be a visible measure of the true state of public morale, but also that it could lead to a stampede, Churchill and many other ministers were set against the scheme.

One of the first groups of 90 children sailed on 1 July from Liverpool for Quebec on the liner *Arandora Star*. Also on board were over 700 Italian internees and 473 Germans, including 100 captured merchant seamen, who were being carried to internment in Canada. Meanwhile, Gunther Prien was at the end of a successful patrol in which he had sunk seven ships in convoys inbound from Gibraltar and Canada. He was returning to base and had only one torpedo left when he sighted the *Arandora Star* around 100 miles west of Malin Head in the early hours of 2 July. At 0713 hours Prein's last torpedo struck the liner amidships and she began to sink.

The Canadian destroyers *Skeena* and *St Laurent* were detached from the Home Fleet to her aid, as were the Royal Navy destroyers *Echo*, *Walker*, *Jason* and *Firedrake* which sailed from the Clyde along with the rescue tugs

The Chief Petty Officer's mess in HMS Gleaner, *the fleet mine-sweeper responsible for the destruction, off Arran, of U33. Conditions aboard the tiny, overcrowded North Atlantic escort vessels were rarely as civilised as this photograph, taken in harbour, would indicate. Winds could, and frequently did, reach hurricane force, causing mountainous seas. In the winter, and particularly on the Murmansk run, driving snow and ice were additional hazards. One particularly severe gale in mid-January 1942 left a trail of wrecked vessels from Mingulay to the Mull of Galloway. Convoys became scattered in storms, with lone vessels falling easy prey to prowling U-boats.*
(TRUSTEES OF THE IMPERIAL WAR MUSEUM, LONDON)

Englishman and *Schelde*. Sunderland 'K' of 209 Squadron, piloted by Flight-Lieutenant Phillips, took off from Oban in driving rain to carry out an air-sea search and quickly located the lifeboats. Phillips' crew dropped first-aid kits, food and cigarettes to the survivors and signalled their position to HMCS *St Laurent*.

St Laurent picked up 857 survivors who had been in the water for seven hours. They were landed at Greenock in the early hours of the following morning. Unfortunately, 821 died, including 714 deportees, 37 guards and four crewmen. Some 66 evacuees were drowned. Worse was to come.

Disgraceful and wholly untrue propaganda was circulated to the effect that the high loss of life had been due to the internees fighting amongst themselves for places in the boats. Many of the internees were Jewish refugees of undeniable probity who had escaped from Germany only to find themselves being rounded up and forcibly deported from Britain amid the hysterical orgy of alien-baiting which followed military defeat in Europe. Churchill himself minuted on the report of the sinking that 'The case of the German who saved so many raises the question of special treatment – by parole or otherwise.'

One operation, conducted in the utmost secrecy, reveals that real doubts about Britain's chances of survival in mid-1940 were not confined to the minds of anxious parents. One morning in July, a case fell on Greenock docks and a shower of gold sovereigns burst across the cobbles. Amid tight security, Britain's bullion reserves were being brought north to Glasgow in unmarked railway vans. They were stored in the vaults of the Royal Bank of Scotland in the city's Royal Exchange Square while awaiting a ship which would take them to safety in Canada.

Under the curious code-name 'Operation Fish', the first shipment of £130 million in gold bullion left Greenock on 24 June in the cruiser HMS *Emerald*. The largest shipment, of £440 million, left the Clyde on 2 July. Locked in compartments all over the battleship *Revenge* was £160 million in bullion and negotiable securities. HMS *Bonaventure* and the Polish liner *Sobieski* had £60 million aboard and the rest was in the liners *Monarch of Bermuda* and *Batory*. This convoy passed two empty lifeboats from the *Arandora Star* as it hastened across the Atlantic. In all, well over £1,800 million in gold and securities was spirited out of the Clyde, much of it to a vault under the Sun Alliance building in Vancouver.

The tanker *Scottish Minstrel* was 150 miles west of Tiree, inbound with 9,200 tons of fuel oil on 16 July, when she was torpedoed. The rescue tug *Englishman* sailed from Greenock to assist and a Sunderland took off from Oban to search for survivors. Burning fiercely, the *Scottish Minstrel* foundered before the *Englishman* could reach her. Although 37 survivors were picked up, nine of her crew died. Early the next day, the same U-boat sank the SS *Fellside*, outbound in ballast for Sydney, killing nine of her crew.

The first convoy carrying Anzac troops arrived in the Clyde on 16 June 1940. It comprised the liners Queen Mary, Aquitania, Empress of Canada, Andes, Mauretania *and* Empress of Britain. *To the left of the* Empress of Britain, *pictured here off Greenock, can be seen the twin funnels of the battle-cruiser* Hood, *part of the convoy's escort. The* Empress *and HMS* Hood *were destined to become two of the war's most significant maritime casualties.*
(TRUSTEES OF THE IMPERIAL WAR MUSEUM, LONDON)

Inbound convoy HX55 had split up by the evening of 17 July, some of the ships heading north for the Pentland Firth and ports on the east coast. The SS *Manipur* was sunk six miles off Cape Wrath at 2315 hours when a torpedo exploded in number 4 hold, followed 30 seconds later by another which struck her stokehold. She rolled over and sank in less than five minutes. She lost 14 of her crew; 64 survivors were rescued by HMCS *Skeena*. Two other ships, one a Norwegian, were sunk in the North Western Approaches before the week was out.

The last two weeks of July 1940 saw the Luftwaffe make its first attempt at mining the Clyde approaches. A lone aircraft passed over the Kyles of Bute in the early hours of 16 July and dropped two mines off Tighnabruaich. One exploded on hitting the water, the other detonated at 2245 hours the following day. Two more mines were dropped from a JU88 off Kempock Point, Gourock, at around 0120 hours on 20 July. These were dealt with by mine-sweepers later that morning.

Convoy OB188 was outbound from the North Channel on 26 July when the liner *Accra* and the SS *Vinemoor* were torpedoed. Over 400 survivors were picked up from the *Accra*, which later sank. SS *Vinemoor* stayed afloat despite having had her stern blown off and the *Englishman* was sent from Greenock to bring her in. The destroyer *Jason* and HMS *Gleaner* sailed on 27 July to search for the offending U-boat just as the 5,260-ton SS *Sambre* was torpedoed. The Dutch rescue tug *Schelde* left Campbeltown to go to her aid. The agony of OB188 continued when the 10,000-ton SS *Tiara* was torpedoed. The rescue tug *Brigand* sailed from Kirkwall to take her in tow. Meanwhile, the destroyer *Hurricane* was conducting an anti-submarine sweep of the North Channel, ordered after HM trawler *St Loman* had sighted a periscope.

The 5,472-ton banana boat *Jamaica Progress* was inbound for Holyhead from Kingston, Jamaica, at 2200 hours on 30 July, when she was torpedoed and sunk 45 miles west of Tiree. One lifeboat with 18 survivors aboard reached Castlebay, Barra, at breakfast-time on 1 August. A 210 Squadron Sunderland from Oban spotted the other lifeboat five miles west of Barra Head and the 30 survivors in it were rescued by the trawler *Newlands* and taken to Fleetwood. Eight of the *Jamaica Progress*'s crew died.

Meanwhile, also west of Tiree, the *Jersey City* had been sunk. The destroyer HMS *Walker* signalled at 0112 hours on 2 August that she had picked up 42 survivors. Two of the *Jersey City*'s crew had been killed. The same U-boat sank the small Swedish steamer *Sigyn*, inbound from Halifax for the Clyde with pit props. *Hurricane*, *Jason* and *Gleaner* were sent on an anti-submarine sweep after a U-boat was sighted on the surface close to the *Sigyn*'s last position. *Hurricane* gained fleeting contact with a submarine which it depth-charged without success. An Oban Sunderland sighted 23 survivors from the *Sigyn* in two boats and guided the destroyer *Warwick* to the rescue.

Three tankers, *Strinda*, *Lucerna* and *Alexia*, were all torpedoed just as they left the North Western Approaches in convoy OB191 during the early hours of 2 August. All three survived and were brought in to the Clyde by rescue tugs.

The terrible harvest of shipping continued in the early hours of 3 August when the MV *Statira* was bombed and set on fire off Cape Wrath, and the Swedish steamer *Atos* was torpedoed and sunk 40 miles west of Colonsay. The *Statira* was still burning when towed in to Stornoway. The 5,408-ton *Boma* blew up after being torpedoed 100 miles west of Islay in the evening of 5 August. The 14 survivors of the SS *Geraldine Mary*, one of three ships torpedoed on 4 August, landed at Brenish on the west coast of Lewis on 7 August. Two other boats with 37 aboard were still missing.

The AMC *Transylvania* was torpedoed by *U56* 120 miles west of Islay just after midnight on 10 August. She sank four and a half hours later, before the rescue tugs *Salvonia* and *Englishman* could reach her. The destroyer *Havelock* picked up 43 officers and 229 ratings. More than 80 of her crew did not survive. The *Transylvania* had been requisitioned in September 1939 and the Anchor Line received £950,637 16s 10d in compensation for her loss.

A Dornier reconnaissance aircraft was seen circling over Tobermory

Watched over by a 210 Squadron Sunderland from Oban, inbound troop convoy TC6 approaches the Clyde on 31 August 1940. In the left-hand column, furthest from the camera, are, from left, the Empress of Australia, *the* Monarch of Bermuda *and the* Samaria. *Leading the centre column is the battleship HMS* Revenge, *and nearest the camera is the* Duchess of York. *TC6 had sailed from Halifax, Nova Scotia, on 23 August.*
(TRUSTEES OF THE IMPERIAL WAR MUSEUM, LONDON)

shortly before midnight on 11 August and a U-boat was seen by a Coastal Command aircraft off the coast of Northern Ireland early the following morning. Four destroyers were ordered on a sweep and HMS *Anthony* attacked a contact at 2014 hours without success. Enemy aircraft were detected while mine-laying over the Clyde between Port Glasgow and Dumbarton Rock at 0230 hours on 13 August. Other aircraft dropped mines off the entrance to Loch Ryan.

Four of the crew of the Swedish timber ship *Nils Gorthan* were killed when she was torpedoed 60 miles west of Islay on 13 August. The anti-submarine trawler *St Kenan* signalled at 2350 hours two days later that she had picked up nine survivors. A Sunderland sighted a raft with another eight survivors and HMS *Anthony* went to pick them up.

A single aircraft returned to drop more mines off Bowling at 0010 hours on 14 August and the British steamer *Betty*, inbound from Saigon with rice, was torpedoed west of Islay.

138

A 210 Squadron Sunderland on convoy patrol over the North Western Approaches that afternoon was attacked by a Focke Wulf Condor. Flight-Lieutenant Parry-Jones's crew returned fire and both aircraft sustained damage before making for home. The Sunderland landed safely at Oban at 1555 hours. (Less than a month later, however, on 2 September, Parry-Jones and his crew of ten failed to return from a convoy patrol.) HMS *Anthony* attacked another U-boat contact west of Islay that evening, again without success.

Thursday, 15 August 1940, was one of the worst single days for losses off the west coast of Scotland. The *Empire Merchant*, the Swedish steamers *Hedrun* and *Warjo*, the Dutch motor ship *Alcinious* and the SS *Clan Macphee* were all torpedoed. Flight-Lieutenant 'Ginger' Baker, up from Oban in a 210 Squadron Sunderland to escort OA198, was looking for survivors from the *Empire Merchant* when his crew sighted a U-boat on the surface 300 miles west of Tiree. He attacked at 1415 hours and his first depth-charge blew the U-boat, which had started to crash-dive, back to the surface. His second depth charge exploded around ten feet from the conning tower and blew the U-boat right out of the water, after which it rolled over and sank from view trailing oil and bubbles. The Commodore of OA198 signalled, 'Well done, hope you get your reward.'

Meanwhile, Flight-Lieutenant Frame in another 210 Squadron Sunderland had sighted some of the *Empire Merchant*'s boats. At 2030 hours that evening, the tanker *Sylvafield* reported sighting a U-boat on the surface. She was torpedoed at 2230 hours. An Oban Sunderland signalled the Fleetwood trawler *Newlands* to pick up 16 survivors adrift in a lifeboat off Barra Head on 18 August. These she landed at Tobermory.

One of the two U-boats responsible for the attacks on convoy OA198, and that damaged by 'Ginger' Baker's depth-charges, was Kapitanleutnant Dietrich Knorr's *U51*. The U-boat was limping back to base at Lorient on 19 August when her signals were intercepted and her position plotted. Meanwhile, HM S/M *Cachalot*, a large mine-layer built by Scotts of Greenock, had sailed from the depot ship HMS *Cyclops* in Rothesay Bay on 16 August. She was to lay mines off the new U-boat bases in the Bay of Biscay. On 19 August, having laid the mines, Lieutenant-Commander David Luce received a signal that a U-boat, thought to be making for Lorient, had been detected in his area. *Cachalot*'s lookouts sighted *U51* at 0111 hours the following morning. Luce fired a full salvo of six torpedoes, two of which appeared to hit their target, and the U-boat was blown apart. There were no survivors.

The rescue tug *Salvonia* sailed from Campbeltown that afternoon to bring in the *Alcinious* which was on fire but still afloat. She was diverted to pick up five survivors from the *Empire Merchant* who had been spotted by a Sunderland. The SS *Kelet* reported picking up 51 survivors from the *Clan*

Officers of 210 Squadron, Coastal Command, outside their station headquarters at Dungallan House, Oban, at the end of August 1940. From left to right: F/O 'Shorty' Evison, F/O Parry Jones (lost with his ten-man crew in Sunderland F/210 while returning from convoy escort duty on 2 September 1940), F/O Stan Baggott, F/O Phillips, P/O Swain, F/O Bowie, F/Lt Gibson, F/O Chapman, F/O Robertson (who took part in the rescue of the survivors of the City of Benares*), F/O Frame (who found over 30 survivors from the torpedoed* Empire Merchant*), F/Lt P. E. Lombard, F/O Jones, F/O Ivor Meggitt, F/O Pusey, F/Lt Ernest 'Ginger' Baker (who dropped the depth-charges which damaged U51 and led to her sinking five days later by HMS/M Cachalot) and F/Lt Paul (killed later in the war while serving with a Typhoon squadron). On the right is Sqdn/Ldr Fergus 'Crasher' Pierce with his dog Susie, the squadron mascot.*

RAF Oban was officially opened, initially as part of 18 Group, Coastal Command, by Group Captain J. H. O. Jones on 2 October 1939. Wing Commander Wrigglesworth and P/O Pain brought the first of 209 Squadron's aircraft into the new base five days later. The serviceability record of 209's Stranraer and Lerwick flying boats was appalling. In January 1940 they had just two aircraft operational and no spares had arrived for the Lerwicks which were suffering from 'much trouble' caused by throttles breaking and magnetos failing. This was somewhat disconcerting in an aircraft which demonstrated time and again its reluctance to fly on one engine. By mid-1940 both 10 and 210 Squadrons were operating Sunderland flying boats from Oban. These were replaced by American-built Catalinas in April 1941.

Evidence of increasing American involvement in the Battle of the Atlantic came with the attachment to RAF Oban, in May and June 1941 and six months prior to Pearl Harbor, of four US Navy officers.

Macphee and a Yugoslavian ship rescued 22 of the crew of the *Empire Merchant*. Although nine of her crew died, 21 survivors from the *Hedrun* were picked up. HMS *Warwick* reported picking up another 12 from the *Empire Merchant* that afternoon, just as reports came in that the SS *Ampleforth* had been torpedoed and sunk 180 miles west of Tiree.

The Greek timber ship *Leonidas M Valmas*, inbound for Dublin, was torpedoed in the North Channel on 20 August. Owing to the particular nature of their cargo, timber ships are usually very hard to sink. Unfortunately, 16 of the crew panicked, abandoned ship and were needlessly lost. Tugs brought the *Valmas* into the Clyde at the end of the month.

At least one U-boat managed to get in amongst an outbound convoy 60 miles west of Islay in the evening of 23 August and, within five minutes, torpedoed the 11,000-ton SS *Cumberland* and the 5,407-ton steamer *Havildar*. At 0736 hours the following morning the 5,610-ton steamer *St Dunstan* was torpedoed 40 miles west of Islay. Fourteen of her Lascar crew panicked and were drowned while trying to launch a lifeboat.

The *Cumberland*'s stern had been blown off, despite which she remained afloat long enough to be taken in tow by the rescue tug *Englishman*. The efforts at salvage proved to be in vain as she sank seven miles north of Malin Head at 1230 hours the following day. The *Salvonia* sailed from Campbeltown to go to the aid of the *Havildar*, also still afloat, and brought her safely to Greenock.

Having got the *Havildar* in to Greenock, the *Salvonia* put back to sea to assist the Dutch tug *Schelde* with the salvage of the steamer *St Dunstan*. This ship had been struck in the bows, her back was broken and she was taking water through her number 2 collision bulkhead. She sank off Whiting Bay in Arran on 27 August.

Amid tight security, on 28 July 1941, a 210 Squadron Catalina flew from Oban, via Iceland, to Archangel in the Soviet Union. It carried Harry Hopkins, Averell Harriman, Admiral Ghormley, Major-General Chaney and Brigadier-General Lee, emissaries sent by Roosevelt to London and Moscow in preparation for the momentous 'Atlantic Charter' meeting at Argentia, Newfoundland, which took place the following month. The arrival, from mid-1941, of long-range, land-based Liberator bombers from America meant that RAF Oban began to lose its front-line convoy escort role, and the focus of operations shifted to airfields such as Stornoway and Benbecula. At the end of February 1942, 210 Squadron left to operate from Sullom Voe and the station became increasingly involved in training. RAF Oban was reduced to Care and Maintenance status on 28 April 1945.
(TRUSTEES OF THE IMPERIAL WAR MUSEUM, LONDON)

Two U-boats were operating off the west coast and torpedoed three ships on 25 August: the *Stakesby* 23 miles north of the Butt of Lewis, the *Jamaica Pioneer* 140 miles west of Barra and the tanker *Pecten*, inbound in convoy HX65B, 40 miles west of Tiree. That evening, a lifeboat containing 17 survivors from the tanker *La Brea*, torpedoed while inbound for Dundee, landed at Loch Boisdale. Another boat with another 14 of *La Brea's* crew landed at Islivig on the west coast of Lewis the following evening.

The *Jamaica Pioneer* finally sank, despite the efforts of her crew, at 0100 hours on 26 August. A Sunderland from Oban sighted two of her boats the following morning and signalled their whereabouts to HMS *Anthony*. Almost 40 survivors from the *Stakesby* were landed that morning at Stornoway by the Norwegian *SS Cetus*. *Stakesby* was beached at Glumach Bay, Stornoway, the following day. She was still on fire in four holds. Another lifeboat from the *Jamaica Pioneer*, containing her master and 13 of her crew, was found by HMS *Wanderer* that afternoon.

The 9th Destroyer Flotilla sailed on 28 August to search for the two U-boats off the North Channel. One of these had sunk the Finnish steamer *Elle*, inbound for Ardrossan with spoolwood, at 0312 hours, killing two of her crew. HMS *Gleaner* reported, at 0445 hours on 29 August, that three ships had been torpedoed in the outbound convoy OA204.

A U-boat was heard signalling from a point almost 200 miles west of Mull at 2210 hours on 30 August. The 15,434-ton Dutch liner *Volendam* passed through this position just over an hour later and was torpedoed. The *Volendam* was carrying 884 passengers including 317 evacuee children. The evacuation of children had been temporarily halted following the sinking of the *Arandora Star*, but pressure to restart the programme had intensified with the threat of invasion. *Salvonia* and *Englishman* were ordered to sea 'with all despatch' and HMS *Warwick* closed the stricken liner. The *Volendam* stayed afloat despite having number 1 and 2 holds flooded; the tugs had her off Toward Point on the evening of 1 September. All her passengers were taken off by other vessels, 251 of them by the Norwegian steamer *Olaf Festenes*, and landed at Greenock.

The tanker *Andarra* and the Greek steamer *San Gabriel* were torpedoed at 0400 hours on 31 August by the same U-boat responsible for the attack on the *Volendam*. The tug *Thames* sailed from Stornoway and brought the *San Gabriel* in to beach her at Cardross in the Clyde on 3 September. The *Andarra* reached the Clyde in tow of the *Schelde*. The 7,461-ton Belgian steamer *Ville de Hasselt*, outbound independently at 14 knots for Boston, was sunk west of Lewis at 1713 hours on 31 August. One lifeboat was picked up by the Icelandic ship *Hilmir* the following day, while another was found 12 miles west of St Kilda that evening by the Belgian trawler *Transport*. The rest of the *Hilmir's* crew were reported safe after being picked up; 21 of them were landed at Roag, Lewis, on 7 September by the trawler *Ben Aden*.

Seventeen survivors from the SS *Ulva*, torpedoed west of the Hebrides at 0215 hours on 3 September, were landed at Castlebay two days later. Another ten survivors landed at Leverburgh in Harris that day from the SS *Severn Leigh* which had been torpedoed almost two weeks earlier while outbound for St Johns in convoy OA200.

Kapitanleutnant Hans-Gerrit von Stockhausen in *U65* reported sighting the 53 ships of the inbound slow convoy SC2 at the beginning of September. Three other boats, including Gunther Prien's *U47*, were sent to reinforce him and formed one of the first wolf-packs. Despite the presence of seven escort vessels and constant Coastal Command patrols, seven ships were sunk northwest of Ireland on the night of 7 September. U-boat sightings were reported by Coastal Command aircraft the following day and one was bombed unsuccessfully. The SS *Mardinian* and the Greek steamer *Poseidon*, both inbound, were torpedoed and sunk that night off Barra Head. More than 70 survivors were picked up from rafts by HM trawler *St Apollo* and the destroyer *Anthony*. Anti-submarine defences in the North Western Approaches were considerably denuded that night when, in response to the invasion scare, six destroyers were sent south to Portsmouth.

The rescue tug *Marauder* sailed from Greenock on 11 September after the SS *Harpenden* and the Dutch ship *Maas* were torpedoed west of Islay. The *Maas* sank with the loss of all but two of her crew. *Harpenden* reached the Clyde in tow of the *Marauder* on 15 September. The latter put back to sea immediately after the SS *Hird*, a straggler from HX70, was torpedoed south of Iceland.

The tanker *Coronda*, and the steamships *Regent Lion* and *West Harshaw* were bombed and strafed in the North Channel at 0700 hours on 15 September. The *Coronda* was disabled and the *Superman* sailed from Greenock to bring her in. That night the Norwegian steamer *Lotos* was torpedoed and sunk 15 miles north-west of Rockall. Eight survivors came ashore on Berneray after five days in a lifeboat. The 8,323-ton *Aska* was bombed and set on fire in the North Channel at 0250 hours on 16 September and went ashore on Cara Island, still burning, later that day. Some 75 survivors, including 65 French colonial troops, were landed at Larne.

Hitler had declared unrestricted submarine warfare in the waters around Britain on 17 August 1940. Despite this, and the torpedoing of the *Arandora Star* and *Volendam*, the Children's Overseas Resettlement Board continued to send its 'seavacs' abroad. When she sailed from Liverpool on 13 September in convoy OB213, 96 children were aboard the 11,081-ton Ellerman liner *City of Benares*, 90 of them under the government scheme. She was torpedoed 600 miles out in the Atlantic by Kapitanleutnant Heinrich Bleichrodt in *U48* at 2000 hours on 17 September. The destroyer *Hurricane* was despatched to pick

143

Boat No. 12 from the City of Benares *alongside HMS* Anthony *after being spotted by Oban-based Sunderland flying boats of Coastal Command. No. 12 had been adrift for eight days with 46 survivors aboard, six of whom were 'seavac' children.*
(THE SCOTSMAN)

up survivors and her captain signalled angrily that the *Benares'* lifeboats had been rushed by panic-stricken Lascar crew members and that many had capsized as a result.

Boat number 12 with 46 survivors aboard and commanded by the *Benares'* Fourth Officer, 22-year-old Ronnie Cooper of Invergowrie, was adrift for eight days until, on 25 September, it was spotted by Squadron-Leader Garing in a Sunderland of 10 Squadron, Royal Australian Air Force. Garing had just handed over the escort of HX73 to 'Ginger' Baker in his 210 Squadron Sunderland and was on his way back to Oban when he sighted the boat. Garing was short of fuel so he returned to the convoy and signalled the lifeboat's whereabouts to Baker, who then dropped food to the survivors – among them six children – and guided the destroyer HMS *Anthony* to the rescue.

Sadly, 134 passengers, including 77 children, died in the *Benares* disaster, along with 119 of her crew. All of the survivors were landed at Greenock.

Distraught parents wrote to the Ellerman Line offices in Glasgow seeking reassurance that their children had died instantly. Despite the fact that this was manifestly not the case, such reassurances were invariably given. Others wrote asking for brochures on the *Benares*. Among them were Robert and Mary Dixon of Sunderland who had lost their only daughter in the tragedy. They said, 'It would be comforting if we could see where our little darling spent the last five days of her life.' The sinking of the *Benares* led to the long overdue abandonment of the official overseas evacuation scheme.

Gunther Prien sighted the 37 ships of the slow inbound convoy, HX72, on 20 September. Donitz reinforced Prien, who had only one torpedo left, with Kapitanleutnant Joachim Schepke in *U100*, and Otto Kretschmer and Heinrich Bleichrodt. A wolf pack was formed which inflicted terrible losses on the convoy, 11 ships being sunk in seven hours. Schepke alone accounted for seven ships in four hours after both he and Kretschmer managed to get inside the columns of ships.

Four ships of the outbound convoy OB216, the *Empire Adventure*, the former whaling factory-ship *New Sevilla*, the tanker *D. L. Harper* and the Ellerman liner *City of Simla* were torpedoed 50 miles west of Islay that night. The *Salvonia* took the *New Sevilla* in tow with the intention of beaching her in Kildalloig Bay at the entrance to Campbeltown Loch, only for her to sink nine miles west of the Mull of Kintyre the following evening. The *Superman* took the *Empire Adventure* in tow, but she too sank on the way into the Clyde.

The *City of Simla* sank by the stern within 20 minutes of being torpedoed. The Fleetwood trawler *Van Dyck* picked up 32 survivors. A further 146 passengers and crew were rescued by SS *Guinean* of the United Africa Trading Co, and taken to Gourock. Two passengers and one crew-member died.

145

The Third and Fourth Officers and the Saloon Steward of the *Simla* earned the special praise of many passengers for their bravery and calmness during the evacuation of the ship. This contrasts sharply with reports from many passengers of panic among the Lascar crew. Two women and a child were kicked off ladders by Lascars trying to get to the boats. Another woman was left in the water after crew-members refused to let her into a lifeboat. Her 12-year-old son was hit across the knuckles as he tried to hold on to the boat, by a Lascar wielding an oar.

Having signed contracts they were unable to read, Lascar seamen found themselves sailing into the North Atlantic and a war few of them understood. Many mutinied and the first 55 were sentenced to four weeks' imprisonment in November 1939. Over 100 Lascar crew-members on the troop-ship *Karanja* mutinied at Gourock in May 1941 and were sentenced to 60 days in Barlinnie Prison Military Detention Centre. A British seaman tried for desertion on the same day was fined three pounds.

In prison the Lascars were described as 'a happy and contented crowd', despite the fact that they had no suitable clothing and were shivering with cold. The *Karanja* was normally employed by the General Steamship Navigation Co on the India to East Africa run, and her crew were on their first trip into British waters.

With Britain's battle for survival at its height, the War Cabinet were greatly concerned over the effect such incidents were having on public opinion in the United States and in India, where the independence movement was becoming increasingly influential. The *Karanja's* crew were released early on the direct instruction of the War Cabinet. Within hours they had been hustled out of the country.

A lone enemy aircraft on a reconnaissance mission to the western anchorages appeared over Oban at 1535 hours on 24 September 1940. It dropped an auxiliary fuel tank into Station Square before continuing on south. Hurricanes of 615 (County of Surrey) Squadron and 245 Squadron were scrambled to patrol over Kintyre and the Clyde estuary but made no interception. It is said that the station headquarters at RAF Oban received a number of telephone calls from irate locals asking why the lumbering Sunderland flying boats had not been scrambled to intercept!

The liner *Oronsay*, with 3,100 troops aboard, was damaged by a long-range Focke Wulf 200C bomber on the morning of 8 October while 200 miles west of Islay. Though both her engines were disabled, she was able to repair one and make for the Clyde under the escort of HMS *Arrow*, HMCS *Ottawa* and the anti-aircraft cruiser *Cairo*. Four of those aboard died and 12 were injured. The inbound convoy SC7 suffered grievously at the hands of a wolf-pack of 11 U-boats which lay in wait for it off the Rockall Bank in mid-October. Seventeen ships were sunk in two nights of unrelenting attacks. SC7 lost 21 ships in all, nearly 60 per cent of its strength.

Another inbound convoy, HX79, was intercepted the following night and Gunther Prien and Englebert Endrass – Prien's First Lieutenant at Scapa Flow and rapidly acquiring ace status himself – sank a further 15 ships between them. Two JU88s were detected minelaying at the Tail o' the Bank at 0500 hours on 25 October.

The Focke Wulf 200C was a conversion of the pre-war Kondor four-engined airliner. As such it proved a singularly inadequate warplane, being underpowered, slow, poorly armed and notoriously fragile. The former passenger accommodation was filled with extra fuel tanks and this gave it its one advantage, namely the range to operate far out into the Atlantic from bases in Norway and France. In the days prior to the advent of the escort carrier, these aircraft could shadow a convoy, unmolested, signalling its position, course and speed to U-boat headquarters at Lorient in France.

The 26-year-old Oberleutnant Bernhard Jope took off for his first operational patrol in a Kondor from the KG40 base at Merignac near Bordeaux at 0400 hours on Saturday, 26 October 1940. At 0920 hours a meteorologist in his crew sighted a large, three-funnelled vessel steaming eastwards about 70 miles off the Irish coast. The Kondor carried four 250kg bombs and, in a remarkable piece of beginner's luck, Jope managed to hit the ship at the first attempt. His target, the 42,348-ton Canadian Pacific liner *Empress of Britain,* was to become the largest single Merchant Navy casualty of the Second World War.

The *Empress* had been launched from John Brown's Clydebank yard on 11 June 1930 by the Prince of Wales, an event notable for the proceedings having, for the first time, been broadcast to the Empire. The very last word in luxury travel, she was one of the finest, most beautiful ships ever to carry the British flag. She sailed from Suez on 23 September, homeward-bound via the Cape and the North Channel for Liverpool. The acute shortage of escort vessels and the *Empress*'s speed led to her being sailed independently at 22 knots. She was carrying 645 passengers and crew, 150 of them service personnel and their families.

Jope's first bomb crashed through the upper deck between the second and third funnels and exploded in the Mayfair Lounge. A fierce fire started immediately which spread rapidly along passageways lined with richly varnished wood panelling. The ship's fire mains failed completely, making it impossible to fight the blaze. Meanwhile, Jope continued to pass over the ship, strafing the upper deck and bridge area and dropping his other three bombs, one of which struck the ship near the stern. Within half an hour it became plain to Captain Charles Sapsworth that the fires had become uncontrollable and his ship was doomed. He gave the order to abandon ship.

The destroyers *Echo* and *Burza*, a unit of the Polish Navy, were detached from an inbound troop convoy to go to the rescue. The tugs *Thames* and *Marauder* sailed from Campbeltown, the tug *Seaman* put out from Londonderry and the cruiser *Cairo* left Greenock to provide anti-aircraft cover. As the rescue ships converged on the burning liner, and aircraft circled overhead, the huge column of smoke rising from her fires could be seen from 40 miles away.

Many of the lifeboats had been burned, and others had been damaged by bombs and gunfire. The ship was still making way when the first boats hit the water and, often half empty, they were quickly left far behind. One of the two motor lifeboats, which should have been used to shepherd the rowed boats to where they were most needed, was holed and sank. The other had not been properly maintained and it took four vital hours before its engine could be persuaded into life. Meanwhile, over 300 people were trapped on the foredeck and the last of these did not leave until around 1630 hours, just as the *Echo* and *Burza* hove into sight.

Commander Stanley Spurgeon in *Echo* signalled at 1640 that the *Empress* was abandoned, gutted but floating on an even keel. The destroyer set about picking up the survivors from the boats which had become scattered over a wide area. The anti-submarine trawlers *Drangey*, *Cape Argona* and *Paynter* arrived at 1750 hours and picked up another 250 survivors, bringing the total rescued to 598. Sadly, 47 people died. *Echo* and *Burza*, having taken aboard all the survivors, sailed for the Clyde and arrived at Gourock at 0830 hours on the following morning.

Meanwhile, the destroyers *Broke* and *Sardonyx* had arrived. A party from the former went aboard the hulk to secure hawsers for the tugs at around 1000 hours on 27 October and the latter reported at 1300 hours that the tow had commenced at five knots. First Lieutenant in *Sardonyx* was newly promoted Peter Scott, son of polar explorer Captain Scott, and a famous naturalist in his own right. Meanwhile, the anti-submarine trawlers, being short of fuel, had been forced to sail for home.

At 0205 hours the following morning the *Marauder* reported that the *Empress* had rolled over and sunk in under ten minutes after two explosions had been seen on her port side, immediately under the twisted remains of her bridge. Although lookouts on board *Sardonyx* had seen what they thought were two torpedoes being fired from about six cables off the liner's port quarter, nobody could be certain about what had happened. The reason for the sinking was confirmed that evening when the Admiralty signalled *Broke* to the effect that an enemy broadcast claimed the *Empress* had been torpedoed.

The final twist in the tale of the *Empress of Britain* was yet to come. She had been torpedoed by Oberleutnant Hans Jenisch in *U32*. Shortly after midday on 30 October, Jenisch shelled a small freighter, the SS *Balzac*, a straggler from convoy SL51. The *Balzac* escaped unharmed after her distress calls brought the destroyers *Harvester* and *Highlander* racing to her aid. *Harvester* maintained Asdic contact on the submerged U-boat while Commander William Dallmeyer in *Highlander* dropped an accurate pattern of depth-charges. *U32* was seriously damaged and forced to the surface, whereupon Jenisch ordered his crew to abandon ship. By this time *Highlander's* main and secondary armament was riddling the U-boat and a number of her crew were killed while going over the side. *Harvester* picked up 29 of her crew and *Highlander* eight. *U32* was held in the beam of *Harvester's* searchlight as she sank slowly, stern first. Six of her crew had died.

Two seamen were drowned earlier that day when the destroyer HMS *Sturdy* became a total loss after running aground in fog on Tiree.

U31, commanded by Kapitanleutnant Wilfried Prellberg, was first sighted west of Barra Head early on 31 October by the steamship *Achilles*. The U-boat was heard signalling the following day and listening stations were able to get a fix on the transmission which placed it around 120 miles west of Tiree. The destroyer *Antelope* was escorting convoy OB219 when she gained Asdic contact on *U31* at 1133 hours on 1 November. Following a number of depth-charge attacks, *U31* struggled to the surface shortly after 1400 hours. As the German crew made to abandon their crippled charge, *Antelope* suffered damage as she laid herself alongside in an unsuccessful effort at boarding. *U31* sank shortly afterwards leaving her crew of five officers and 38 men as prisoners-of-war.

The British steamer *Cape St Andrew* was torpedoed and sunk west of the Bloody Foreland on 12 November after falling behind her convoy. Fourteen of her crew died. The 5,587-ton steamer *Planter*, another straggler, this time from SL53 inbound from Freetown, Sierra Leone, was torpedoed and sunk as she entered the North Channel on the morning of 16 November. Twelve of her crew were lost. HMS *Witherington*, one of the escorts, attacked an Asdic contact immediately after the *Planter's* sinking. Despite this, the Swedish SS *Veronica*, inbound for Barrow with iron ore, and the little MV *St German*, 1,044 tons with a cargo of pit props, were torpedoed that evening. Seventeen of the *Veronica's* crew died.

The *St German* did not sink until 18 November and, that evening, a Sunderland on patrol out of Oban sighted a U-boat on the surface near Rockall. Another Sunderland, commanded by Flight-Lieutenant Lombard, left Oban early the next morning. Lombard found *U104* still on the surface, and dropped a depth-charge less than 50 feet from her bows. This failed to explode and the U-boat crash-dived before a second attack could be carried out. A large volume of signals were heard from *U104* that afternoon and on the afternoon of 20 November, Kapitanleutnant Jurst and his crew were sent to the sea bottom south of Rockall by the corvette HMS *Rhododendron* on 21

The 37 ships of convoy HX84 were inbound for the North Channel from Halifax, Nova Scotia, on 5 November 1940. HX84 comprised a mixed bag of vessels, most coming from American ports with munitions, some from as far afield as the Pacific with cargoes mainly of foodstuffs. Their sole escort was the armed merchant cruiser HMS Jervis Bay, formerly an emigrant liner on the Australia run, and owned, prior to being requisitioned, by the Aberdeen and Commonwealth Shipping Line. Capable, at a stretch, of 15 knots, she was punily armed with some elderly 6" guns.

At around 1800 hours they blundered into the German pocket battleship Admiral Scheer, commanded by Captain Theodor Krancke, a sister ship of the more famous Graf Spee. With extraordinary gallantry, Captain Fogarty Fegen and the crew of Jervis Bay turned their ship towards the enemy on what could be nothing more than a suicide run. The Scheer's 11" guns soon demolished Jervis Bay and she sank by stern, her white ensign still flying, having been nailed to the main top mast in traditional fashion after the original had been shot away. Just 65 of her crew survived. Among the dead was Captain Fegen who was awarded a posthumous VC. Jervis Bay's action gained vital

November. This was the 32nd and last U-boat to be sunk until March 1941.

The late summer and autumn of 1940 were acknowledged as the U-boat crew's first 'happy time'. Losses of Allied merchant shipping had been appalling – 300,000 tons were lost to U-boat attacks in October alone. U-boat attacks fell away in November, due in part to the winter weather in the North Atlantic and to the exhaustion of both crews and their boats. When the submarine campaign was restarted in earnest, early in 1941, Donitz moved the focus of his operations westwards to the area south of Iceland. But sinkings in the North Western Approaches never again reached the catastrophic levels of late 1940.

As U-boat activity lessened, so the Luftwaffe began to make its presence felt over the west coast of Scotland. A single JU88 carried out a reconnaissance of the western anchorages at lunch-time on 8 December. It was chased out over the Farne Islands by Spitfires of 72 Squadron.

Shipping was bombed off Port Ellen in Islay on 19 December and off Rathlin Island three days later. The most concentrated raid took place amid heavy rain and a strong south-westerly wind in the Firth of Lorne on 23 December 1940. Five Heinkel IIIs came up the Irish Sea looking for targets. At 1800 hours they found five vessels lying in the convoy assembly anchorage in Oban Roads. The 2,092-ton Danish steamer *Flynderborg* was struck by two bombs and strafed. She was not seriously damaged, though her wireless operator was badly injured. A bomb entered the foc'sle of the 5,117-ton SS *Dan y Bryn* but failed to explode. The 6,941-ton Dutch steamer *Breda* was seriously damaged by a near miss and, despite efforts to beach her, sank in 13 fathoms in Ardmucknish Bay. Another Dutch vessel, the 4,652-ton *Tuva*, had to be hurriedly beached after a bomb exploded in her number 3 hold, killing seven of her crew. She was refloated and beached again in a more sheltered spot in Camas Nathais on the afternoon of Christmas Day. Only then was an unexploded bomb discovered sticking out of her starboard quarter. The *Tuva* was eventually patched and refloated. The harbour service drifter *Lupina* was also damaged in this attack.

minutes for the other vessels in the convoy and all but five escaped certain destruction. One of the ships struck by the Scheer's shells was the Eagle Oil Company's tanker San Demetrio, *which was carrying 11,200 tons of petrol. Set on fire, she was abandoned until, two days later, one of her own lifeboats came upon her and, as the fires had largely burned out, the survivors reboarded her. Lacking charts or a compass, Second Officer Arthur Hawkins and Chief Engineer Pollard along with 14 of her crew managed to raise steam and bring their charge, with all but 200 tons of her desperately needed cargo intact, to the west coast of Ireland. From there they telephoned for an escort to the Clyde, where this photograph was taken.*
(RALSTON COLLECTION, STRATHCLYDE REGIONAL ARCHIVES)

The San Demetrio, *under the starboard bridge wing.*
(RALSTON COLLECTION, STRATHCLYDE REGIONAL ARCHIVES)

The sunken *Breda* was bound for Bombay via North America with 3,000 tons of cement and other general cargo on board including aircraft parts and some of the Aga Khan's racehorse stud. All of her 42 crew and 12 passengers survived. After dark, one of the terrified racehorses staggered ashore, whinnying loudly, only to be confronted by an equally frightened rifle-wielding Benderloch Home Guardsman shouting, 'Who goes there?'

Two JU88s conducted reconnaissance flights over the North Channel on 2 January 1941. One was seen over Prestwick before going north over Inveraray and out to sea. A section of Spitfires from 602 (City of Glasgow) Squadron was sent up to intercept the other Junkers as it passed over Airdrie and Glasgow. No contact was made. At 1355 hours, a burst of machine-gun fire from this aircraft damaged buildings off Garscube Road in Glasgow. One bullet embedded itself in woodwork in the bedroom of Jessie Griffith's top flat at 62 Doncaster Street, while others hit a workmen's brazier at the corner of Napiershall Street and North Woodside Road.

The rescue tug *Seaman* was attacked by an enemy bomber south of Rockall on 11 January. The bombs missed, and return fire from the *Seaman* brought the bomber down. Three of its crew were picked up and landed at Greenock. The next attack was nothing if not spectacular. On 15 January a JU88 roared down a rainswept Great Glen to drop a large bomb near the entrance to the Caledonian Canal. No damage was done.

The steamship *Tregarthen* arrived in Oban with an injured crewman at lunch-time on 21 January. She had been bombed 20 miles west of Colonsay while in the inbound convoy HX101. Also that day the rescue tug *Englishman* was bombed and sunk off the North Channel.

Fourteen enemy aircraft were plotted operating over the Irish Sea between 2128 hours and midnight on Sunday, 9 February. Eight mines were dropped in Campbeltown Loch, two of which exploded on land at Askomil on the north shore damaging nearby houses, killing two people and injuring 15. Bombs and incendiaries also fell near Machrihanish airfield, and the Stranraer to Larne Ferry, *Princess Maud*, was attacked but suffered no damage.

Prompted largely by the dreadful losses experienced towards the end of 1940, a major administrative and tactical shake-up in Western Approaches Command took place in February 1941. A new headquarters was set up at Derby House in Liverpool and a new commander, Admiral Sir Percy Noble, was appointed with effect from 0200 hours on 17 February. Of perhaps greater lasting importance was the passing, in April 1941, of effective operational control of Coastal Command from the RAF to the Navy. Now, at last, there was a chance of proper co-ordination between the Command's aircraft and the ships they were to protect. Convoy routes were shifted northwards and increased cover was provided by aircraft based in Iceland.

There were other indications of better days to come for Western

Approaches Command. Escort vessel crews were receiving vastly improved training, most notably at HMS *Western Isles* in Tobermory, and tactics were being refined. On 8 March Gunther Prien, the 'Bull of Scapa Flow', was part of a wolf-pack attacking OB293 south of Iceland. The assembled U-boats, including Prien in *U47*, Kretschmer in *U99*, Matz in *U70* and Eckermann in a new experimental boat, attacked. Immediately, the escort led by Commander J. M. Rowland in the destroyer *Wolverine* began a vicious counter-attack. Severely shaken, Kretschmer crept away from the convoy. Matz was depth-charged to the surface and forced to abandon. *Wolverine* and the destroyer *Verity* then commenced repeated depth-charge attacks on a submerged contact and were rewarded with the unusual sight of an orange glow under the sea and the sound of a U-boat breaking up. Gunther Prien, the darling of the German press – though not of his crew to whom he was an insufferable martinet – was dead. Two months later, as described in Chapter One, Fritz-Julius Lemp, the man who sank the *Athenia*, also met his end.

Sporadic aircraft attacks on convoys near the coast continued. The trawler *Samurai* was bombed and strafed while 30 miles north-west of St Kilda on 23 March 1941. Two weeks later, on 10 April, the steamship *Thirlby* was damaged by bombs 140 miles north-west of the Butt of Lewis. HMS *Umtali* brought the survivors of the grain ship SS *Mount Park* into Oban on 26 April. She had been hit in the engine-room by a bomb while 300 miles west of Tiree. A Dornier 17 reconnaissance plane was shot down over the North Channel on the evening of 13 May. Another reconnaissance flight was detected over the Firth of Clyde on 28 May. It was intercepted by Flight Lieutenant Du Vivier and red section of 43 Squadron and shot down 13 miles south of Hawick at 1415 hours. Two of its crew were killed and two were taken to Jedburgh Police Station as PoWs.

The neutral Swedish motor vessel *Venezuela* was torpedoed and sunk north of Ireland by *U123* on 17 April 1941. All of her crew died. The destroyer *Hurricane* arrived at Greenock in the late afternoon of 1 May with survivors from the Ellerman liner *City of Nagpur*. This ship had sailed from the Clyde on 25 April and was torpedoed in the early hours of 28 April. Many of the survivors were taken to the Central Hotel in Glasgow. Others, uninsured and destitute after losing everything they possessed, made desperate appeals for help to the Ellerman Line.

A sighting report of convoy OB329, transmitted by Kapitanleutnant Wetjen in *U147*, was intercepted at 1100 hours on 2 June. At 1917 hours that evening Wetjen attacked, torpedoing the 5,000-ton Belgian steamer *Mokambo* in the bows. The *Mokambo* stayed afloat and made her own way to the Clyde escorted by the corvettes *Gentian* and *Freesian*. *U147* was depth-charged by HM ships *Wanderer* and *Periwinkle* and sank almost immediately. Meanwhile, the trawler *Arran* was on her way to Oban with 40 survivors from the *Prince Rupert City*, bombed and sunk off Cape Wrath at 0145 hours that morning. HMS *Veteran* picked up 27 survivors after the *Ainderby* was torpedoed 300 miles west of Islay on 10 June.

The string of disasters continued. The trawler *Strathgairn* was blown up on a mine 20 miles south-west of Barra Head on 1 July. Four days later another trawler, the *Goldfinch*, was damaged by a mine in the Solway Firth. The naval tender *Celeno* detonated a mine in the Clyde on 9 July. Three naval ratings and three civilians were killed, the latter all from one family.

The fleet tug *Freebooter* sailed from Stornoway at 1015 hours on 8 February 1942 to assist the SS *Anna Knudsen* which had been torpedoed 125 miles south-west of the Faroes. *Freebooter* reached the Clyde, with the *Anna Knudsen* in tow and with rescue tug *Tenacity* assisting, on 14 February. A sour note had been struck the previous summer by allegations that the crews of the rescue tugs had looted vessels in their care. The Navy was forced to take steps to ensure that there were 'no unfounded allegations against the rescue tugs'.

RT *Tenacity* was credited with saving 24 ships of various nationalities. The brand new RT *Prosperous* was on her first trials trip just before Christmas 1942 when she was ordered to sea to help the Dutch tanker SS *Jan van Goyen*, damaged 1,000 miles out in the North Atlantic. The tow back to the Clyde took a week in dreadful weather, and the recovery was accorded special praise by Flag Officer in Charge, Greenock.

The North Atlantic convoys were bedevilled by appalling weather; severe gales in the second week of January 1942 caused many ships to run ashore on the west coast. Eleven ships were stranded on 20 January alone, seven of them from convoy ONC58. Bad weather caused the *Navada II* to run ashore on the north end of Coll at 2330 hours on 19 July 1942. She was quickly beyond salvage, but her cargo, which included 500 tons of bombs, was removed in something of a hurry.

The Coastal Command airfield on Benbecula was opened in 1942 to extend the precious miles of air cover available to the North Atlantic convoys. The station's first victory came on 15 January 1943 when a Flying Fortress of 206 Squadron piloted by Flying Officer Clark sank Kapitanleutnant Ruweidel's *U337* 600 miles out in the Atlantic. Flying Officer Robert Cowey's 206 Squadron Fortress sank *U710* on the evening of 24 April 1943. The third U-boat taken by 206 Squadron from Benbecula was *U417*, which was sunk by Wing-Commander Thomson's Fortress on 11 June 1943. Thomson's aircraft was damaged by return fire from *U417* and he was forced to ditch. A first attempt at rescue by an American Catalina from Iceland failed. Thomson and his crew were eventually picked up by an RAF Catalina from 190 Squadron.

The 'non-aggression' pact between Stalin and Hitler had been ripped apart when the Wehrmacht marched into the Soviet Union on 21 June 1941. Just over a week later, in place of his passive hostility to British interests, Stalin sent Churchill his first request for military aid. This initial list included hopelessly unrealistic requests for 3,000 modern fighters, a similar number of bombers and 20,000 anti-aircraft guns. Aware of the absolute necessity of keeping the Soviet Union in the war, Churchill gave the sending of supplies the highest priority. The grim series of convoys which followed culminated in the unnecessary massacre, in the middle of 1942, of convoy PQ17. This last demonstrated the folly of attempting to run a convoy from a desk in London.

Convoys from Loch Ewe heading west to Iceland then north of Norway to the Soviet port of Murmansk were in full swing by the end of 1942. JW51B, made up of 14 ships, had the misfortune, in a snowstorm on 31 December 1942, to run into the pocket battleship *Lutzow*, the battle-cruiser *Hipper* and their screen of destroyers. The tiny force of destroyers escorting JW51B managed to hold off the vastly superior German vessels until the cruisers *Sheffield* and *Jamaica* arrived. HMS *Achates* was sunk, as was the mine-sweeper *Bramble*. HMS *Onslow*, with all but two of her guns iced up and useless, was struck repeatedly by the *Hipper's* main armament and left a burning wreck. Her commander and senior officer of the escort, Captain Sherbrooke, continued to direct operations despite the loss of an eye, and was awarded the Victoria Cross. JW51B was saved.

JW54B sailed from Loch Ewe on 20 December 1943. A return convoy, RA55A sailed from Murmansk three days later. Each convoy was escorted by ten British and Canadian destroyers and, with the ever-present threat posed by the German battle-cruiser *Scharnhorst* in mind, the Commander-in-Chief, Home Fleet, Admiral Sir Bruce Fraser, was at sea in the battleship *Duke of York*. Additional cover was provided by a squadron of cruisers led by Vice-Admiral Burnett in HMS *Belfast*.

When JW54B was sighted by German aircraft on 22 December, the *Scharnhorst* and her attendant destroyers left their lair in Altenfjord in northern Norway. Aware of German intentions thanks to 'Enigma' decrypts, Fraser was able to use the convoy to lure the *Scharnhorst* into a trap. The ensuing action, which began at 0930 hours on Boxing Day, is now known as the Battle of the North Cape. Fraser's ships reduced the *Scharnhorst* to a burning, sinking ruin. Just 36 of her crew survived.

HMS *Bulldog*, one of the ships which had caught Fritz-Julius Lemp, destroyed U719 250 miles west of Islay on 26 June 1944. U300, a new type VII boat, operated off the west coast during July 1944. On 5 July the trawler *Noreen Mary* was shelled and sunk by U300 14 miles west of Cape Wrath. Two survivors were picked up by HM trawler *Lady Madeleine*.

By the end of August 1944 Donitz had lost the use of the French bases and was operating his U-boats from Norway, some of them against Scottish coastal waters including the Moray Firth, the Pentland Firth, the Minches and

Survivors from the cruiser HMS Trinidad *after landing at Greenock.* Trinidad *had been part of the escort of the Murmansk convoy PQ13 when it came under attack from three German destroyers. One of her own torpedoes ran wild in the severe weather, turned a half circle and struck the cruiser in the engine-room. She stayed afloat and was escorted into Kola Inlet by the destroyers HMS* Eclipse *and HMS* Fury. *After being patched up, she sailed for home via Iceland on 13 May 1942 only to be caught and set on fire by two JU88s. She was abandoned and sunk by a torpedo from the destroyer HMS* Matchless.*
(TRUSTEES OF THE IMPERIAL WAR MUSEUM, LONDON)*

the North Channel. The type VII boats had by then been fitted with *schnorkels*, breathing tubes which allowed them to operate their main diesel engines and charge batteries while still submerged.

Kapitanleutnant Hartmut Graf von Matuschka brought *U482* to the North Western Approaches at the beginning of September 1944 on an operational voyage of 2,729 miles, more than 90 per cent of which, thanks to the *schnorkel*, were travelled submerged. His first victim was the 10,200-ton American turbine tanker *Jacksonville*, bound for Loch Ewe in CU36, which he sank 20 miles west of Portnahaven, Islay, at 1600 hours on 30 August. The *Jacksonville* was laden with 14,300 tons of petrol. She blew up and just two of her 78 crew survived.

A Coastal Command Liberator sighted *U482*'s conning tower 100 miles west of Islay early on the morning of 1 September and the new Castle-class corvette HMS *Hurst Castle* was directed to this position only to be herself torpedoed. The frigate HMS *Helmsdale* picked up 105 survivors.

Kapitanleutnant Matuschka intercepted ONS251 160 miles west of Colonsay and sank the Norwegian collier *Fjordheim*, outbound for Halifax with anthracite, at 0020 hours on 3 September. Two days later, Churchill sailed from the Clyde on the *Queen Mary* for the summit conference with Roosevelt at Quebec. On 8 September Matuschka brought *U482* back to a position 70 miles west of Islay and, at 0600 hours, he sank the 15,702-ton tanker *Empire Heritage* with two torpedoes. The tanker, inbound for the Clyde, sank in less than five minutes. Half an hour later the little rescue ship *Pinto* had stopped to pick up the tanker's survivors. She too was torpedoed, sinking in just 90 seconds. More than 130 men died in the double sinking. Forty-five survivors were picked up by HM trawler *Northern Wave*.

A new anti-submarine striking force, Force 33, had been formed to protect the North Western Approaches at the end of August, but Matuschka's successful patrol, taking place as it did in home waters, came as something of a shock. Anti-submarine sweeps began immediately and *U743*, commanded by Kapitanleutnant Helmuth Kandzior, was found 250 miles offshore by HMS *Porchester Castle* and HMS *Helmsdale* on the morning of 9 September. Both ships opened fire on the U-boat after *Porchester Castle*'s first attack blew her to the surface. Further depth-charges were dropped when *U743* submerged again – whereupon oil, wreckage and grisly human remains came to the surface. Another submarine, *U484*, was also destroyed that day 40 miles west of Tiree by the Canadian corvettes *Dunver* and *Hespeler*.

The 19th Escort Group were on patrol seven miles off Cape Wrath at 0948 hours on 6 December 1944 when a torpedo slammed into HMS *Bullen*. Some 97 survivors were picked up and the frigate *Loch Insh* and sloop *Goodall* rounded on and destroyed Kapitanleutnant Aldegarmann's *U297*.

The increase in U-boat activity in home waters brought with it occasional reconnaissance flights to the North Western Approaches by Luftwaffe aircraft based in Norway. One, a JU88 of 1(F)/120 based at Stavanger Sola, crashed into Little Loch Broom following engine failure in the early hours of 29 December 1944. One crew member survived and was taken prisoner.

Hartmut von Matuschka brought *U482* back to the Clyde approaches in January 1945. His first victim on this patrol was the Norwegian tanker *Spinanger*, bound for the Clyde from Londonderry and torpedoed close to the Clyde light vessel at lunch-time on 15 January. Three of the *Spinanger*'s crew died and their ship was beached in Kames Bay. Matuschka got his second victim less than half an hour later when one of his *Zaunkonig* acoustic homing torpedoes tore a 30-foot hole in the starboard quarter of the American-built escort carrier HMS *Thane*. Twelve sailors were killed and a number of others were injured or burned. An immediate result of this attack was the provision of an escort of destroyers for the Stranraer to Larne ferry. *U482* was found sitting on the bottom off Machrihanish on 16 January and was destroyed by ships of the 2nd Escort Group, among them HMS *Amethyst*, which later became famous for her part in the 'Yangtse Incident'.

HMS *Thane* steamed slowly upriver to the Gareloch under heavy escort whereupon she was secured to a buoy and hurriedly evacuated. The torpedo had struck next to her main magazine. Lieutenant James Woodrow, a naval mines disposal officer, and Lieutenant-Commander Edward Seager, the Staff Officer, Intelligence, at naval headquarters in St Enoch's Hotel, rowed out to *Thane*. They found that 100,000 Bofors and 5" shells had been displaced in the magazine and that many of the soft-nosed Bofors shells had been primed by the concussion. It was indeed a miracle that the ship had not been blown apart in one massive explosion. She was in a most dangerous condition. As they rowed ashore, a somewhat shaken Seager reminded himself to mind his own business in future.

Lieutenant Woodrow, a scion of the Bridge of Weir civil engineering family, returned on board *Thane* with a specially trained team of ratings and petty officers. As the ammunition hoist had jammed, they were forced to carry each shell on deck; and, in one heart-stopping moment, Woodrow slipped and fell into the piles of ammunition. The shells were loaded into a puffer which made a number of trips to drop the shells in 95 fathoms of water between Ardrossan and Brodick. Woodrow himself carried the most dangerous Bofors shells on deck and, after checking there was nobody nearby, threw them over the side where they exploded on hitting the water. *Thane* was deemed not to be worth repairing and was broken up at Faslane later in 1945.

Six months earlier, the dry summer of 1944 had exposed a land-mine dating from the raids of 1941 in a reservoir above Dumbarton. Woodrow made that safe. He was also called in when the *Empire Heywood Stanhope* arrived in the Clyde with time bombs hidden among her cargo of oranges. These had been placed there by enemy agents in Spain and had begun exploding while she was still at sea, though the blast had been absorbed by the fruit. One bomb, however, was discovered very close to her side where it would have done considerable damage. As the cargo was hurriedly rolled down chutes into waiting lighters, many oranges fell into the sea and were washed up on nearby beaches to the delight of locals. A child, who could only have had the vaguest memories of oranges was reputedly overheard saying, 'If it bounces, it's a ba'.' His friend replied, 'If it explodes, it's a bomb.'

James Woodrow's extraordinary courage earned him a George Medal and bar.

U1014 was destroyed in the North Channel on 4 February by the 19th Escort Group. Other contacts were attacked in the North Channel by both ships and aircraft throughout February. A torpedo narrowly missed the Dutch liner *Nieuw Amsterdam* two days later, and 15 died when the steamship *Dettifoss* was sunk west of Corsewall Point on 21 February.

The small steamer *Inger Toft*, inbound from Reykjavik, was sunk by *U722* three miles west of Neist Point in Skye on 16 March. The American destroyer USS *Thornhill* attacked a submerged contact 15 miles south of Islay the following evening. *Thornhill* carried out four attacks and reported that these were followed by two explosions after which a large quantity of wreckage, including a desk to which hair and flesh were adhering, floated to the surface. Among the debris were German documents dated 12 December 1944. German records do not show any U-boats as having been lost on 17 March. It would appear that *Thornhill* had attacked the hulk of *U1014*, sunk by Royal Navy frigates and corvettes on 4 February.

As the war drew to a close, the waters off the west coast of Scotland were becoming increasingly hazardous for U-boats. *U1003* was rammed and sunk in the North Channel on 20 March by HMCS *New Glasgow*. HMCS *Thetford Mines* picked up 33 survivors. *U965*, commanded by Kapitanleutnant Unverzagt, was sunk 28 miles east of the Butt of Lewis by HMS *Conn* at 1245 hours on 27 March. The following day saw Kapitanleutnant Reimers' *U722* fall victim to depth-charges from the frigates *Byron*, *Redmill* and *Fitzroy* 20 miles east of the entrance to Loch Boisdale.

HMS *Rupert* and HMS *Conn* attacked a submerged contact off the Point of Stoer on Friday, 30 March 1945. The contact was detected on the bottom at 1839 hours and further attacks made at 1440 hours the following day brought a large quantity of wreckage from *U1021* to the surface.

U218 laid 13 mines in the Firth of Clyde on 18 April, a mere three weeks before the end of the war. These were found to be of a new type, code-named 'Oboe', after one was caught in the nets of the drifter *Fairview*. A mine was responsible for the destruction on 20 April, off the entrance to Loch Ryan, of the trawler *Ethel Crawford*. Most of her crew were killed.

The code-word '*Regenbogen*' (rainbow) went out from U-boat headquarters at 0134 hours on 5 May 1945. U-boats were to be scuttled before their crews gave themselves up. The order for destruction was, however, rescinded just eight minutes later. On 8 May, Allied commanders ordered that all U-boats should immediately surface, fly a black pennant and report their position in plain language. Not all U-boat commanders heard the orders, and others chose to ignore them. Seven surrendered U-boats were under the watchful eye of Captain M. J. Evans in HMS *Philante*, formerly the luxury yacht of Tommy Sopwith, in Loch Eriboll by the evening of 10 May. Another four had surrendered at the Kyle of Lochalsh. Their crews were taken aboard British ships and their torpedoes removed.

A surfaced U-boat was attacked by Coastal Command aircraft 110 miles west of Islay at 1330 hours on 11 May. Another attack was carried out on a

The new escort carrier HMS Vindex *on trials in the Clyde. In August 1944* Vindex *sailed, with 825 Squadron embarked, from Loch Ewe as part of the escort for convoy JW 59 bound for Murmansk. One of her aircraft damaged U394 which was later finished off by escort vessels.*

Despite initial teething problems, the escort carriers made an invaluable contribution in closing the mid-Atlantic air gap over the convoys.

schnorkelling U-boat 70 miles west of Islay by an aircraft of 172 Squadron at 1700 hours that afternoon. It was the last anti-submarine attack of the European war.

In all, 49 U-boats had been gathered in Allied ports by 22 May, 14 of them in Loch Eriboll while one, *U293*, remained at Kyle of Lochalsh. By November 1945 110 U-boats had been concentrated at Loch Ryan and at Lisahally in Lough Foyle, Northern Ireland. These had all been expended as targets by the following February in 'Operation Deadlight'.

A total of 8,223 merchant navy survivors were landed in the Clyde between April 1941 and the end of 1942. All came under the care of the Renfrewshire ARP service and, from the Island Site first-aid post at Gourock Pierhead, the wounded were taken on to hospitals in Glasgow, at Hairmyres and Mearnskirk.

Along with the Mersey, the Clyde, as one of the eastern termini of the lifeline, was of vital importance. An emergency port scheme was put into operation in September 1940, Thames barges were brought north to increase lighterage capacity and huge new port facilities were created at Faslane and Cairnryan. Accommodation for 4,000 men was provided in eight camps around Number 2 Military Port, Cairnryan. At Number 1 Military Port, Faslane, the road from Helensburgh to Garelochead had to be diverted up the hill and a spur two and three-quarter miles long constructed from the West Highland Railway. Shandon Hydropathic Hotel was requisitioned to provide accommodation for essential personnel. Quays were constructed and cranes were brought north from docks at London, Deptford and Southampton, all of which were effectively closed due to enemy action. Movements were controlled from the Merchant Ships Operations Room at Marymount, Barrhill Road, Gourock.

Clyde Navigation Trust pilots moved more than 500 million tons of shipping during the war, 52 million tons of cargo was handled and something of the order of four million troops were embarked or disembarked. The average turnaround period for merchant vessels of over 300 tons was only four days by the end of 1942. During that year 3,960 merchant vessels and 6,650 coasters used the port, and 607,550 tons of cargo was discharged overside.

The terrible slaughter in the North Atlantic lasted almost six years from the moment when Fritz-Julius Lemp's torpedo struck the *Athenia*. The Second World War was always going to be won by the side with both the preponderance in resources and the ability to manage them to best effect. Despite relentless attacks, the vital supply lines to the United States and the Soviet Union had been kept open and the huge troop and supply convoys so essential to military operations in North Africa and Europe had won through. In the final analysis, the Battle of the Atlantic was won by a combination of

British intelligence-gathering, tactics and technology, American shipbuilding capacity, air power and the extraordinary contribution of the Royal Canadian Navy which grew from 11 ships in 1939 to 350 in 1945. The maintenance of the Atlantic lifeline was Britain's largest single contribution to eventual victory.

The sea-bed was littered with wrecks and millions of pounds worth of cargo. Over 2,450 ships with a total displacement of 12.8 million tons were lost during the Battle of the Atlantic. Tens of thousands of men, women and children had drowned, had been choked and burned alive in blazing oil, frozen to death on the Murmansk run, or simply blown to pieces.

Once the coast of France was in German hands, the North Channel became the main route for the transatlantic traffic and, both in 1940 and 1944-45, the Kriegsmarine made determined efforts to close it. Had they succeeded in 1940, Britain would have lost the war.

Chapter Six

For a Noble Purpose

British fortunes were at a particularly low ebb at the beginning of 1941. The German bombing of British cities was at its height, morale was at its lowest and the country was in the grip of severe winter blizzards. Britain's strategic position had collapsed into military impotence.

The re-election of President Franklin Roosevelt in November 1940 had brought neither the open-ended financial aid, nor the American entry into the war hoped for by many and already widely recognised as a prerequisite of victory. The American government was quite unable to understand that Britain was, in fact, desperately close to bankruptcy and would soon be unable to pay for arms shipments ordered in the United States. The Americans were, not unnaturally, quite unwilling to use their considerable financial might to prop up the British Empire, an institution they regarded as, at best, anachronistic.

Among those on board a special train which left King's Cross on the night of 14 January 1941 were Winston Churchill, his wife, Lord and Lady Halifax, and Harry Hopkins, Roosevelt's newly arrived Special Envoy. The party were on their way north to see Lord Halifax off in his new role as Ambassador to Washington and to conduct a whistle-stop tour of fleet bases.

The Prime Minister's apparent solicitude towards the new Ambassador was a sham. For some months, there had been growing feeling in the country against Halifax, last of the pre-war appeasers in the War Cabinet. Churchill was also aware that Halifax had, following the defeat in France, exceeded his authority in making peace overtures through neutral Sweden without War Cabinet approval. The death of Lord Lothian, the previous Ambassador, also an appeaser, gave Churchill the opportunity to sack Halifax as Foreign

Secretary and shunt him off to Washington. In doing so, he also removed the only remaining threat to his own position as Prime Minister.

After taking the reluctant Ambassador to Scapa Flow, from where he crossed the Atlantic in the battleship *King George V*, Churchill returned south on Friday, 17 January, to visit the dockyard at Rosyth. Calling at Edinburgh they picked up Tom Johnston, then the Regional Civil Defence Commissioner, and Norman Duke, Johnston's Principal Officer.

The train drew into Glasgow's Queen Street Station at lunch-time and, despite the visit not having been given any pre-publicity, was greeted by a large crowd through which the party had to fight its way to the City Chambers. Around 200 guests, including a number of reporters invited by the publicity-conscious Lord Provost Paddy Dollan, awaited in the City Chambers. Though hampered by a heavy cold, Churchill rose to the occasion and made an impromptu speech which ended thus: 'My one aim is to extirpate Hitlerism from Europe. The question is such a simple one. Are we to move steadily forward and have freedom, or are we to be put back into the Middle Ages by a totalitarian system that crushes all forms of individual life and has for its aim little less than the subjugation of Europe and little more than the gratification of gangster appetites?

'Do not suppose that we are at the end of the road. Yet, though long and hard it may be, I have absolutely no doubt that we shall win a complete and decisive victory over the forces of evil, and that the victory itself will only be a stimulus to further efforts to conquer ourselves and to make our country worthy in the days of peace as it is proving itself in the hours of war.'

That evening Tom Johnston entertained the Prime Minister and Hopkins to dinner in Room 21 at the North British Hotel in George Square. At the end of the meal, Johnston stood up and addressed Hopkins with these words: 'We have tonight with us a friend from overseas. If he cares to say a word to us we shall be delighted. This is quite an informal gathering, no press representative is present. More particularly, I do welcome Mr Hopkins for the sake of his old grandmother from Auchterarder.'

Hopkins, a frail and dishevelled figure whose recurring ill-health brought about his early death, aged 56, in 1946, rose to reply. He looked directly at Churchill and he said: 'I suppose you wish to know what I am going to say to President Roosevelt on my return. Well, I'm going to quote you one verse from that Book of Books in the truth of which Mr Johnston's mother and my own Scottish mother were brought up: 'Whither thou goest, I will go; and where thou lodgest, I will lodge; the people shall be my people, and thy God my God.' Quietly he added. 'Even unto the end.'

Lord Moran, Churchill's doctor, was present and wrote that he was surprised to find the Prime Minister in tears. 'Even to us,' wrote Moran, 'the words seemed like a rope thrown to a drowning man.'

'It will be a splendid episode in the history of the Empire if Australian, New Zealand and Canadian troops defend the Motherland against invasion.' (Winston Churchill in a hand-written minute of 27 May 1940.)
Two officers of the 28th (Maori) Battalion, New Zealand Expeditionary Force, at Princes Pier, Gourock, on 17 June 1940. They were part of the newly arrived 5th New Zealand Infantry Brigade.
(TRUSTEES OF THE IMPERIAL WAR MUSEUM, LONDON)

This somewhat theatrical event has been portrayed, particularly in Glasgow, as a turning point in the war. It was no such thing. Harry Hopkins had no authority to make any commitments on behalf of the President, his role being purely that of an observer. Earlier, he had made it clear to Churchill that not more than 15 per cent of all Americans were in favour of active participation in the war. Hopkins had, however, just experienced his first week in the emotionally charged atmosphere which surrounded the Prime

Minister, and had fallen completely under his spell. Anglo-American relationships were far too complex to be materially altered by an exchange at an unimportant dinner-party in Glasgow. In any case, the 'Lease-Lend' legislation which was to throw Britain its transatlantic lifeline had been evolving for some months and was already beginning its passage through Congress.

One lasting side-effect of that evening in the North British Hotel was the strong impression that Tom Johnston made on the Prime Minister. Just three weeks later, on 9 February 1941, he was offered the position of Secretary of State for Scotland, a post not hitherto known for the dynamism of its incumbents.

Johnston, the MP for West Stirlingshire, was instinctively anti-war but was in no doubt as to the probable course of events in Europe. In March 1939 he went against many of his Labour Party colleagues by supporting both an economic boycott of Germany and the development of civil defence. Johnston was, as a result, the only non-establishment figure invited to become a Regional Civil Defence Commissioner in May that year. This post brought him into direct conflict with the many Labour-controlled local authorities opposed to civil defence preparations as a means of protesting against conscription. In appointing him Secretary of State, Churchill believed that, with Johnston in St Andrews House, the chances of labour problems disrupting war production in Scotland would be considerably reduced.

Johnston's achievements were considerable; he is still considered by many to be the best Secretary of State Scotland has had. He developed a system of governing Scotland by committees and quangos responsible to London. This still functions 50 years on and is anathema to the devolution-minded.

Johnston's dynamic régime at St Andrews House contrasted sharply with that of his immediate predecessors, Sir John Colville and Ernest Brown. Once the initial flurry of activity surrounding the evacuation scheme and the internment of enemy aliens had died down, Scottish Office war diary entries regularly read: 'Summary of Important War Action for week ending . . . Nil.'

The only department really busy with war-related work in John Colville's Scottish Office was the Public Relations department. One of their first tasks, in November 1939, was to furnish the Foreign Office 'with particulars regarding the internment and treatment in Barlinnie Prison, Glasgow, of the Acting German Consul in Glasgow and the Porter at the Consulate, and, in Duke Street Prison, Glasgow, of the Acting Consul's Lady Secretary.' This material was used to reply to a German broadcast which had alleged that the Acting Consul and his small staff were being treated like common convicts.

Later that month, Public Relations department staff took an American journalist to see Scotland's war effort. He was shown Women's Voluntary Service centres, the Women's Land Army at work, and 'something of our air defences'. After a meeting with Provost Dollan in Glasgow, he toured some shipyards and education facilities for evacuees. Despite the fact that he had seen little of a particularly warlike nature, he gave his assurance that 'Scotland's war effort will receive quite a lot of space in his newspapers'.

Central to rightist mythology surrounding the British at war is the image of a nation unshakably united under inspirational leadership, single-handedly saving the world from tyranny. More potent for the left is the view that an heroic and downtrodden working class, let down by the establishment, rescued Britain from defeat. Both these misinformed, propagandist self-images continue to influence British political life more than half a century later. Unable to come to terms with either the shock of effective defeat in 1940, or their sharp decline in the years thereafter, the British have tended to take refuge in belief in their own propaganda. The reality of wartime Britain was considerably more complex and refreshingly human than the myth allows.

Scottish working-class attitudes in the early months of the war were largely conditioned by memories of the savage depression of the 1930s. Unemployment, poverty and events on the international stage, most particularly the Spanish Civil War, had served to increase Communist Party membership and influence in the west of Scotland during this period. The left were thrown into confusion by the Nazi-Soviet pact of 1939 as a result of which Stalin was able to join Hitler in the rape of Poland. Stafford Cripps, a prominent figure on the Labour left, wrote that the subsequent Soviet invasion of Finland was a necessary defensive move, sentiments which *Tribune* was pointedly unable to endorse. The intelligentsia of the left were deeply distressed by what they saw as both the immorality of war and a retreat from human values.

The Scottish National Party retreated into anti-war rhetoric. Party Chairman Douglas Young fought a long legal battle with the authorities after refusing to register either for military service or as a conscientious objector. In 1942 he produced a pamphlet in which he windily bemoans the 'intrusion of outside influences', and rails against the 'religionists' and the aristocracy. He refers to the Duke of Argyll and the Duke of Hamilton, amongst others, as 'The Scottish Quislings'. He was released from Saughton Prison in March 1943 after spending eight months inside for refusing to register.

Young believed that the Germans would win the war and advocated that Scotland should make a separate peace. In view of his comments about the aristocracy, it comes as something of a surprise to discover that he saw the SNP acting as a Vichy-style government in a Nazi-dominated Scotland. At a parliamentary by-election in February 1944, Young came close to winning the Kirkcaldy Burghs seat.

The Scottish Office was moved, in January 1940, to establish a small committee to counteract fascist, communist and pacifist propaganda in

Glasgow and the west of Scotland. As the so-called 'Phoney War' dragged on, in January 1940 tax increases and the introduction of rationing demanded proportionately greater sacrifice from the less well-off. Over 2,000 people attended meetings organised by the Scottish Peace Council in Glasgow at which the speakers included Willie Gallacher, the Communist MP for West Fife. Sir Hugh Roberton, the Director of the Glasgow Orpheus Choir and a committed pacifist, addressed a pro-peace meeting in Barrhead. A Christmas broadcast by the Orpheus Choir was quietly cancelled by the BBC. Amid widespread resentment over the rising cost of living and apathy over British war aims, communist and pacifist anti-war slogans began to appear on walls in and around Glasgow in early April 1940. Meanwhile, members of the Anarchists Foundation, said to have been working against the prosecution of the war, were jailed.

It would be reasonable to assume that, following the German invasion of Norway and, subsequently, the Anglo-French defeat on the Western Front, attitudes would have hardened almost overnight. There is strong evidence that this was far from being the case. Public opinion surveys showed that anti-war groups were still strong even after Dunkirk and were benefiting from the deep depression and widespread anger at the time. Soldiers of the BEF returning from France brought stories of poor leadership and equipment, and a broadcast at the end of May which appealed for 12-bore cartridges was said to have had a most unsettling effect.

Listening to enemy broadcasts, notably those from 'Radio Caledonia', was on the increase in June 1940. Those which referred to working-class conditions in Scotland were believed to be having some effect and there were a number of recorded cases of workers stating that they would have nothing to lose under Hitler.

The BBC was reduced, on Friday September 1939, from seven broadcast programmes to a single, national network, known as the Home Service. This was done as the Air Ministry feared that the Luftwaffe would use BBC transmitters as navigation aids. All Scottish Regional Service programmes disappeared and the reception of the national service was notoriously poor north of the border.

The Home Service got off to a singularly bad start in Scotland, not least because of the incessant and tactless playing, in the first days of the war, of the song, *There'll always be an England!* Tom Johnston, as Regional Commissioner, was particularly indignant when, on two occasions at the end of November 1939, the BBC refused to carry items of importance to Scotland as they were 'crowded out with more important matters'.

Whenever he needed to get his own way with a recalcitrant London bureaucracy, all Johnston had to do was to raise the spectre of Scottish nationalism. In February 1940 the BBC position with regard to the resumption of a single weekly programme entitled *The Week in Scotland* was that they would only put such a programme on 'if the Cabinet, i.e. the Ministry of Information, was prepared to endorse Tom Johnston's view that the political

In 1939 Britain imported all of her oil, most of her raw materials and half of her food. The economy, and with it the nation's survival, were therefore desperately vulnerable to attacks on the trade routes by surface raiders and, above all, by U-boats.
In order to cut down on imported goods and ensure fair shares for all, rationing was introduced. Imports of food were reduced by almost a third, from 23 million tons in 1938 to 16 million tons by the end of 1940. In addition, every effort was made to cut down on waste. This Glasgow Corporation cart reminded already hard-pressed house-wives to save kitchen waste for use as pig swill. Such campaigns found little in the way of a receptive audience among the poorer communities where waste was, in any case, anathema.
Britain's economic plight in 1945 served largely to ensure that rationing and shortages continued for years after the war.
(GLASGOW MUSEUMS: THE MUSEUM OF TRANSPORT)

171

circumstances in Scotland require a concession of a weekly talk devoted to Scottish news'.

Meanwhile, the Ministry of Information was reporting that Scottish listeners to the BBC were becoming thoroughly fed up with hearing the whole of Britain referred to as 'England' and that a newsreel which referred to Douglas Farquhar, the commanding officer of 602 (City of Glasgow) Squadron, as an 'English' airman was booed in Glasgow cinemas.

Matters did begin to improve after Moultrie Kelsall was appointed Acting Programme Director for the BBC in Scotland in mid-1940 and the transmitter was split that October. Among the figures employed by Kelsall were the writer Neil Gunn and a young actor called John Laurie whom, on one occasion, he described rather waspishly as 'a ham actor in a ham part'. A variety programme entitled Under Your Tin Hat in July 1941 featured artists drawn from the civil defence services throughout Scotland. These included Walter Pert, a first-aider from Dumbarton who played Scottish tunes on the accordion. Miss Mary Smith, a VAD from Helensburgh, sang Scottish songs, and Walter Jackson of Glasgow Auxiliary Fire Service gave 'a novelty turn' entitled 'That Man is Gone!'

Very much alive to the volatility of morale, the government made strenuous efforts to both measure and control public opinion. Telephone calls were bugged and thousands of letters, particularly those between Glasgow and Ireland, were opened and read. Information was also gathered from the BBC, the WVS, Citizens' Advice Bureaux, Chief Constables, the Regional Information Office in Edinburgh and the Scottish Unionist (Conservative) Party Whip's office. Additional material came from the Mass Observation social survey organisation employed by the Ministry of Information which also operated its own 'Anti-Lie Bureau'. For evidence of the volatility of morale it is only necessary to consider the hatred and violence, much of which was inspired by fear, that was directed against the Scottish Italian community following Mussolini's declaration of war in July 1940.

The Glasgow Information Committee was formed, under the auspices of the Ministry of Information, at the end of June 1940. Chaired by cinema proprietor Alex King, it had 23 members drawn from the political parties, trades unions, local authorities, the WVS, Glasgow University and George Outram & Co, the newspaper publishers. Their remit was to consider 'the ways and means of circulating the right kind of propaganda', in the west of Scotland.

The committee's primary role was to organise a series of 'War Commentary' meetings at which carefully selected speakers would give morale-boosting addresses on the progress of the war. A recording of the Prime Minister's wireless speech of Sunday, 27 April 1941, was played to a sizeable audience in the Odeon Theatre, Ayr, on the following Sunday night. Glasgow's Lady

Provost Agnes Dollan was in attendance at the Elder Cinema when the women of Govan were treated to a WVS film stirringly entitled *Britannia is a Woman*. Even church ministers were enlisted to pitch their sermons towards the maintenance of morale.

'War Commentary' speakers were required to report back to the committee with any pieces of gossip picked up during and after each meeting, particularly those which would identify defeatism. The speakers themselves were carefully watched. One was severely reprimanded after allowing a meeting in Kilmarnock in October 1941 to stray into a discussion of Glasgow's municipal problems.

Not surprisingly, it proved impossible to keep politics out of the War Commentaries. The Labour Party found a convenient excuse not to share the platform at a meeting addressed by Ayr MP Sir Thomas Moore in November 1941. Moore's pre-war amity towards Hitler and the Nazis was widely known.

An internal committee paper on the maintenance of public morale fell into the hands of the Scottish Unionist Chief Whip, Sir James Stuart MP, later Viscount Stuart of Findhorn, in August 1940. Stuart, a strong supporter of appeasement, was outraged to discover that the paper suggested that photographs of Neville Chamberlain walking in the park, carrying an umbrella, failed to suggest energetic leadership in time of war. To the intense anger of the Unionist old guard, the paper stated that the public wanted a scapegoat for the resounding military defeats suffered in Norway and on the Western Front.

The paper pointed out that it was 'quite irrelevant whether or not some members of the previous government were incompetent. They have become the focusing points of widespread suspicion and criticism, and there seems little likelihood of any publicity by them, or on their behalf, being favourably received.'

This perfectly reasonable and well-argued submission had been prepared, at the committee's request, by one of its members, Dr Philip Vernon, the head of the Department of Psychology at Glasgow University. The implicit criticism of Chamberlain's régime moved Stuart to write a strongly worded letter of complaint to Duff Cooper, the Minister of Information.

Immediately it became apparent that the paper had aroused the wrath of the Unionist establishment, the rest of the committee wasted no time in disowning Dr Vernon. Desperately watching his own back, Regional Information Officer Niven McNicoll sent Duff Cooper a toadying letter in which he absolved himself and other committee members of any responsibility, and even went so far as to name the paper's author. Duff Cooper, whose idleness and incompetence as Minister of Information led to his early dismissal, compounded the error by 'unofficially' naming Vernon in a mollifying reply to Stuart.

The committee provided confirmation, if it were needed, of its proscription by accepting, 'with regret', Philip Vernon's resignation in January 1941.

Vernon's astute assessment of morale in late 1940 was echoed throughout the Scottish educational establishment. In November it was reported that, 'In academic circles in Scotland, gloomy predictions are reported; the view is not that Hitler will win, but that there is little prospect of his being beaten.' Surveys in mid-1941 showed that over 40 per cent of Scots believed that Britain could not prevail without the entry of America into the war. 'Lend-Lease' had just completed its passage through Congress and it was reported that over 70 per cent of those questioned in Scotland believed America would declare war on Germany.

In the factories, war workers had begun to feel remote from the war. Life had become a dull and flavourless mix of numbingly repetitive tasks, long hours and fatigue. The 'Twenties' (women born in 1920) were required to register for employment in war work in April 1941. The Employment of Women (Control of Engagement) Order extended this requirement to women between 18 and 40. Social etiquette dictated that, despite 12-hour shifts in the factories, women also carried out all the household chores. Clothing was rationed from June 1941, and women were encouraged to 'make do and mend' by faintly ridiculous propaganda figures like 'Miss Sew and Sew'. Rationing brought coupons, points and ration books. Shopping became an exhausting round of rising prices, shortages and queues in the cold and the pouring rain. This, allied to heavy bombing and the constant strain of uncertainty about relatives in the fighting forces, led to a sharp increase in illness and a resultant drop in productivity. Tom Johnston, an admirer of Beveridge, was being visionary when he introduced free medical for war workers care in Emergency Medical Service hospitals.

Apart from a brief period of stability during the summer of 1940, industrial relations in Scotland, and Britain as a whole, continued to be dogged by the pre-war attitudes of class-consciousness and mutual suspicion. Fatigue and irritability had begun to set in by the autumn of 1940. Wages disputes were common; much official concern was expressed when 200 women at the Barr and Stroud works in Caxton Street, Glasgow, went on strike for higher pay at the beginning of June 1941. Amongst other things, Barr and Stroud were manufacturing vital rangefinders and submarine periscopes.

Riveters at John Brown's Shipyard went on strike for three days over the activities of a shipyard detective brought in to deal with an epidemic of pilfering. Much ill-feeling, and the occasional strike, was generated by the introduction of Polish refugees into the factories and mines. Other workers refused to work alongside conscientious objectors. At the instigation of MI5, the government implemented Order 1305 in July 1940. This made binding

The success or failure of the Allied invasion of Normandy was always going to depend on the ability of the invading forces to bring a preponderance of men and material to bear in the shortest possible time. It was believed (correctly, as it turned out) that the Germans would be equally aware of this and defend ports such as Cherbourg with a will. Plans for the 'Mulberry' floating harbours were completed in November 1943 and construction was begun at top speed. Here, on 17 February 1944, a 'Whale' floating roadway section has just been launched at Cairnryan. Pontoon bridge sections were being built not far away at Garlieston near Wigtown. Two 'Mulberries' were planned, one at the American 'Omaha' beach and one at Arromanches in the British/Canadian sector. Much of the American harbour was lost in a severe storm a few days after D-Day. 'Mulberry B' at Arromanches survived and remained in use for eight months instead of the planned three months.

(TRUSTEES OF THE IMPERIAL WAR MUSEUM, LONDON)

arbitration in an industrial dispute compulsory, thus effectively outlawing strikes. It did little or nothing to improve matters on Clydeside.

As one official report put it in 1941, 'Tales of slackness in war production, of defects of supply, and faults of management are common in the Scottish industrial areas.' There were recurring reports of men playing cards throughout nightshift working. The majority of workers were willing to respond to the Government's exhortations for higher production but were often frustrated by shortages of raw materials. Patrician managers were unwilling to communicate with workers other than by edict, and failed to inform workers that many of these raw materials were lying at the bottom of the North Atlantic.

Skilled workers often found themselves being wasted on routine tasks without explanation. The 12-hour shift was the norm in 1940 and seven-day working weeks were common. The restricted wartime public transport service led to many people experiencing unforeseen difficulties in reaching work on time. Much bitterness and resentment was caused when men but a few minutes late through no fault of their own were locked out for as much as half a day.

The Soviet Government was, in early 1941, still in tacit alliance with Nazi Germany and had denounced the British government for conducting an 'imperialist' war. This conveniently ignored the fact that Stalin had joined Hitler in the conquest of Poland and had overrun much of Finland. The British Communist Party slavishly followed the Moscow line, despite the misgivings of many influential members. A Scottish edition of the *Daily Worker* was launched in November 1940 and both CP membership and influence increased steadily.

There were widespread feelings that, following their absorption into the coalition War Cabinet, the leaders of the Labour Party had ceased to represent the interests of the working class. Ernie Bevin, formerly the strong man of the TUC, had been appointed Minister of Labour in Churchill's government. This was done very much on the basis of employing a former poacher as gamekeeper. In December 1940, he convened a series of meetings in Glasgow in an attempt to improve worsening industrial relations. A communist-inspired 'People's Convention' was held in Manchester in January 1941 and was followed almost immediately by the suppression of the *Daily Worker*. The annual conference of the Scottish Mineworkers' Federation in 1941 passed a motion praising the 'Soviet Union's policy of peace' by 37,000 votes to 12,000.

Support for a Communist candidate in the Dumbarton by-election of March 1941 reached 15 per cent and coincided with a wave of strikes by apprentices throughout Scotland. The Apprentices' Committee which organised these strikes was a mysterious body, composed almost entirely of young communists, which proved to be somewhat elusive when attempts were made to negotiate a settlement. The strikes ended with a spontaneous return to work on the morning of 14 March 1941, the day after the first heavy raid on Clydeside. The Communist Party changed their stance overnight following the German invasion of the Soviet Union on 22 June 1941 and became enthusiastic advocates of the war.

Nowhere in Scottish industry were industrial relations worse than in the coal mines where decades of low pay, poor working conditions and frequent, lengthy periods of unemployment had left a legacy of bitterness among the workforce.

The fall of France in June 1940 was followed by a slump in demand for coal as overseas markets collapsed. Younger miners left the industry in large numbers for the services and many older men left for the munitions factories where both wages and working conditions were markedly better. Domestic demand increased in line with war production but, by early 1941, production per man-shift was decreasing sharply. Absenteeism was increasing with around a quarter of miners being regular poor attenders. This was particularly worrying as Scottish pits tended to be mechanised to a greater degree than their English counterparts, and the absence of one key man would have a disproportionately serious effect on production.

Of the 65 recorded disputes which took place in the Scottish mining industry during the first three months of 1941, 58 occurred in Lanarkshire and West Lothian. Most of the disputes concerned wages and working conditions. Bad feeling between managers and miners was particularly strong in Lanarkshire and conciliation machinery broke down in an atmosphere of mutual suspicion.

Priory Colliery at Blantyre had been notorious for its appalling record of industrial relations for many years. Meetings convened jointly by the National Union of Mineworkers and the Ministry of Fuel and Power in an effort to resolve the situation had only served to expose all the old mutual hatreds and distrust between miners and coalmasters. Local union officials defied their national colleagues by stating that any attempt to change working practices and improve production would result in the pit immediately going on strike.

A mines inspector wrote: 'I am bound to say that a spirit of indifference prevails among the majority of the workmen on all three shifts, although it is more pronounced on the backshift.

'Many incidents savouring of sabotage in the workings have taken place in the last year such as:

The bolts of hanging glands slackened off.

Stone dust put in turbo-pump bearings.

Pit props jammed into conveyors.

Destruction of permanent lights.

Interference with electrical apparatus.

The deliberate derailing of tubs and consequent damage to rail tracks.'

Scottish mining villages were self-contained, closed communities, largely impervious to outside influences. Frequent surveys for and by the Ministry of Information told the same story: that miners remained apparently unaware of or indifferent to the main issues of the war. As one report put it, 'More important is the deep-seated hostility to the management or owners, and the suspicion of all the latter's recommendations. "The owners wouldn't be for the war if it didn't pay them," is a common remark, and many of the younger and relatively irresponsible men are much more bitter against the "class enemy" than they are against the Nazis.'

In an attempt to identify the mining communities with the war effort, the Ministry of Information subjected them to a campaign of propaganda and publicity. Tom Johnston and Joseph Westwood, the Under-Secretary of State, spoke at meetings. Pithead War Commentaries were held, films were shown and leaflets, imaginatively entitled 'Workers under Nazi Gangsters', were distributed.

The fundamental problems, however, remained throughout the war. A dispute over 'heat money' sought by two machine men at Priory Pit in June 1943 flared up into a prolonged strike which was followed by a lock-out. Appearing at Hamilton Sheriff Court charged with breaking wartime regulations on unofficial strikes, 182 men were fined one pound each and 14 were fined ten shillings (50p). Priory Pit was taken over, and effectively nationalised, by the Ministry of Fuel and Power the following month. Coalmasters were still offering incentive bonuses to men able to prove themselves non-union in 1944. Coal output in Scotland slumped from 30.5 million tons in 1939 to 21.4 million tons in 1945. During the same period, the workforce in the industry declined from 88,000 to 80,000.

Many of Scotland's mines were played out by the end of the war and the National Coal Board, formed on nationalisation in 1947, was already planning the phased closure of much of the industry over the ensuing 20 years.

The Second World War reversed, almost overnight, the seemingly relentless economic decline of the inter-war years. For a brief period, a highly interventionist government organised a planned economy which worked. The depression of the 1930s had brought about the extinction of many of the great names of Clyde shipbuilding. Beardmore's at Dalmuir had closed in 1931, Barclay Curle's suffered a part closure of their yard in 1932, D & W Henderson's at Meadowside closed completely in 1933 and the great Fairfield yard at Govan was only saved by the intervention of James and Henry Lithgow in 1935. The closed yards were bought up by National Shipbuilders' Security Ltd, a cartel of the major surviving shipbuilders, which, in their own euphemism, 'sterilised' them, thus effectively ensuring a sizeable pool of long-term unemployed.

The former Napier and Miller yard at Old Kilpatrick was used to fabricate sections of the Mulberry Harbour vital to the success of the D-Day landings. Before this could take place, the yard had to be reopened by special Government decree as it was still the subject of a National Shipbuilders' Security bond. The former D & W Henderson yard at Meadowside was also reopened for the production of landing craft by Redpath, Brown & Co.

Sir James Lithgow served in the wartime Government as Controller of Merchant Shipping and Repairs. The famous yard which bore his name produced 1,200,000 tons of shipping during the war. John Brown's yard at Clydebank constructed the battleships *Duke of York* and *Vanguard*. The former was launched, in pouring rain, by the Queen on 6 January 1941. The latter, destined to be the Navy's last capital ship, went down the ways on St Andrew's Day, 1944. Stephen's of Linthouse built the carrier *Ocean* and the fast mine-layers *Manxman* and *Ariadne*.

The largest vessels built by Fairfield's were the 35,000-ton battleship *Howe* and the 26,000-ton carrier *Implacable*. Much of Fairfield's work was with smaller vessels including the Dido-class cruisers, *Phoebe* and *Bellona*, as well as 18 destroyers, two sloops and numerous landing and assault craft. The yard also undertook a considerable amount of repair and conversion work.

The Denny yard at Dumbarton constructed two merchant aircraft-carriers, the *Empire McAndrew* and the *Empire McDermott*. These hybrid vessels were designed to carry grain and were fitted with a small flight deck from which Swordfish aircraft could be operated. McGruers, the yacht-builders, produced motor launches and motor torpedo boats at their yard on the Gareloch.

Prefabrication of the Loch-class frigates and Castle-class corvettes was carried out using techniques pioneered on the Clyde. A specialist team of 30 naval architects was installed in Glasgow and created designs based on around 1,300 composite parts which could be prepared outwith the shipyards, thus considerably speeding up construction and easing demand on yard space. John Brown's were the lead yard and launched the first frigate, HMS *Loch Fada*. Parts of frigates, along with sections of Mulberry Harbour, were built by Motherwell Bridge Engineering Ltd on what is now Strathclyde Park.

Despite both antiquated plant and its heavy dependence on imported ore and scrap, production by the Scottish steel industry held up better than the coal industry. An average of almost two million tons were produced annually between 1940 and 1944. The workforce at the Alex Findlay steel plant in Motherwell jumped from 700 in 1939 to 1,700 in 1945.

The first large contract placed with the Scottish Co-operative Wholesale Society sheet metal works at Sheildhall was for 140,000 2" naval rockets attached to 480 feet lengths of steel cable. During the Battle of Britain, these devices were sited along the edges of airfields in the south of England. The rockets were fired vertically upwards in salvoes of nine or more and, at around 600 feet, the top of its trajectory, the cable was released and

*General Sir Bernard Montgomery visited the SCWS Sheet Metal Works at Sheildhall on
21 April 1944. Here he appears fascinated by the workings of a machine which pressed
out tin cans. While the war did bring about full employment, much of the work in the
factories was repetitive and numbingly boring.*

*The inspirational little General was, by 1944, if anything more popular than the Prime
Minister. Churchill found Montgomery's assiduous publicity-seeking distasteful and his
growing interest in politics most unwelcome. Though the BBC were ordered to reduce
his invitations to broadcast, Montgomery chose to ignore Churchill's requests that he
should cut down on his tours.*

suspended from a parachute, hopefully directly in front of an approaching bomber. Should the enemy plane be unfortunate enough to fly into this device, another parachute opened at the bottom of the suspended cable and the bomber was dragged down out of control.

More conventionally, an average of three hundred 500lb bomb casings were produced weekly at the SCWS sheet metal works. Thousands of 150-gallon drop tanks for American Thunderbolt fighters were fabricated, many of which, after the war, found their way into Glasgow's parks where they did duty as children's boats. Another interesting weapon produced at Sheildhall was the 'Bomb Demolition No.1 40lb Mk.2'. Better known as the 'Flying Dustbin', this thin-cased bomb was designed to be fired from a Churchill tank, specially equipped with a mortar in place of its more usual gun. Around 230,000 of these weapons, designed to destroy concrete emplacements during assault landings, were produced.

Also at Shieldhall, the SCWS cabinet factory manufactured bridging pontoons, 10,261 bomb cases, 8,000 cordite cases, 55,000 bunks for Anderson shelters, as well as large quantities of 'Utility' furniture.

The SCWS boot and shoe factory turned out 607,500 pairs of boots for the services and reconditioned thousands more. The hosiery factory made 1,835,270 items including underwear, socks, woollens, uniforms and flying suits. The SCWS sundries department at Shieldhall filled 63,360 tins of Calf's Foot Jelly, 742,248 tins of powdered egg and 1,137,672 tins of milk powder in addition to making up thousands of emergency ration packs. Millions of SCWS cigarettes were produced for the forces.

The SCWS motor body and cartwright department in Scotland Street, Glasgow, delivered 750 tank transporters which were to prove their worth in the defeat of Rommel in North Africa. The building department constructed hundreds of air-raid shelters, two British restaurants for Glasgow Corporation and built an extension to the Hoover works at Cambuslang. Hoover required the extra space to expand their production of aircraft parts. Even a German prisoner-of-war writing home would find 'SCWS Ltd' at the bottom right-hand corner of his letter form. They were produced by the Society's paper and print department at Eastfield, Cambuslang.

By 1943 the Royal Naval Torpedo Factory in Alexandria was producing torpedoes to the value of £15 million pounds annually. This apparently

On 7 April 1944, exactly two weeks before this photograph was taken, Montgomery had been present at the historic meeting in St Paul's School, London, when the detailed plans for the D-Day invasion were presented to 111 people, including Churchill, all of whom had been sworn to the strictest secrecy.
(TRUSTEES OF THE IMPERIAL WAR MUSEUM, LONDON)

healthy output concealed the fact that the work of the RNTF research and development department at Fort Matilda, Greenock, was grossly underfunded. Only £50,000, about 0.3 per cent of gross manufactured value, was being spent on new development work. 'ULTRA' decrypts had revealed that the Germans were well advanced in the development of the *Zaunkonig* (Wren) acoustic homing torpedo. A major shake-up was ordered.

Scotland's first, largest and best known wartime industrial import was the Rolls-Royce plant at Hillington, west of Glasgow. The decision to develop a 'shadow' aero-engine factory near Glasgow was taken in 1938 and construction work began in mid-1939. The recruiting of staff began in May 1939 and the first two blocks of the new factory were being completed just as war broke out in September. By 1941, Merlin engines, which had operated for 240 hours, were being reconditioned and over 100 new Merlins were being produced every week, all by 26,000 employees. Factory space had expanded beyond the two million square feet at Hillington to include the W. D. and H. O. Wills tobacco factory on Alexandra Parade and a former lace factory at Thornliebank. Production continued to expand and, by the end of the war in 1945, around 30,000 Merlin engines had been supplied and tested.

The wartime dispersal of industry was not carried as far, geographically, as is often believed. In the event, Scotland got only 32 government factories and this contributed to the maintained dependency on traditional heavy industries. These saw their fortunes boosted by short-run wartime demand but the war also brought in major scientific and technical advances such as nuclear power, the jet engine, antibiotics and computers.

The British economy was in ruins by 1945 and the Treasury concluded that the country was facing 'an economic Dunkirk'. Forecasts of unemployment figures approaching three million and a massive balance of payments deficit served only to reaffirm the unpalatable fact that Britain had only survived the war courtesy of American economic support and financial strength. This led to the austerity programme of 1945 to 1947 which saw unemployment in Scotland rise to almost 80,000. Further American aid was desperately needed, and, though huge dollar loans were made available, this was only at enormous political cost. Britain was forced to agree to the ending of her role as a world power and accept a post-war world dominated by the United States. An immediate humiliation was the American insistence on independence for India, first intimated in 1942. The final collapse of British influence on the world stage was clearly signalled by the debacle at Suez and the retreat from empire.

Dollar-funded post-war reconstruction allowed the comparative domestic prosperity to continue up to the end of the 1950s but, by then, time was running out for much of Scotland's creaking, Victorian industrial base.

The first German emissaries arrived at Field Marshal Montgomery's TAC headquarters on Luneburg Heath at 1130 hours on Thursday, 3 May 1945. That lunch-time, the City Business Club met in the Ca'doro Restaurant, in Gordon Street, Glasgow, and were addressed by Malcolm Hime on 'Fluorescent lamps and their post-war application'. The *Glasgow Herald* was scarcely able to conceal its contempt in reporting the visit, to Dr Edouard Hempel, the German ambassador in Dublin, of the Prime Minister of Eire, Eamon de Valera, who wished to express his condolences at the death of Hitler. The papers also contained much debate on the damage being done to both salmon fisheries and the environment by hydro-electric schemes in the Highlands. Battle lines for the first post-war election were already being drawn.

Webster Booth and Anne Ziegler were appearing that week at the Alhambra Theatre in *Sweet Yesterday*, a production described by the *Glasgow Herald* critic as 'The kind of nonsense we used to have when musical comedy was musical comedy'. Verdi's *Il Trovatore* was being presented by the Carl Rosa Opera Company at the Theatre Royal and *The Merry Widow* was on at the King's. Dave Willis and Jimmy Plant were in the musical presentation *Spring Serenade* at the Pavilion and among those appearing at the Empire were Nosmo King, Vic Percy and ventriloquist Peter Brough with 'Archie Andrews'.

The announcement of a complete German capitulation was expected daily and a suggestion from the Government that local authorities should permit an extension of normal licensing hours on VE day was deplored by the Assembly of the Congregational Union in Scotland. Two thousand people had packed into the Coliseum Cinema in Eglinton Street on Friday, 5 May, for the evening showing of *The Constant Nymph* starring Charles Boyer and Joan Fontaine. A cartoon had just finished when David Stewart, the General Manager of Associated British Cinemas in Scotland, walked on to the stage and announced that the German armies in the west had surrendered to Field-Marshal Montgomery. As one, the audience rose to their feet and cheered. By the time the main feature started, most had left to join the celebrations in the streets outside.

A foretaste of the new world order came on the Saturday when both the British and American governments expressed their anger at the arrest, by the Soviets, of 16 leading Polish politicians. The death in a Japanese internment camp of the Reverend Eric Liddell was announced that Saturday. Liddell won the 400 metres at the Paris Olympics in 1924 after refusing to compete in an earlier event as it took place on a Sunday. He had also played rugby for Scotland in 1922 and 1923. The first annual review of the Boy's Brigade since 1939 took place that afternoon on Queen's Park Recreation Ground. General Andrew Thorne, GOC Scottish Command, took the salute as 4,000 boys marched past and the massed bands belted out 'Onward Christian Soldiers' and the National Anthem.

Queen's Park was also the venue for Glasgow's May Day Parade on Sunday, 7 May. Ten thousand marched from George Square to hear Abe Moffat, the General Secretary of the National Union of Mineworkers, indulge in a little rabble-rousing hyperbole when he told them that, 'but for the valiant services of miners and transport workers throughout the country, Britain would not now be on the eve of celebrating the defeat of the German armies'.

Victory celebrations in Glasgow had begun in earnest immediately after the nine o'clock news on Saturday, 6 May, when it was announced that Monday, 8 May, would be VE day. Around 320 extra cattle were slaughtered to meet expected demand for beef in Glasgow over the VE day public holiday. Bonfires were lit in city streets in defiance of dire warnings from Chief Constable Malcolm McCulloch. McCulloch had also warned against decorating buildings with too many flags as they might fall on horses in the streets below and cause accidents. Thousands made for George Square only to be disappointed as official celebrations were not to take place until the following night. Many gathered around a large bonfire on waste ground in North Frederick Street. Effigies of Hitler were burned and the fire service answered 70 calls to bonfires which had got out of control in the city.

Promptly at midnight on 7 May, searchlights on naval vessels stabbed the night sky over the Tail o' the Bank and a cacophony of noise began as ships sounded · · · – morse code for V, on their sirens. Hundreds of coloured Verey lights criss-crossed the sky over Campbeltown, Paisley Abbey was floodlit and, in Kilmarnock, a huge crowd heard the Town Hall bells rung for the first time since 1939.

Pubs and restaurants in Glasgow had sold out of alcohol by the early evening despite which they were still being besieged by thirsty revellers. Thousands of joyful people crammed into George Square, among them hundreds of wide-eyed children. Congas wound their way through the crowd and many joined in the 'Palais Glide' being danced outside the City Chambers which, along with Glasgow University, was floodlit. George Square was bedecked with hundreds of coloured lights. Sailors attempted to bareback ride equestrian statues in the square and a Dutch seaman burlesqued Hitler from the Duke of Wellington's statue in Royal Exchange Square. Two policemen who attempted to put out a bonfire in Townhead were attacked by a crowd and a number of youths were charged with the theft of wood. Three tons of empty bottles were picked up in the vicinity of George Square the following morning.

George Square was the setting for a more solemn occasion on the afternoon of Wednesday, 10 May, when a victory thanksgiving service was held. Concluding his address, Lord Provost James Welsh said: 'Let us remember that we stand here as free men and women primarily because of the bravery, resolution and self-sacrifice of our fighting forces, and the skill and courage with which they have been directed and inspired. Let us use this freedom, and the power that comes with it, for a noble purpose – to build a civilisation in which war will be made impossible and the peoples of the world live together in peace and concord.'

Acknowledgments

The volume of material, much of it hitherto untouched, that is available on the west of Scotland during the war years is considerable. I am most particularly grateful to Strathclyde Regional Council Archives. Without access to their vast storehouse of primary source information, this book would have been impossible. Also in Scotland, I must express my considerable indebtedness to the Scottish Record Office, the National Library and the Central Library, all in Edinburgh. In Glasgow, both the Mitchell Library and the Business Records Department of Strathclyde University Library provided invaluable facilities. Particular mention must be made of the assistance provided by both Clydebank District Council Libraries Service and Inverclyde District Libraries.

The staff of the Department of Photographs at the Imperial War Museum in London were, as ever, most helpful. Valuable source material was made available by the British Newspaper Library at Colindale.

No book of this nature could be written without access to the colossal resources of the Public Record Office at Kew. Here, as always, the staff were most courteous and helpful. As before, I am eternally grateful to all those who took the trouble, often in most uncomfortable and trying circumstances, to compile reports and war diaries.

To pay tribute to all those individuals who have helped in the compilation and production of this book would be quite impossible. I must, however, make a particular acknowledgment of the assistance given by the late Group Captain George Pinkerton OBE DFC, Jack Smith, the staff of the Scottish Cooperative Wholesale Society, Neil Owen, Curstan Terris, Paul Kemp, Pat Malcolm, Vanora Skelley, Lesley Cooper-White and Ron and Wilma Milne. To them, and everyone else who contributed, my deepest gratitude.

Selected Bibliography

PUBLISHED SOURCES

Richard Baxter, *Stand By to Surface* (Cassell, 1944)

Prof William Boyd, *Evacuation in Scotland* (University of London Press, 1944)

Ewart Brookes, *Destroyer* (Jarrolds, 1962)

Ewart Brookes, *Prologue to a War* (Jarrolds, 1966)

Angus Calder, *The People's War* (Jonathan Cape, 1969)

Angus Calder, *The Myth of the Blitz* (Jonathan Cape, 1991)

Dugald Cameron, *Glasgow's Airport* (Holmes McDougall, 1990)

Max Caulfield, *A Night of Terror* (Frederick Muller, 1958)

The Clydebank Blitz in Pictures (Clydebank Libraries, 1980)

Sir John Colville, *The Fringes of Power* (Hodder & Stoughton, 1985)

Peter Cremer and Fritz Brustat-Naval, *U333: The Story of a U-boat Ace* (Bodley Head, 1984)

John D. Drummond, *A River Runs to War* (W. H. Allen, 1960)

A. S. Evans, *Beneath the Waves* (William Kimber, 1986)

Peter Fleming, *Operation Sealion* (First published as *Invasion 1940* by Rupert Davies in 1957)

M. R. D. Foot, *SOE 1940-46* (BBC Publications, 1984)

Norman L. R. Franks, *Search, Find and Kill – Coastal Command's U-boat Successes* (Aston Publications, 1990)

John S. Gibson, *The Thistle and the Crown* (Edinburgh, 1985)

Martin Gilbert, *Finest Hour – Winston Spencer Churchill, 1939 to 1945* (William Heinemann, 1983)

Donald Gilchrist, *Castle Commando* (Oliver & Boyd, 1960)

Michael Glover, *Invasion Scare 1940* (Leo Cooper, 1990)

Paul Harris, *Glasgow at War* (Archive Publications, 1986)

Prof. F. H. Hinsley and C. A. G. Simkins, *British Intelligence in the Second World War* (Vol IV: Security and Counter Intelligence) (HMSO, 1990)

Air Vice Marshal Sandy Johnstone, *Spitfire into War* (William Kimber, 1986)

Geoffrey Jones, *Submarines versus U-boats* (William Kimber, 1986)

Geoffrey Jones, *U-boat Aces* (William Kimber, 1988)

Prof R. V. Jones, *Most Secret War* (Hamish Hamilton, 1978)

Francois Kersandy, *Norway 1940* (Collins, 1990)

Richard Lamb, *Churchill as War Leader – Right or Wrong* (Bloomsbury, 1991)

Bruce Lenman, *An Economic History of Modern Scotland 1660-1976* (Batsford, 1977)

Lloyd's War Losses (Lloyds of London, 1989)

Captain Donald Macintyre, *The Battle of the Atlantic* (Pan, 1983)

Alexander McKee, *Black Saturday* (Souvenir Press, 1966)

Dr I. M. M. Macphail, *The Clydebank Blitz* (Clydebank, 1974)

Charles Messenger, *The Commandos 1940-46* (William Kimber, 1985)

Robin Neillands, *The Raiders* (Weidenfeld & Nicholson, 1989)

Clive Ponting, *1940 – Myth and Reality* (Hamish Hamilton, 1990)

Winston Ramsay (ed.), *The Blitz Then and Now*, vols I to III (After the Blitz Publications, 1989)

Jack Mallman Showell, *U-boat Command and the Battle of the Atlantic* (Conway Maritime Press, 1989)

Robert Seamer, *The Floating Inferno* (Patrick Stephens, 1990)

David Smith, *Action Stations 7* (Patrick Stephens, 1983)

S. E. Smith (ed.), *The United States Navy in World War II* (Ballantine, New York, 1966)

Prof T. C. Smout, *A Century of the Scottish People* (Collins, 1986)

John Terraine, *The Right of the Line* (Hodder & Stoughton, 1985)

Dan van der Vat, *The Atlantic Campaign* (Hodder & Stoughton, 1988)

Fred M. Walker, *Song of the Clyde* (Patrick Stephens, 1984)

C. E. T. Warren and James Benson, *Above us the Waves* (Harrap, 1953)

Nigel West, *M15* (Bodley Head, 1981)

NEWSPAPER FILES

The Glasgow Herald

The Bulletin

The Daily Record

The Scotsman

The Greenock Telegraph

The Clydebank Press

The Times